PREHISTORIC POTTERY
in
BRITAIN & IRELAND

To the memory of Professor George Jobey, DSO, University of Newcastle Upon Tyne, who steered my undergraduate researches towards prehistoric pottery, and to Jane, Frances and Ben who have suffered accordingly

PREHISTORIC POTTERY
in
BRITAIN & IRELAND

Alex Gibson

First published in 2002 by Tempus Publishing

Reprinted in 2011 by
The History Press
The Mill, Brimscombe Port
Stroud, Gloucestershire GL5 2QG
www.thehistorypress.co.uk

Reprinted 2012

Copyright ©Alex Gibson, 2002, 2011

The right of Alex Gibson to be identified as the Author
of this work has been asserted by him in accordance with the
Copyrights, Designs and Patents Act 1988.

All rights reserved. No part of this book may be reprinted or reproduced or utilised in any
form or by any electronic, mechanical or other means, now known or hereafter invented,
including photocopying and recording, or in any information storage or retrieval system,
without the permission in writing from the Publishers.

British Library Cataloguing in Publication Data.
A catalogue record for this book is available from the British Library.

ISBN 978 0 7524 1930 5

Typesetting and origination by
Tempus Publishing.
Printed and bound in Great Britain.

Contents

List of illustrations	6
Acknowledgements	8
1 Introduction. Why pots?	9
2 Aspects of manufacture and ceramic technology	33
3 Decoration and surface treatments	51
4 The earlier Neolithic: 4000–3000 BC	69
5 The later Neolithic and the earlier Bronze Age: 3000–1000 BC	83
6 From Bronze to Iron: 1000–600 BC	109
7 The Iron Age: 600 BC to the Roman conquest	117
8 Postscript	137
Glossary	141
Bibliography	147
Index	155

List of illustrations

Text figures

1 Representational art on European prehistoric pottery
2 Some objects other than pots made from ceramics including loom weights, spindle whorls and perforated slabs
3 'Cheese mould' or bunsen burner in action
4 The terminology of pottery
5 Constructing a relative chronology
6 Bowls in wood and metal with their contemporary ceramic counterparts
7 Some possible skeuomorphic decoration
8 Some fibre impressions in pottery
9 Distribution of Hembury Ware and Trevisker Ware
10 Distribution of Malvernian Ware
11 Diagram showing the frequency of quartz in Welsh Peterborough Ware
12 Photomicrograph of grog in pottery
13 Photomicrograph of flint inclusions in thin section
14 Pinching out a pot
15 The related techniques of ring building (right) and strap building (left)
16 Bronze Age Food Vessel from Northumberland clearly showing the rounded break typical of poorly-bonded rings or straps
17 Beaker vessel from Northon made in two directions
18 Sections through a firing pit at Leicester
19 Typical firing graph from an open firing in southern Romania
20 Black patchy surface of an experimental open-fired pot
21 Spalled early Neolithic pot from Eilean Domhnuill
22 Highly decorated Beaker from Erriswell, Suffolk
23 Durotrigian pots and their distribution set against a map of southern British territories
24 Fingernail rusticated Beaker and Iron Age scratched pot
25 Careless decoration on a Bronze Age Collared Urn from Otford, Kent
26 Incised decoration through the ages
27 Some 'tooled' decoration on IA ceramics
28 Beaker period bone combs for pottery decorating from Northton, Harris
29 Rouletted decoration on Iron Age pottery
30 Various fingernail and fingertip impressions
31 Applied decoration through the ages
32 Burnishing facets on an Iron Age bowl from Hambledon Hill, Dorset
33 The work of the same Northumbrian potter?
34 Carinated Bowls from England, Scotland and Ireland
35 Developed bowls and baggy pots of the earlier Neolithic
36 Some early Neolithic decorated bowls of around 3500 BC
37 Multi-carinated Hebridean jars and Unstan Ware
38 British Impressed Wares
39 Irish Impressed Wares
40 Grooved Ware from Britain and Ireland
41 A Beaker grave group from Roundway, Wiltshire
42 Beaker sequences from Britain
43 Beakers from Northton, Harris, showing range of size
44 Beakers on the periphery? Kilellan Jars, Shetland stone house pottery and Irish Vases
45 Food Vessels

46 Collared Urns of Longworth's Primary and Secondary Series
47 An illustration of the size ranges of Collared Urns
48 Enlarged Food Vessels
49 Cordoned Urns
50 Miniature vessels
51 Deverel-Rimbury pottery
52 Undecorated Barrel and Bucket urns of the Middle Bronze Age
53 Late Bronze Age Pottery from north and western Britain and Ireland
54 Later Bronze Age jars from southern and eastern England
55 Late Bronze Age pottery from the south of England
56 Bulbous jars of the later Bronze Age
57 Early Iron Age pottery from southern England
58 Saucepan pots
59 Glastonbury Ware
60 Atrebatic pottery
61 Scratched jar from Breedon-on-the-Hill
62 Early Iron Age pottery from the Thames Valley area
63 Early Iron Age pottery from East Anglia
64 Frilsford and Hunsbury Bowls from the Midlands
65 Iron Age pottery from Lincolnshire
66 Bulbous jars from the Thames estuary
67 Early Iron Age bowls from Staple Howe, Yorkshire
68 Coarse ware jars from Yorkshire
69 The Clickhimin sequence, Shetland
70 Pottery from the Brochs of the Western Isles
71 Belgic Pottery from south-eastern England

Colour plates

1 Excavation of a pottery cache in pit in the Walton Basin, Radnorshire
2 Plaited cord decoration on a Northumbrian Food Vessel
3 Grain impressions in a Food Vessel from Wether Hill
4 A selection of pots and other experimental pieces made by Romanian school children
5 Black core and oxidised surfaces in an experimental open-fired vase
6 Pots in an experimental open fire
7 Experimental vase with characteristic spalling and distortion
8 Fingernail impression on a Neolithic Impressed Ware vessel from the River Thames
9 Well-executed comb impressed decoration on a late Neolithic Beaker from Monkton-Minster in Kent
10 Breakdown in the decoration of the same vessel
11 Twisted cord impressions on a Food Vessel Urn from Goatscrag, Northumberland
12 Whipped cord 'maggots' on a Food Vessel Urn from Goatscrag, Northumberland
13 'Birdbone' impressions on a Peterborough bowl from Sarn-y-Bryn-Caled near Welshpool, Powys
14 Poor decoration on a Beaker from Manston, Kent
15 Food Vessel from Haugh Head, Northumberland
16 Collared urn from Carneddau
17 Enlarged Food Vessel from Goatscrag, Northumberland
18 Trevisker urn from Kent
19 Later Bronze Age pottery from Runnymeade
20 Later Bronze Age shouldered bowl from Runnymeade

Acknowledgements

I would like to thank all the specialists, particularly members of the Prehistoric Ceramics Research Group, with whom I have discussed aspects of prehistoric pottery over the last 30 years. I am grateful to John Cotton, Stuart Needham, Alison Sheridan, Derek Simpson, Peter Topping, Jacqui Wood and Ann Woods for providing illustrative material. I would also like to thank the Clwyd-Powys Archaeological Trust for allowing me to reproduce photographs of some of the pots from my Welsh excavations. Peter Kemmis Betty has been most understanding as this book was severely delayed due to a job and house move. The Huxley passage in chapter 2 is from *Brave New World*, originally published by Chatto & Windus. It is reprinted by permission of The Random House Group Ltd © the estate of Mrs Lauren Huxley. Finally, mostly, and as always, I owe an enormous debt to my wife Jane for putting up with a paper-strewn kitchen and a somewhat distracted husband. I promise I'll finish the bathroom now!

1 Introduction. Why pots?

Why Pottery?

This book is dedicated to the memory of the late George Jobey, my prehistory tutor at Newcastle University. George had an uncanny habit of throwing (sometimes literally) an artefact at you when you called at his office followed by the question 'what do you make of this then?' George was, to his students, a warm friendly character as well as a truly inspiring teacher and casual enquiries at his office often turned into impromptu tutorials. I remember one day calling on George to discuss my final year options and in so doing was typically given and asked to comment on a strangely decorated piece of pottery. It had what I described at the time as 'string marks' on it and I was later to realise that it was cord-impressed Food Vessel of the early Bronze Age. There proved to be more to our meeting that day than simply my first face to fabric encounter with Food Vessels outside of museum cases. I ended up agreeing there and then that one of my third year options would be a study of the Bronze Age pottery from the north-east of England.

I got my own back on George several years later when, after a ceramics-based PhD, I was taking a tutorial at Leicester University. George had arrived early for an evening guest lecture so in his honour the tutorial took the form of an artefact handling session accompanied by a glass of wine. Undergraduates can often be shy to express an opinion on artefacts in case they appear ignorant in front of their peers but George's gentle and friendly manner (and the wine) helped put them at their ease. However, a piece of pottery stumped them all, including George though he did suggest that it might be Neolithic. He was, of course, correct. I expanded on his identification and told them all that it was a fragment from a middle Neolithic Ebbsfleet bowl. The tables were turned and it was now the master's turn to be the student. But in a typically gentle and humorous way that I shall never forget, George looked at each individual student with his slightly bulging eye, wagged a paternal finger at them and said 'So this is Ebbsfleet. Well m'dears this is the first time I've seen this stuff.' Then he chuckled 'But it hasn't stopped me lecturing about it for 30 years.'

It was also at Leicester that I met and learned a lot from Ann Woods who was studying ceramic technology. Ann, through a number of controlled experiments and the use of thin section analysis, was able to throw some serious criticisms at established theories. She highlighted inaccurate terminologies and a real lack of understanding of the mechanics of pottery production by many leading archaeologists and artefact 'authorities'. Ann and I were able to carry out many controlled experimental firings and this nurtured my interest in the manufacture of prehistoric pottery and gave me an insight into the technology and, more importantly, the people behind the pots.

For me the study of pottery has been and is still fascinating. There is always something new to see. Often I am asked to report on small featureless sherds of pottery that leave me stumped. 'It is definitely pottery and possibly quite old' has become a stock reply. The analysis of pottery is subjective and we cannot always be too proscriptive about the identifications we make. There must always be room for the acknowledgement of one's own limitations, of the limitations of the data, and for the informed opinions of others. It can be a complex subject and this complexity can put people off. It is a great regret that few archaeology departments in British universities actively teach Ceramic Studies and we are in danger of losing ceramics specialists to identify and report on material found in future excavations.

However this book is not intended to be a manual for would-be specialists. Experience can only be gained from handling the material, not from reading books. Instead it is intended to be an introduction to prehistoric pottery, to raise some questions about the ceramic record and above all to remind ourselves that pots were made by people.

What is Pottery?

Earthenware, china, porcelain, terracotta and stoneware are just five examples of a large range of fired clays that are generically known as ceramic or pottery. Pottery is the product of a potter, a person who makes pots and who normally works in (just to be confusing) a pottery – a place where pots are made. The term is a blanket one to cover a variety of products with a variety of appearances. Finely decorated bone china prestige table wares differ considerably from more rustic earthenware bowls and jugs just as dense-bodied stonewares differ obviously and dramatically from, for example, softer and more porous terracotta field drains. Yet all may be described under the term 'ceramic'. Neither is all ceramic utilitarian. Some plates, such as those commemorating a coronation, a local or national event, or even a seaside holiday may never have been intended for any use other than display. Scarcely a house in the developed world is devoid of some small ceramic ornament – a figurine, a bowl of flowers or a wall decoration (including tiles). Some of these can command considerable market values, others values of a more personal nature. What unites these multifarious objects, however, is that they all involve the transformation of clay by fire. In each case, they are fashioned from clay, allowed to dry and then heated to such a degree as to alter chemically the physical nature of the clay particles from which they are made. This process is irreversible: once clay has been heated to this extent, it will turn ceramic and remain so.

As mentioned above and described in more detail in chapter 2, the manufacture of pottery involves the physical transformation of clay. through a chemical process brought about by fire. While the Neolithic has been described as the first agricultural revolution as a result of the introduction of farming at this time, perhaps, as it also coincides, at least in Britain, with the adoption of ceramics, the earliest Neolithic period should also be termed the first industrial revolution. While in the preceding Mesolithic and Palaeolithic periods fire had been used for cooking, warmth, light and the hardening of wooden points, now it was being used physically to transform a natural material. Fire was being controlled in an industrial process. Too much fire too quickly would result in the explosion of the pots while too little heat would not transform the clay into the permanent containers required. This is a learned skill. Today, traditional potters hand down their skill to apprentices and future masters. They also instinctively know when the crucial stages in the firing process have been reached (chapter 2 below).

In bonfire firings, the 200° C stage can be recognised visually as the pots begin to steam and smoke (the water-smoking stage). The ceramic change (typically around 700°C) can also be detected visibly as the pots begin to redden or even glow, but also audibly as the pots begin to 'sing' or 'tinkle' as the chemical water escapes. In kiln firings, however, these visual stages cannot be observed unless the kiln had a window (a very modern feature). Yet there are other ways of recognising these crucial stages. Traditional kiln-using potters in southern Romania, for example, can tell when the water-smoking stage has been reached by the heat of the wasters used to cover the kiln and by the colour of the fire in the kiln. For this reason, firings are often undertaken at night. This, though, is a skill, even reaching the status of an instinct, engendered from training and very much a competence that could not be satisfactorily described in words by the potters themselves: they just 'know'. Neolithic potters, as proven by the surviving products of their craft, also 'knew'. They knew how to control this fiercest and most consuming of natural of forces. They tamed it and exploited its properties of transformation. Just this process led, almost 2000 years later in these islands, to the development of metallurgy and Britain's second industrial revolution.

Ceramic objects

On the prehistoric European mainland, pottery is not only used for making vessels. It is also used for *objets d'art* or religious iconography or paraphernalia. Small figurines may be found widely in the Neolithic of eastern Europe; these may be highly stylised but generally represent women or sexually ambiguous figurines. Animals may also be fashioned out of clay, again often stylised, and sometimes embodied into pots (**1**). In western Europe too, animal images may be found incorporated into vessel designs. Some people made representations of their temples and houses in clay. In the Iron Age ceramics of Europe, human and animal representations may be found on pottery. There are, for example, women weaving on vases from Sporon in Slovenia and funeral processions and games on the Geometric wares of Greece. From an earlier age there are octopuses on Minoan ceramics from Bronze Age Crete, and the famous marching warriors on a Bronze Age vase from the citadel of Mycenae (**1.5**).

In Britain, this representational art is absent from the ceramic repertoire and indeed in almost all media (with the notable exception of wood) from the Neolithic to the

Introduction. Why pots?

1 *Representational art on European ceramics. 1 – model cart from Transylvania (mid-second millennium BC); 2 – model of a house from Moravia (fourth millennium BC); 3 – statuette of a seated man from Hungary (fourth millennium BC); 4 – female figurine from Romania (late second millennium BC); 5 – warrior painted on a vase from Mycenae (late second millennium BC); 6 & 7 – woman spinning and two pugilists incised on pottery from Hungary (mid-first millennium BC); 8 – bowl with bull's head from the Netherlands (late sixth millennium BC). Not to scale. 1-4 & 6-7 after Piggott 1965, 5 after Osgood, Monks & Toms 2000, 8 after Modderman 1971*

later La Tène Iron Age. This absence is interesting, puzzling even, but despite this it is a phenomenon that is rarely considered. While it is certainly true that the occurrence of figurative ceramic art becomes less frequent as we move further west in prehistoric Europe, nevertheless, the small figurines and statuettes are easy to make. We might therefore expect them to be amongst experimental works or even 'apprentice pieces'. For example, it was interesting to observe that, while undertaking experiments into open firings at the University of Leicester in the early 1980s, the University of Oxford in the mid-1990s and, more recently, with school children in Romania, the less competent or less confident potters invariably ended up making small animals and people. The end results were 'primitive' (almost stylised) representations of their subjects. These proto-potters were experimenting with the clay before attempting something more ambitious. They were getting to know the clay, finding out how it worked, noting how plastic it was and what pressures were needed to mould it. Some of these experimental objects clearly had the appearance of toys. However, to date, nothing quite like this has been found in British prehistory. Even the 'duck-stamped' pottery of the Iron Age in the southern Welsh Marches is named after the *similarity* of the impressions to swimming ducks rather than the potters' intention at zoomorphic representation. Potters in prehistoric Britain seemed to be concerned only with the manufacture of receptacles, though very occasionally spoons and items of adornment have also been found. In all cases of decoration, the potters focused on abstract or geometric designs. Perhaps, as in contemporary Islamic societies, likenesses were taboo and forbidden.

Exceptions to the containers are, as already mentioned, spoons, loomweights, spindle whorls and a small number of other unusual objects. Occasionally, low-fired moulds for metal artefacts are also found, but these tend to be of clay fired by the heat of the molten bronze or copper rather than ceramics made specifically for casting. The majority of spoons appear to be Neolithic in date. They are simply-designed objects apparently made from a single piece of clay (**2.1, 2.2**). The two from Nether Swell in Gloucestershire are perhaps the best known and date to sometime before 3000 BC. The longevity of the artefact, however, is demonstrated by the recovery of a similar object from Beaker contexts in midden material buried in the sand dunes at Luce Bay in south-west Scotland, and a scoop or spoon from later prehistoric contexts at Staple Howe (**2.2**). Loom weights tend to be later prehistoric in date coming especially from the later Bronze Age and Iron Age settlements. Cylindrical types are common in the earlier period, being replaced by triangular forms in the later Iron Age (**2.5**). Spindle whorls are also used in the textile process and comprise small ceramic discs, each with a central perforation, which are assumed to have given weight to hand-held spindles used in the spinning of yarn (**2.6**). These are fairly common on Iron Age sites but are rare in the Neolithic and Bronze Age. This is rather peculiar for we know from the cord impressions in pottery that spinning was also taking place in these earlier periods. Perhaps unfired clay was being used to give weight to the spindle.

From the later Bronze Age large thick slabs of fired clay are found on settlement sites (**2.4**). These are often two or more centimetres thick and are perforated with multiple circular holes, each over 1cm in diameter. They are generally found in association with

Introduction. Why pots?

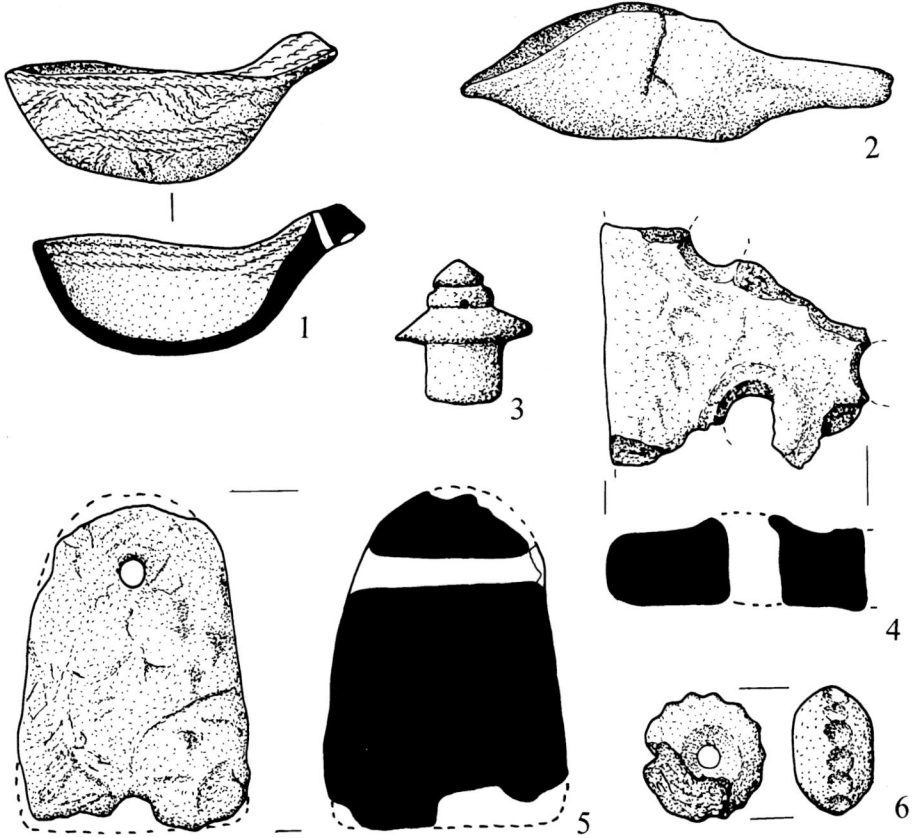

2 *Some examples of ceramic objects other than pots. 1 – early Bronze Age scoop from Longstock, Hampshire. Scale 1:4; 2 – Iron Age spoon or scoop from Staple Howe, Yorkshire. Actual size; 3 – pottery stopper from Hengistbury Head, Dorset. Scale 1:6; 4 – perforated slab from Runnymede, Berkshire. Scale 1:2; 5 – loom weight from Staple Howe. Scale 1:3; 6 – spindle whorl from Runnymede. Scale 1:2.*
1 after Manby 1995; 2 & 5 after Brewster 1963; 3 after Cunliffe 1987, 4 & 6 after Needham 1991

hearths and are therefore labelled oven plates because they are assumed to have had something to do with cooking processes. In truth, however, their precise function is not known although similar artefacts from Chalcolithic eastern Europe have been interpreted as kiln plates or floors, some even being found *in situ*.

In the Iron Age, a peculiar ceramic object enters the archaeological record. This is a conical object with multiple perforations through the walls (**3**). They resemble conical sieves, but the perforations are too large for this to be a serious interpretation. They are conventionally labelled cheese moulds used for separating the curd and whey, but again little practical consideration was given to the size of the holes, which are clearly too large to have functioned in this way. Absorbed residue analysis on these objects has furthermore failed to find any traces of milk residues or fats that might be expected had they indeed been cheese moulds. Experimental work

Introduction. Why pots?

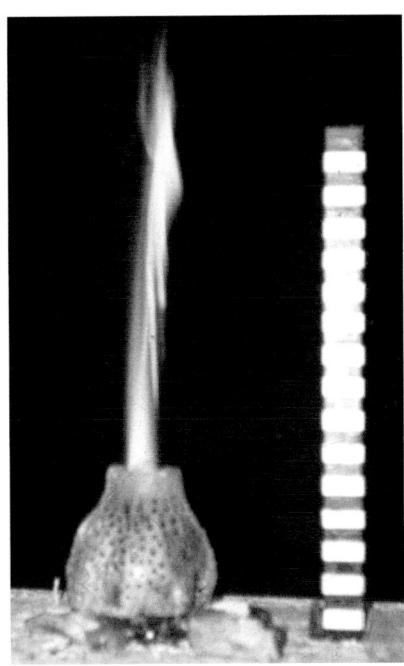

3 *'Cheese mould' or Bunsen burner in action.*
Reproduced by courtesy of Jacqui Wood

by Jacqui Wood, however, has shed new light on these old objects. They were not strainers or containers, but instead were a form of 'Bunsen burner'. They were filled with fuel such as dried reed, placed point-upwards on a surface and the reeds were lit. The holes took in air to allow the fuel to burn and a hot pencil-like flame burned out of the top of the object. Wood argues that this hot directable flame would have been essential in the fine metalworking and jewellery manufacture of later prehistory.

The terminology of Pottery

Pottery reports in academic journals and excavation reports are full of technical terms that may often be confusing to a non-specialist reader. These terms are labels that are used as a type of shorthand to help avoid complicated and unnecessarily long descriptions. For example 'a flattened and/or moulded surface inside and immediately below the rim' is called a 'bevel': thus one word can describe the concept. Other terms may be used to avoid ambiguity. For example the term 'carination' (derived from the Latin *carina* meaning the keel of a ship) may be used to describe a sharp change in direction in the pot's profile. 'Shoulder' might also be used if there is only one carination but some vessels, such as the Hebridean Bowls of the Neolithic, may have multiple carinations and in such cases the term 'shoulder' would be inappropriate. Some of these terms are explained in the glossary, but it is hoped that this current section will illustrate the most commonly used terms (**4**).

'Rim', for example, is self-explanatory. But there are various forms of rim, such as moulded, internally bevelled, beaded, rounded, pointed, inturned or everted.

Introduction. Why pots?

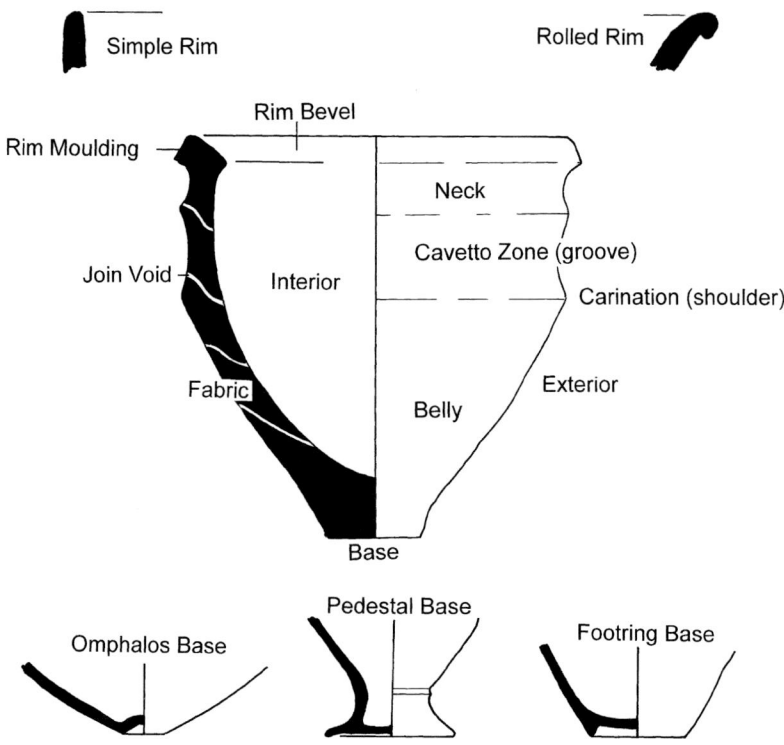

4 *The terminology of pottery*

There are also various sorts of bases such as simple, protruding foot, footringed or omphalos. These again are largely self explanatory with, perhaps, the exception of omphalos. This is the Greek word for navel and refers to a boss on the inside of the base. These are only encountered from the later Bronze Age in Britain. The neck of a vessel, as with the body of a person, is the area above the shoulder, the belly is the area below. Shoulders may be 'sharp', if they are marked by a distinct carination, or 'slack' if they are more rounded. Some vessels may have small knobs of clay or 'lugs' protruding from the wall while others may have similar features or 'stops' set within grooves. These grooves are normally rounded in section and relatively deep and are sometimes called 'cavetto zones'. This type of feature is most common in the Food Vessel pottery of the early Bronze Age.

These terms are most frequently used in chapters 4-7 and the illustration (**4**) may be used as a quick guide.

Pottery as a dating tool

Pottery is a great survivor. Once clay has been turned to ceramic, it will last indefinitely in a relatively unaltered state. Much Prehistoric pottery is found in a fragmentary condition having been deliberately buried in pits or ditches (**colour plate 1**) yet, on excavation, it can often be hard and solid despite its 2000-6000 years' burial. Only grinding or crushing will destroy the sherd. As a result, pottery is a frequent find on archaeological sites, including those from prehistory, and sometimes it is found in great quantities. Combine this durability with the changes in pot design and decoration that take place over time, and pottery becomes of great use to the archaeologist as a tool for dating the past. At a basic level of relative chronology, we know from the flint artefacts with which they are associated as well as from more recent radiocarbon dates that undecorated round-based Carinated Bowls do not occur beyond the earlier Neolithic. Beakers mark the transition between the ages of stone and bronze because they are found with the earliest copper and bronze tools. Collared Urns were current during the earlier Bronze Age because they are occasionally found with bronze daggers and stone battle axes. Saucepan pots are found with ironwork of the middle Iron Age and Belgic imports from Europe herald the end of the prehistoric period in Britain. Because pottery changed over time, sequences can be identified and refined within this broad, open framework and relative chronologies can be constructed (**5**). For most of the twentieth century, pottery was our main dating tool in the study of British Prehistory. The advent of radiocarbon dating allowed us to anchor this relative chronology within an absolute time-frame.

However, the arrival of radiocarbon dating and other absolute dating techniques did not diminish the importance of pottery as a dating tool, but rather refined its use. This is especially so in the Neolithic and Bronze Age. For example, it was conventionally believed that Peterborough Ware was late Neolithic in date and that within this tradition there was a chronological development from the Ebbsfleet style through the Mortlake style to the flat-based Fengate style that strongly influenced the development of the Collared Urns of the Bronze Age (see below, chapters 4 & 5). This perfectly workable and accepted sequence has now been challenged by systematic radiocarbon dating that has conclusively proven that all three styles of Peterborough Ware were in concurrent use by 3000 BC. This means that Fengate Ware is now known to be up to a millennium earlier than Collared Urns and it is therefore difficult to see how the theory that the former influenced the latter can be maintained. What we are uncertain of at present is the date for the demise of the Peterborough tradition; but it is nevertheless difficult to envisage that such an impractical and esoteric form as Fengate Ware might have lasted, unchanged, for a millennium. Despite the growing body of radiocarbon dates for British prehistory and the refinements to chronology that this has allowed, there are still major questions to be asked.

When dealing with Radiocarbon dates, however, we need to ask ourselves what it is that we are actually dating. With Food Vessels in particular, the majority of dates have been obtained from the bones of the individual and, presumably, the date of deposition of the remains. However, if we assume that the pot had already been made before the person died, then this date only gives a *Terminus Ante Quem* for the Pot. We certainly know that many pots had had use-histories or were old and broken when deposited. Unfortunately we cannot translate this into a real time frame. We are only dating the period during which these pots appeared in graves, not the time-span of the pots themselves. We need more dayes for pottery from non-funerary context, but unfortunately these are very few and far between and may not have survivng organic associations.

Introduction. Why pots?

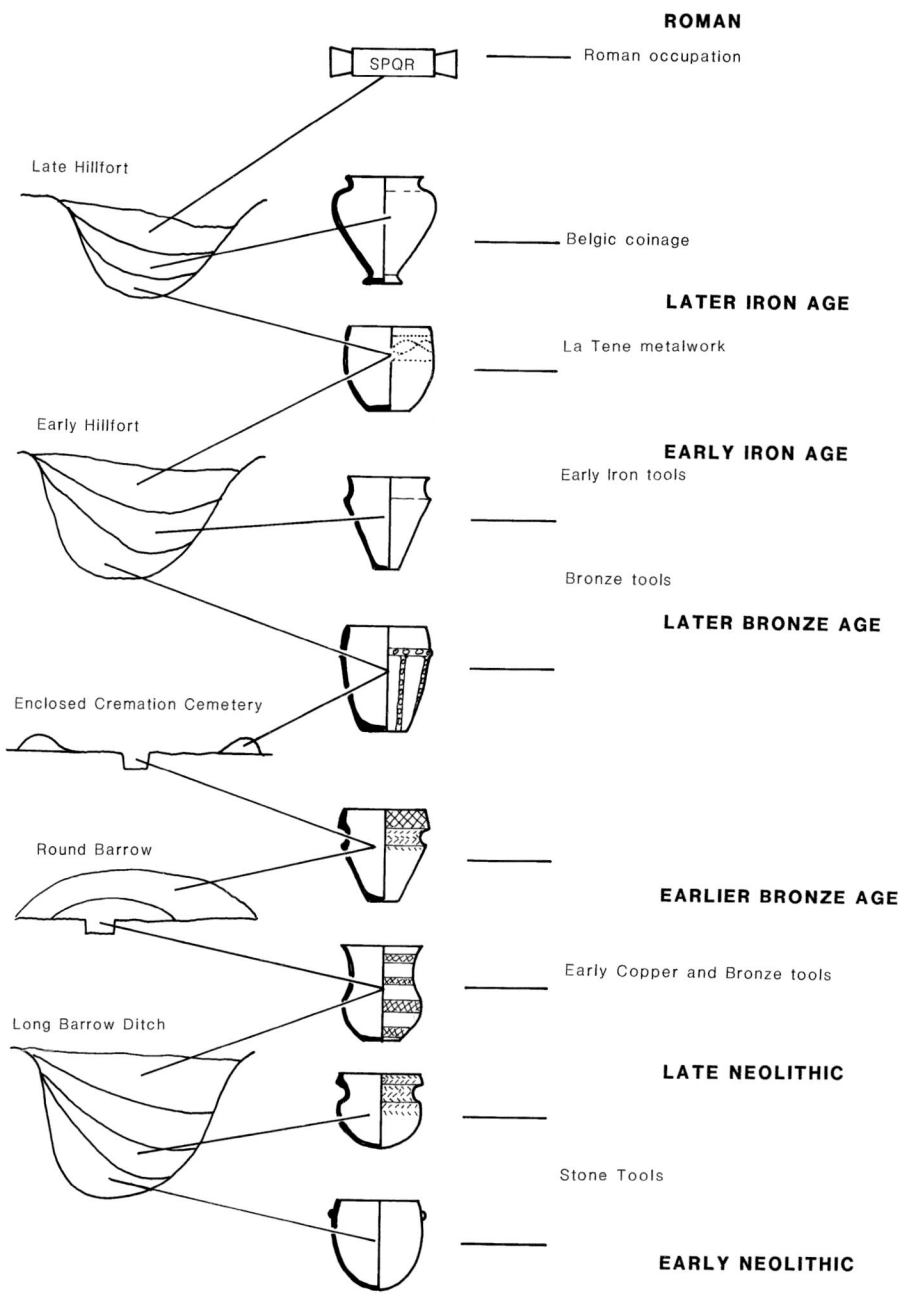

5 *Relative chronology chart.* From Gibson & Woods 1997

Pottery as an economic indicator

Too often archaeologists can focus on the typology of pottery for its own sake. For some, the refining of typologies can be an end in itself without it being asked what this really means. Generally, this process is directed towards tightening chronologies or identifying and defining regional variations but at other times it appears to be purely an academic exercise of some interest but little application. However, pottery is an artefact brought about by human agency. Pots are made by people as part of their holistic life system. It is only one facet of a rich, varied and no doubt colourful material culture, much of which was organic and survives extremely rarely only in exceptional preserving environments.

The light that pottery can shed on other aspects of material culture and economy is a facet of ceramic studies that deserves much wider consideration and recognition. Since the pioneering studies of pottery in the earlier twentieth century, it has often been assumed that pottery must have developed from somewhere and therefore now-invisible organic objects were called upon to account for various formal and decorative traits. Small simple, round-based bowls, for example, were considered to mimic the gourds that, it was considered, had formed the main containers in the pre-ceramic societies of the Fertile Crescent between the rivers Tigris and Euphrates whence all things Neolithic were considered to have generated. The herringbone pattern on Peterborough Ware and the cordoned and filled triangle decoration on some Grooved Ware vessels were considered to have been derived from basketry. The large, 'baggy-profiled' pots from the early Neolithic causewayed enclosure at Windmill Hill were thought to resemble the skin bags that were presumed to have formed an organic part of contemporary material culture. Unfortunately, there is little in the way of surviving archaeological evidence from the British Neolithic to support or indeed refute these earlier assumptions, and consequently they are now regarded as somewhat simplistic explanations. It cannot be denied that organic containers did exist in the Neolithic, but we remain uncertain as to the forms of the majority of them.

Nevertheless, some pots do shed light on forms that existed in other media. The furrowed haematite-coated bowls of the later Bronze Age and earlier Iron Age, for example, have copper-alloy counterparts and the contemporary large, shouldered pots or situla jars are ceramic representations of the large cauldrons entering the metalwork record of the early Iron Age. Here the derivations are easier to ascertain, because the forms survive in both media. There are also chance survivors in other, normally less durable media. Around 2000 BC, for example, there are strange pots, generally with Beaker associations, called 'polypod bowls' because of the presence of four short legs protruding from below a round, hemispherical body. These bowls also survive in wooden form from Irish peat bogs and can be seen to be contemporary with the pottery examples (Earwood 1991/2) (**6.1, 6.2**). Taking a wider view, it seems that the practice of parallel wooden and ceramic forms is a common phenomenon. Caroline Earwood (1989/90), for example, has pointed out the affinities between wooden and metal handled bowls as well as wooden and metal cauldrons in Iron Age Ireland and Scotland. In the Neolithic lake villages of the Jura in eastern

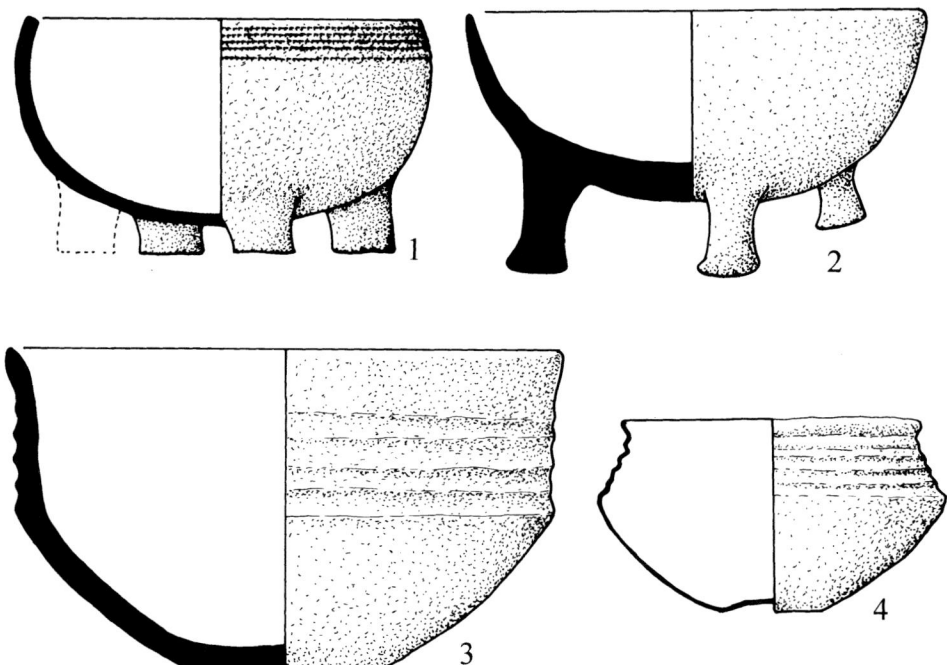

6 *Bowls in wood and metal with their contemporary ceramic counterparts. The forms are similar, but note the size differences. 1 – Beaker polypod bowl from Inkpen Hill, Berks. Scale 1:8. After Clarke 1970; 2 – wooden ploypod bowl from Tinkernaghen, Co. Tyrone. Scale 1:4. After Earwood 1992; 3 – haematite bowl from All Cannings Cross, Wiltshire. Scale 1:2. After Harding 1974; 4 – bronze bowl from Welby, Leicestershire. Scale 1:2. After Harding 1974*

France, where preservation conditions are exceptional, wooden forms of round-based Neolithic bowls have been found. The coexistence of similar artefact forms in wood, ceramic and metal seems therefore, to be a widespread phenomenon.

Manby (1995) has again taken up the issue of the influence of external material culture on ceramics and has suggested that a ceramic scoop found in a Collared Urn from Longstock in Hampshire may, by reason of its practical form, have a leather prototype (**2.1**). The twisted cord decoration on this artefact may well be replicating the reinforcing stitching on leather examples. He also argues that an early Bronze Age Food Vessel from Corbridge in Northumberland may be derived from basketry. Here closely spaced whipped cord impressions on the outside of the vessel certainly do resemble the weaving of basketwork (**7**). On the underside of the vessel, a change in direction of these impressions bears a striking similarity to the effect of a basketry disk having been stitched to an upper cylinder to create a two-part bowl.

The horseshoe-shaped handles on Bronze Age Cornish and Wessex urns as well as the zig-zag relief decoration on some broadly contemporary Food Vessel Urns (**7**) are also occasionally invoked as representing rope or carrying handles or suspension cradles. These arguments are sometimes reinforced by the use of twisted cord to decorate the handles or by the emphasising of the cordons using incision to resemble

Introduction. Why pots?

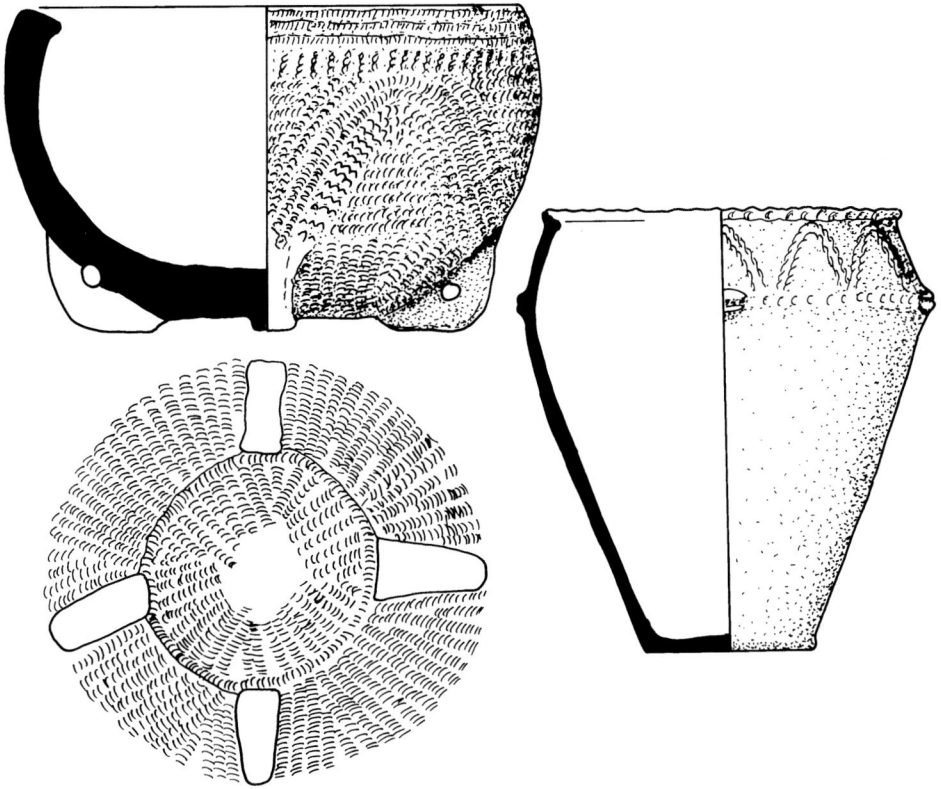

7 *Some possible Skeuomorphic decoration. Left, a Bronze Age Food Vessel from Corbridge (Northumberland), the impressions on the underside of which possibly reflect basketry. Scale 1:4. After Manby 1995. Right, a Bronze Age Biconical Urn from Thickthorn Down (Dorset). Do the cord loops represent rope carrying handles? Scale 1:8. After Tomalin 1995*

stitching. These arguments, as well as those expressed by Manby, are attractive theories but so far concrete proofs of their validity are absent from the archaeological record. Future wetland archaeology may possibly validate these hypotheses.

It is rarely discussed in the archaeological literature possibly because it has not been widely recognised, but Neolithic and earlier Bronze Age pottery actually provides our single largest resource for the study of contemporary fibres. From the impressed wares of around 3000 BC to the demise of cord decoration around 1200 BC actual surviving fibres are rare, though some idea of the variety of material used can be gleaned from the well-preserved impressions that survive on pottery (**8** and **colour plate 2**). Cord impressions at their simplest indicate that single twist fibres have been used. Some have a hard and well-defined internal structure where the actual individual fibre impressions can be seen suggesting the use of a hard material like a modern parcel string. Others are much softer and less regular suggesting a material such as hand-spun wool. Impressions of plaited cord, particularly on the earlier Bronze Age pottery from south-west England indicate the knowledge of this technique to produce stronger and/or more decorative material. Whipped cord, as discussed in chapter 3 below, is produced by wrapping a piece of cord around itself (like a hangman's noose) or around another fibre or core. Once again, evidence for this practice comes from the surviving impressions found on pottery and a variety of coarseness and fineness can be found within the repertoire. These impressions show the knowledge and presence of composite strings at this period, and some are so fine and well defined that a resilient material such as gut or sinew must have been used. Might these finer strings be bowstrings? Or might they even be the strings for musical instruments? Either way, the impressions found on pottery may be the only evidence for such materials that survives in the archaeological record for the prehistoric period in Britain.

Another way in which pottery can shed light on the wider economy is by looking at the impressions that survive both within the fabric of the pottery and on its surface. In particular, seed impressions can be found on pottery of all periods. This was first recognised as an important palaeoenvironmental resource as far back as the 1950s, when it was observed that fired pottery preserved the impressions of grains and seeds which otherwise might survive only in exceptional circumstances. These impressions, dating to the time of the manufacture of the pot, would therefore offer a small window for determining which plants and cereals were being grown by the users of the vessel. These impressions are generally considered to result from the accidental inclusion of such plant material during the manufacture of the pot in a generally agrarian environment such as on a farmyard. This may, in many cases, be a correct interpretation and it is notable that many grain impressions are found on the bases of pots. However, a Food Vessel from Wether Hill in Northumberland contains so many cereal grain impressions both within the fabric of the pot as well as on the surface, that it seems that grains were deliberately added to the clay as an opening agent. Indeed, some actual carbonised grains have been recovered from the fabric of the pot and used to obtain a radiocarbon date. The cereals preserved within this single pot represent one of the largest cereal caches so far discovered in early Bronze Age Northumberland and are therefore important for regional palaeoenvironmental studies. The inclusion of a food resource within the fabric raises important questions as to the symbolism of this. The topic will be discussed in more detail in chapter 2 below.

Plant remains may also be found inside pottery in the form of pollen grains. Analysis has shown that meadowsweet is a common plant type found in association with pottery from Bronze Age burials. This has often been taken to suggest that the pots held some sort of liquid (archaeologists, for some reason, prefer to assume that this liquid would be alcoholic), flavoured with meadowsweet. A re-examination of the material by Tipping (1994) suggests that there are several explanations for the occurrence of pollen in these contexts. Firstly, a Beaker from Ashgrove in Fife contained abundant lime (*Tilia*) pollen despite the fact that lime was not common so far north at this time. He suggested, therefore, that it might have contained imported honey. The presence of cereal pollen in a Food Vessel from North Mains in Perthshire might be taken to be indicative of a food such as a porridge. The abundance of meadowsweet pollen over the grave at

8 *Some whipped cord impressions on Neolithic pottery. Top left, Callis Wold, Yorkshire; top right and bottom left, Marden, Wiltshire; bottom right, Hedderwick, East Lothian*

Sketewan, Perthshire, is strongly suggestive of a floral tribute to the deceased with the blooms more than likely spread over the floor of the grave. Tipping admits that it is unlikely that there would be one single explanation for this widespread phenomenon but future work may well identify patterns and practices in this interesting aspect of Prehistoric ritual.

The discipline of applied chemistry has also contributed greatly to our understanding of the functions of some prehistoric pottery, as well as adding extra information to our knowledge of the prehistoric economy. Prehistoric pottery, being unglazed, is porous and therefore traces of the contents of a pot will be absorbed into the fabric of the vessel. Of course, these organic traces degrade over time so it is unlikely that we would ever recover an exact prehistoric recipe; nevertheless some organics are surprisingly robust and leave chemical traces. These traces or residues can be detected and identified using refined analytical techniques such as gas chromatography-mass spectrometry and (an even bigger mouthful) gas chromatography-combustion-isotope ratio mass spectrometry (see Evershed *et al.* 1997). These techniques detect fatty acids and, since different animal fats have different chemical profiles, by plotting out the fats' chemical signatures, species identification may often be possible. It may also be possible to differentiate between body fats derived from meat and those derived from milk.

Absorbed residue analysis was undertaken at a Neolithic site called Upper Ninepence in the Walton Basin of mid-Wales (Evershed & Dudd in Gibson 1999). Palaeoenvironmental data from this site was very limited due to the acid soil conditions. Soil pollen did not survive, nor did bone. Plant remains survived only when burnt or carbonised. Both Peterborough Ware and Grooved Ware pots were found but in different pits suggesting that there had been two periods of deposition here. Radiocarbon dates confirmed this with the Peterborough Ware dating to around 3000 BC and the Grooved Ware slightly later at 2700 BC. The residue analysis of both pot types told a very interesting story. The fats from the Peterborough Ware had come from grass-eating animals such as sheep or cattle (at that time it was difficult to tell them apart as their diets are essentially the same), while the Grooved Ware pots had held pork. It seems that different economies were being practised and this is supported by animal bone evidence from the chalklands of Wessex which suggest associations of Peterborough Ware with sheep and cattle and of Grooved Ware with pig.

This difference in economy suggested by the residue analysis at Upper Ninepence was supported by the microscopic analysis of the traces of wear on the flint artefacts. Different uses and materials leave different wear signatures, and the flints from the Peterborough phase suggested that they had been used for a complete range of agricultural practices such as meat cutting, woodworking, hide preparation, vegetable cutting and so on. The flints associated with the Grooved Ware phase, however, indicated a preponderance of meat cutting and hide preparation suggesting that a restricted and possibly specialised set of tasks was being undertaken in this phase. Thus at this Welsh site, new scientific analytical techniques have shed important light on the regional economy around 3000 and 2700 BC despite the superficially disappointing range of conventional environmental evidence preserved in the acid soil.

Pottery may also preserve evidence for regional identities. This is not a new idea: pottery was one of the major artefact types used in Gordon Childe's concept of culture. As pottery changes over time and in parallel with other artefact types, so may it change regionally. These regional differences may indicate territorial identity and suggest the existence of cultural or even tribal systems. Many regional differences are observable from the earlier Neolithic, such as the baggy profiled Windmill Hill style of Wessex or the decorated carinated bowls of southern England. In Scotland, the Neolithic Unstan Bowls are largely restricted to the far north and west of the country. In the Iron Age, the regionality of pottery can be set against the tribal divisions documented by Roman geographers. This has been extensively studied by Barry Cunliffe in his seminal work entitled *Iron Age Communities in Britain* (1991). Cunliffe has identified regional styles of pottery coinciding with the documented tribal geographies. The Atrebatic Wares (pottery of the tribe known as the Atrebates) of central southern England, around Hampshire and West Sussex, are characterised by bead-rimmed, high-shouldered jars and bowls. In Dorset and Somerset, the tribe known as the Durotriges produced various jar forms (Durotrigian Wares) of such high quality that they later became exploited by the Roman invaders. Known as Black Burnished Ware to Roman scholars, this ceramic is one of the most commonly found types of pottery on Roman military sites.

Distribution and trade

Related to this issue is the distribution of pots away from their sources of manufacture. This is generally discussed under the term 'trade' but it must be remembered that trade is a two-way system. Trade involves receiving in exchange for giving, but in the archaeological record evidence can only normally be identified for one of these mechanisms. For example, Neolithic polished stone axes made from stone from the Langdale Pikes in Cumbria are found all over Britain and even into Ireland. These are taken to represent trading in this commodity. What went back to Cumbria is more difficult to identify. Perishable commodities such as foodstuffs, animals or even slaves would, of course, leave no trace within the archaeological evidence. There are other mechanisms which can be used to account for these distributions such as gift exchange (trade to strengthen social links rather than for purely economic reasons), bride wealth, tribute or fealty.

Whatever the mechanics involved, the petrological study of the clays from which ceramics have been made can shed light on their place of manufacture and, when considered in relation to their findspots, can help to build up a picture of 'trade' or social networking. As will be mentioned below in chapter 2, prehistoric ceramics contain two types of non-clay inclusions in the fabric. The first comprises material deliberately added to the clay and the second are the minerals which occur naturally within the clay. By studying the latter group, the petrology of the clay can be determined and, if the geology is distinctive enough, an area of manufacture may be identified. The earliest instance of this may be found in the earlier Neolithic in the form

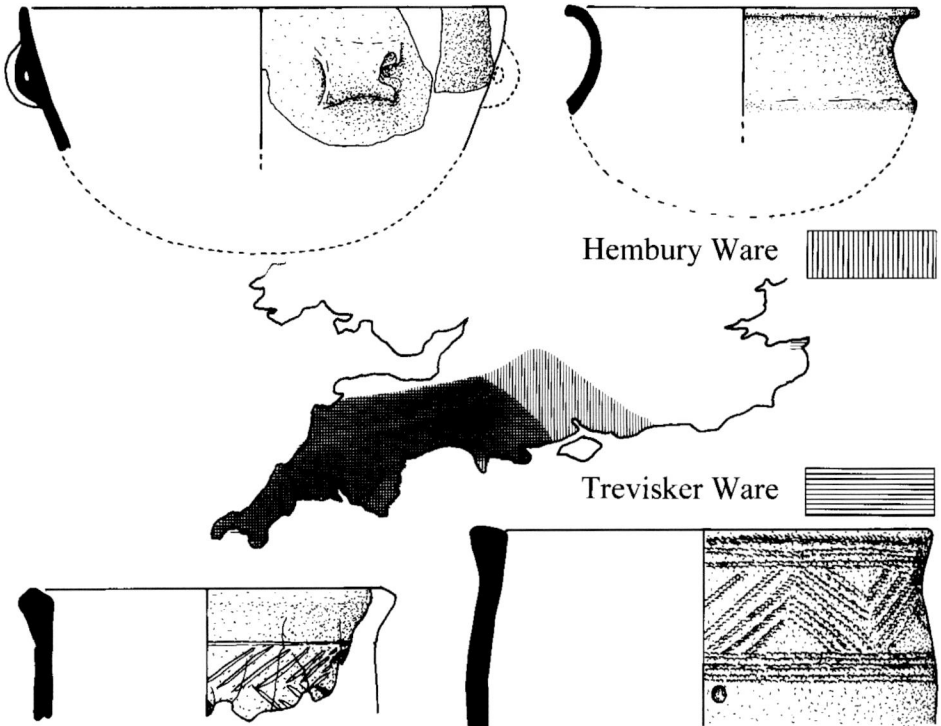

9 *Distribution of Hembury Ware and Trevisker Ware. Hembury (upper) pots from Carn Brae. After Mercer 1981; the Trevisker (lower) pots from Trevisker Round. After ApSimon & Greenfield 1972. Scale 1:4*

of the Hembury wares of Cornwall. Apparently made by specialised craftsmen, these ceramics were made from distinctive high-quality clays outcropping in the Lizard area of Cornwall. Finds of this gabbroic Hembury Ware have been made as far east as Maiden Castle in Dorset (**9**). It is only human agency that can account for the movements of these pots. Archaeologists have discussed whether it was the pots or the clay that was transported. The fineness of the pots and their restricted range of physical attributes suggest the former.

The distinctive gabbroic clay source of the Southwest peninsula was exploited in the Bronze Age as well, and a characteristic style of pottery called Trevisker Ware was also traded away from its source of manufacture (**9**). Generally restricted to south-west England, an example of this form of pottery has also been found in Kent and further afield in Normandy at Mondeville near Caen and at Ile Tatihou off St Vast la Hogue on the Cherbourg peninsula. At this latter site the Cornish origins of the pot have not been established (and indeed the geology of this area of France is very similar to Cornwall) but the style is so similar that strong links between the two regions cannot be denied.

A pioneering study by Peacock (1968) on the 'duck-stamped' pottery from the Herefordshire-Cotswold Area demonstrated that the main source of the clay was in the Malvern region and he concluded that the pottery was then traded out from this area (**10**). Peacock's original study was restricted in geographical area, but

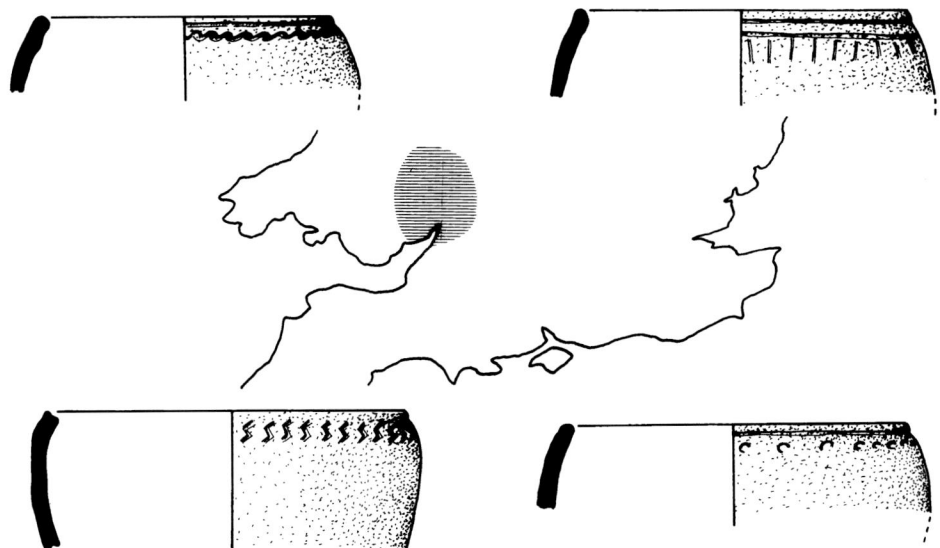

10 *Distribution of Malvernian Ware after Peacock 1968. The bottom left pot is from Cleve Hill, Gloucestershire, the others are from Sutton Walls, Hereford.*
Scale 1:4. After Cunliffe 1991

Malvernian pottery can now be identified further afield such as from the Breiddin in north Powys, Pen Dinas near Aberystwyth on the west Welsh coast and from the Walton basin in central Powys. Once again the term 'trade' is used without any reference to the other commodity being traded but doubtless at least some of the pottery would have been 'bought' in exchange for more perishable goods.

Functions

We have so far been looking at what pottery can tell us of the past and its uses to archaeologists. We have not, as yet, considered its usefulness to prehistoric peoples. It was, after all, prehistoric people who made pottery. They did not make it for the benefit of future archaeologists but rather they must have had a need for it or at least found it useful. It often occurs in large quantities on archaeological sites so it must have been a common artefact type not simply made for display and burial. Much of what is written about the functions of ceramics is assumed theory. It is logically assumed that pots were used for storage and cooking and therefore they are frequently referred to as storage vessels and cooking pots. Occasionally carbonised residues on the surfaces of pots appear to confirm the cooking hypothesis though few of these encrustations have been analysed. It is also worth remembering that there is no direct evidence for pots having been used for storage. This assumption is usually inferred from the large size of some vessels and by analogy with the *pithoi* of the Bronze Age Mediterranean. Claims that some of the large tub-shaped Grooved Ware vessels of Neolithic Orkney functioned as brewing tuns or barley containers are largely speculative though not necessarily implausible.

Pottery is indeed an excellent medium for the transferral of heat. Having already survived the rigours and rapid temperature rises of open fires, the heat of a cooking fire is little but a gentle warming. The round based bowls of the Neolithic, in particular, are well suited to being placed on a bed of glowing embers and the out-turned necks or heavy rims facilitate lifting and their removal from the flame. The flat-based pots of later prehistory are less well suited for this but still would have been able to tolerate direct contact with the heat and would have stood on the embers providing that they were fairly level or flattened by some sort of cooking plate.

The residue analysis described above is, however, now proving that pottery was indeed used for cooking and food preparation. It also suggests the emergence of different cooking processes or strategies in the Neolithic from the preceding periods. In these islands, food had been cooked for millennia prior to the introduction of pottery. Doubtless hunter-gatherers were accomplished cooks using various outdoor techniques such as smoking, cooking with hot stones, spit roasting or even pit roasting using embers, greenwood and fresh foliage. The process of the boiling or stewing of meats and/or plants is less easy to envisage given the lack of fire-proof containers in Mesolithic contexts. Experiments in Ireland have demonstrated that this can be achieved by the addition of hot stones to food placed with water in skin pouches so stews cannot be ruled out of the Mesolithic diet. Certainly, however, this process would have been easier with pottery since, as mentioned above, ceramic allows direct contact with the naked flame. With the introduction of cereals and an increasing reliance on cereal production throughout prehistory, pottery could be used for the preparation of porridges and other cereal-based gruels or broths. This would certainly allow the more economical use of resources once a sedentary lifestyle had established itself. The adoption of pottery amongst the Mesolithic hunter-gatherer groups of the Ertebølle culture of north-west Europe, however, indicates that ceramics and sedentism do not necessarily need to go together but clearly pottery was perceived as useful or desirable; perhaps a tool in new cooking processes essential to a changing economy and lifestyle.

Similarly, processed meats might also have been stored. Smoking and, perhaps to a lesser extent, salting and drying would already have been available as methods for the preservation of meat. Cooked meats and offal are less easily preserved unless they are kept in a sterile anaerobic environment. Pots might have facilitated this preservation. By sealing both the fabric and the mouth of the vessel cooked offal and meats, not dissimilar to a modern pâté or terrine, may have been preserved for future consumption. In this respect, the identification of lipids, and particularly milk lipids, within ceramics might as easily represent a proofing process as a cooking one. By boiling milk inside a pot or by quenching a newly fired pot in milk, the vessel wall would have been sealed with fats. Similarly, traces of beeswax have been found in the upper parts of some later vessels. This may have been to seal the contents in the same way as paraffin wax may be used to seal bottles and pots today. Much more experimental work needs to be done in this field.

One aspect of storage that is rarely considered in this context is of course usually considered in another. That is the long-term storage of human remains or burial. Pots may accompany burials or, in the case of Bronze Age urns, contain the actual remains.

Accessory vessels are normally considered to have contained, physically or symbolically, provision for the afterlife. Some pots may have been made specifically for burial while others may have been removed from the domestic sphere just as the deceased had left the world of the living: they had both been removed from currency.

Display

The display potential of pottery has already been mentioned above. In Prehistoric Britain, ceramics (with the very few exceptions discussed above) take the form of containers – bowls, jars, urns, cups. This is not to say, however, that the pots themselves were purely functional. Some may well have had the display potential discussed above in a modern context. There is a growing body of evidence to suggest, for example, that the complex comb-impressed decoration of the Beaker pottery of the final Neolithic was highlighted with white inlay that would contrast against the generally red colour of the clay body. At first, cases where this white inlay was recognised were generally dismissed as the result of chalk percolation during their period of burial. However, analysis reported by David Clarke in his pioneering work on British Beakers (1970) noted that some chalk had been deliberately crushed, as it contained crushed foraminifera which would not have been present in percolated material. Crushed burnt bone also seems to have been used. In a small Pigmy Cup of the earlier Bronze Age from Breach farm, in Glamorgan, the complex, incised geometric decoration was inlaid with a red pigment (Grimes 1938) which would have contrasted with the black to dark brown colour of the fabric.

In the red-finished wares of the later Bronze Age and Iron Age, white inlay or paint also seems to have been used to highlight the incised decoration and contrast with the red body of the pottery (Middleton 1995). In Kent, polychrome pottery is typical of the early to middle Iron Age. The white decoration, which appears as inlay within red or black panels, seems to have been made using powdered quartz (Macpherson-Grant 1991). These contrasting colours demonstrate advanced aesthetics and yet another labour-intensive process designed to enhance the attractiveness of the vessel. This would doubtless convey prestige, power and, above all, a sense of value or worth.

Pottery may also be displayed for other reasons. Pots may have acquired meaning and personal histories. A trophy taken from an enemy may be afforded pride of place in a dwelling, as may a gift from a particularly powerful or respected leader. Bride wealth may have included particularly prestigious pottery (and possibly the contents of the pot), and some pots may have histories derived from previous owners such as family members now residing amongst the ancestors. In such a way the status of ostensibly mundane and utilitarian objects may be elevated. Particular artefacts attract meaning to their owners; a meaning which may be passed on to heirs, enhanced through time as a tangible link with the past or even die with the owner.

Ritual

We have already touched on the ritual aspects of pottery above. It cannot be denied that prehistoric pottery had more than a simply utilitarian function. It had deep symbolic meaning and may even have been regarded as a prestige artefact. The most easily recognisable way in which the ritual aspect of pottery can be determined is in the presence of pottery in graves.

Perhaps the most famous of prehistoric sepulchral pottery dates to the earlier Bronze Age. Beakers, Food Vessels and Urns are often highly decorated and are assumed to have contained food or drink for the journey to the afterlife. However this is to deny the earlier presence of pottery in the sepulchral record. From the early Neolithic, pottery has been found accompanying human remains in long barrows, chambered tombs and the ditches of causewayed enclosures. These pots are often fragmentary, almost disarticulated like the bones themselves. It is as if it was important to deposit broken and useless vessels incapable of being reconstructed in the same way as individual skeletons were manipulated, taken apart and buried as collections of bones lacking individual identity.

In the Beaker period at the transition between the ages of stone and bronze, pots tend to accompany the burials of individuals. This phenomenon of single accompanied burial continues into the Bronze Age with Urns and Food Vessels dominating the burial record. Both complete and fragmentary pots are present (as indeed are complete and fragmentary skeletons!) suggesting that some of these may have been made specifically for inclusion in the grave while others may have been removed from a domestic realm. This may be especially the case in the middle Bronze Age where the sepulchral barrel and bucket-shaped urns are indistinguishable from those from domestic contexts. The process of burial at this time seems to have had complexities which are only recently being addressed by archaeologists. A small Collared Urn from Carneddau in mid-Wales, for example, contained only a minute amount of burnt bone. It was complete apart from a chunk out of the rim and collar, and it had been placed upside down in the pit. Despite this, it was full of soil. I find it difficult to understand how an inverted pot can be full of soil. Percolation and worm action may be responsible for some of this material, but not for completely filling it. It seems more likely to assume that the pot had previously been buried elsewhere or deliberately filled prior to its final deposition.

Burials associated with pottery are few and far between in the later Bronze Age or post-Deverel-Rimbury period (Needham 1995). A small shouldered bowl from Maidcross in Suffolk is a notable exception and furthermore is an example of a type of bowl with close metalwork affinities. Ceramics accompanying the dead are even more rare in the Iron Age. None of the rich Urnfield burials so common on the Continent are found in Britain, which has lead Cunliffe (1991) to suggest that many bodies may have been deposited in rivers: hence the presence of metalwork in similar contexts. Iron Age burials, where accompanied, tend to be associated with horse-riding equipment and personal ornaments rather than with ceramics. Only with the Belgic influences of the first century BC does pottery make a comeback into the burial record and then in often elaborate and imported forms such as large amphorae or exotic pedestalled jars and so on.

Whether accompanying a burial or not, pottery may be ritually deposited. A bowl found with a pristine polished stone axe at the causewayed enclosure of Hambledon Hill, for example, is interpreted as a discrete depositional episode rather than the disposal of rubbish. Indeed, most prehistorians would now see the deposition of artefactual material in pits as representing a deliberate act. The material may well be derived from the domestic sphere, but its deposition in such a context as a pit represents a deliberate and ritually charged act. At the large Wessex henge monument of Durrington Walls Richards and Thomas (1984) have identified differing depositional patterns amongst the differently decorated Grooved Ware placed within the timber circles and elsewhere. This they suggest may illustrate the relative importance of vessels decorated with specific motifs or schemes. If correct, this interpretation suggests that there is much more to decoration than purely aesthetics.

The site of Upper Ninepence, in the Walton Basin of east central Wales, has already been mentioned above. The pit groups containing Peterborough Ware and Grooved Ware have something in common: they were rapidly filled and contained only fragmentary pottery and/or used artefacts. In this they are typical of Neolithic pit groups. None of the vessels were reconstructable, each represented by less than a quarter of the whole. The flints had been used, often broken, and, importantly, trampled. It seems that this is discarded material that has been selected for deposition in pits. Along with the flint and food remains (burnt bone, carbonised cereal and hazelnut shells), pottery was deposited. It would appear that small 'tokens' were being deliberately removed from a domestic midden and buried in a conscious act. These pastoralist societies will have been aware of basic investment and return strategies. For one seed planted, a whole tree might grow. From one grain sown a head of corn would be produced. By 'planting' small amounts of the earth's produce (flint for tools, clay for pottery, organic material and food remains) one might be returning to the earth materials and produce that have been provided by the earth in an attempt to ensure perpetual fecundity.

The inclusions found within the fabric of pots may also have more than a simply utilitarian purpose. It has already been mentioned above that the presence of cereal grains in pottery may be deliberate rather than accidental as is usually believed. This may also have been the case where specific and often non-local rock types are used. The doloritic inclusions in middle Bronze Age mid-Wales may be connected to the use of such stone for the manufacture of battle-axes, thus imparting symbolic power or strength to the pottery. Quartz is also commonly found in ritual contexts such as in burials or in association with stone circles. It may be no coincidence that it is chosen for inclusion in Peterborough ceramics. This is especially so where there appears to have been no attempt to cover up the inclusions that erupted through the surface of the pots. It seems that the quartz was intended to be seen. The whiteness of quartz and its reflective properties, especially its ability to reflect moonlight, may have imbued it with magical significance and this power may have been transferred to the pottery in which the rock was incorporated. Crushed flint is also frequently used in prehistoric fabrics yet it is a strange choice. The razor-sharp fragments must have made potting an unpleasant and indeed painful task. One can only assume again that the choice was deliberate and more than simply practical.

Introduction. Why pots?

This aspect of manufacture is also discussed below in chapter 2. But it may be said in connection with the choice of opening materials that by far the best material to use was grog or crushed pottery. Yet this material seems to have been used comparatively rarely, and then in good-quality pottery such as Grooved Ware, Beakers, Collared Urns or Belgic fine wares. The fact that it involves the destruction and pulverising of former pots may itself be a symbolical act referencing such concepts as continuity and rebirth.

Pottery then is a complex topic of study. It is important to the study of chronology, settlement and economy, and ritual, in other words all spheres of prehistoric life. Pottery must be seen as more than a simple container and more than a utilitarian artefact. The importance of the symbolism of the pots, their decoration, their inclusions, their contents and the contexts in which they are ultimately deposited cannot be stressed enough. Pots cannot be regarded for pots' sake alone but must be seen as having played a variety of roles within contemporary society. Some of these roles are obvious, others far more subjective.

2 Aspects of manufacture and ceramic technology

'You are fifteen', said old Mitsima . . . 'Now I may teach you to work the clay.'

Squatting by the river, they worked together. 'First of all' said Mitsima, taking a lump of the wetted clay between his hands, 'we make a little moon.' The old man squeezed the lump into a disk, then bent up the edges; the moon became a shallow cup. Slowly and unskilfully he imitated the old man's delicate gestures.

'A moon, a cup and now a snake.' Mitsima rolled out a piece of clay into a long flexible cylinder, hooped it into a circle, and pressed it onto the rim of the cup. 'Then another snake. And another. And another.' Round by round, Mitsima built up the sides of the pot; it was narrow, it bulged, it narrowed again towards the neck. Mitsima squeezed and patted, stroked and scraped; and there at last it stood, in shape the familiar waterpot of Malpais, but creamy white instead of black, and still soft to the touch. The crooked parody of Mitsima's, his own stood beside it. Looking at the two pots, he had to laugh.

'But the next one will be better,' he said, and began to moisten another piece of clay.

To fashion, to give form, to feel his fingers gaining in skill and power – this gave him an extraordinary pleasure . . . They worked all day, and all day was filled with an intense, absorbing happiness.

Aldous Huxley, *Brave New World*

Introduction

Ceramic technology is the term given by archaeologists to the study of how pots are made and of those materials that were used in the manufacture of the vessels. The ceramic technologists do not necessarily concern themselves with the dating, decoration or stylistic properties of a vessel but rather focus their attention on the detailed 'physiology' of the pot, much as a surgeon would regard anatomy irrespective of his subject's age, race or appearance. However, links remain between the styles and dates of some pots and the study of their manufacture. For example, the use of the potter's wheel did not reach these shores until immediately before the Roman conquest and so wheel-throwing techniques have little direct relevance to the prehistorian. Similarly with regard to decoration, the use of a toothed comb to decorate vessels appears to have been a Beaker introduction some time in the late third millennium, before 2000 BC and comb decoration would therefore be irrelevant to the study of, for example, earlier Neolithic ceramic technology. That said, there are other aspects of technology, such as ring or coil building, burnishing and pinch potting which are encountered throughout British Prehistory and even well into the post-Roman period, and the relevance of these aspects is clearly universal in the study of prehistoric ceramics. At the outset, however, it must be stressed that, from the point of view of the pottery, the writer's main area of research is concerned with the Neolithic and Bronze Age. But nevertheless, and as mentioned above, much ceramic technology is relevant to all prehistoric periods and, indeed, often to the historic period too.

In this chapter we will look at the pots themselves, the materials from which they were made and the technology involved in altering the physical state of a vessel from clay to ceramic. The closely related topic of surface treatments, whether decorative or utilitarian or both, will be considered in chapter 3 though it is readily acknowledged that the separation of these topics is not always easy and the two are often intertwined.

Ceramics can be broadly defined as clay items, usually, but not exclusively, vessels, which have passed through the ceramic change so that when in contact with water, they will not revert to their former clay state. The ceramic change involves driving off the water of chemical composition contained in the actual clay molecules through the agency of heat. The ceramic change is usually accomplished at temperatures of around 700°C, though the precise temperature whether lower or higher, will depend on such factors as the chemical composition of the clay and the length of time over which the temperature is maintained.

Clay

Clay, the raw material of pottery, takes two basic forms, residual (or primary) and sedimentary (Gibson & Woods 1990). The residual clay is one which has not moved from its site of geological formation. In the United Kingdom, the best-known example of a residual clay is the china clay of Devon and Cornwall. The large, gleaming white waste tips resulting from the extraction of this material are familiar sights around the south-west edges of Dartmoor and elsewhere on the south-west Peninsula. These clays are generally pure. For example, they contain few naturally occurring organic inclusions. They also tend to have a large particle size. This has the effect of making these residual or primary clays less plastic and consequently generally less suitable for traditional potting than are the sedimentary clays.

This is not to deny that the properties of the china clays were unknown to prehistoric populations. Indeed, the Bronze Age inhabitants of the South-west Peninsula were certainly aware of these china clays and even exploited them. For example, in 1896, in the floor of Hut 7 at the Legis Tor settlement on Dartmoor, R.

Hansford Worth discovered a pot set within a hole in the natural subsoil or 'calm' (pronounced 'callum') as it is known locally. This pot

> had been mended in situ with china clay, by the simple expedient of taking a kneaded mass of that material and pressing it into the bottom of the pot as it stood in the hole. The broken bottom was supported by the ground in which the pot had been sunk, and thus the leaks could be staunched by this internal application of puddle. The mend was made with raw clay and there was nothing in the operation which partook of the nature of pottery manufacture. It is interesting as showing that the hut dwellers were acquainted with china clay, and their failure to use it in the manufacture of pottery was thus a matter of deliberate choice. (Worth 1967, 122)

The clay had obviously been smeared around the inside of the pot while it was set in the ground as Worth thought that the pot was round-based: it probably seemed so from the inside. Conservation of this vessel, however, has demonstrated it to be a flat-based pot of the Trevisker series of the Bronze Age.

Despite this exploitation of the China clay, no evidence has been found to suggest that it was ever used for potting in prehistory. Indeed Worth, in discussing the clays of the prehistoric pottery found on Dartmoor, also observed that 'China clay lacks the necessary plasticity and cohesion for the manufacture of objects as large as the cooking pots, of such thickness, and painfully made by hand moulding.' (By this Worth meant hand-building rather than moulding in the modern sense.)

Sedimentary clays, on the other hand, are clays that have been transported from their original place of formation by geological action such as water, wind or glacial action. As a result of this transportation, they have become broken down, mixed with other non-clay materials and they are therefore correspondingly less pure than are the primary clays. These impurities make these clays easier to manipulate and also mean that they are better suited to the rigours of open firing which will be discussed below. Therefore it is these clays that were widely exploited by prehistoric potters.

Inclusions

Once it has been extracted, or dug out from its source, sedimentary clay can generally be worked with comparatively little preparation to a sufficient standard to allow potting to begin. If the clay is too coarse and contains large non-clay materials such as pebbles, then these excessive naturally occurring inclusions may be easily removed. If, on the other hand, the clay is too fine and the naturally occurring non-clay inclusions are either sparse or of a fine particle size, then other inclusions may be deliberately added. This latter scenario is frequently the case with prehistoric pottery and it is these non-clay inclusions which often give much prehistoric pottery its coarse and crude appearance. These inclusions can vary in size from less than 1mm to over a centimetre across.

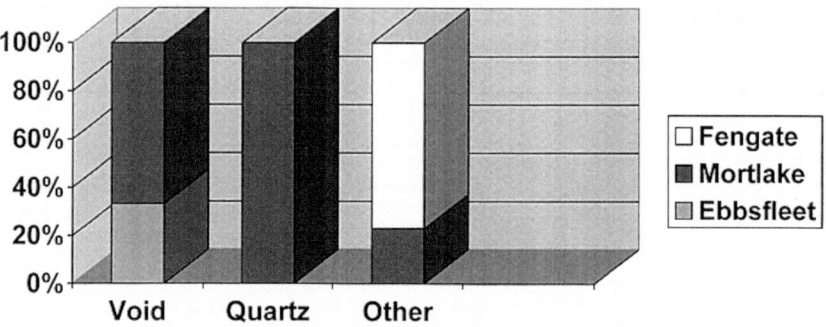

11 *Diagram showing the frequency of quartz as an opening agent in Welsh Peterborough Ware*

Ann Woods (Gibson & Woods 1990) has outlined the two main types of inclusion found in ceramics, particularly prehistoric ceramics. The first type is the *naturally occurring inclusions*, those are the non-clay particles which are found naturally in the clay. The second type is the *deliberately added inclusions* or material intentionally added by the potter during the working of the clay. Woods has also outlined how these two types may be recognised and distinguished from each other in thin section. The former tend to be more rounded in profile having suffered from natural abrasion, while the latter tend to be more angular as they have often been ground or crushed specifically for the purpose. The naturally occurring inclusions are most useful for determining the provenance of a clay because they are naturally present in the clay material and may reflect the original and ultimate geology of the clay source. By contrast, any material, local or foreign, may be deliberately selected for addition to the clay and may not necessarily reflect the geology of the place of manufacture. In the middle Neolithic Peterborough Wares of Wales and the Marches, for example, crushed quartz seems to have been deliberately chosen (**11**).

Nevertheless, the deliberately added inclusions may be interesting in their own right, particularly from the point of view of the choice of material used. Basically, any non-clay material may be added to the clay and will have the effect of reducing plasticity and making it easier to work and fashion; however some inclusions are better suited than others. The most suitable is grog, crushed pottery, which has already gone through the ceramic change and which also absorbs some of the water from the clay being worked (**12**). Hard igneous rocks are also suitable and seem to have been deliberately selected in parts of Wales and elsewhere. In Anglesey, for example, a study of the deliberately added and naturally occurring inclusions has indicated that most of the Bronze Age urns were made from local clays, but that there was a great deal of selection being exercised in the choice of the deliberately added inclusions (Williams & Jenkins 1999).

Organic inclusions may also be naturally occurring or deliberately added. In sedimentary clays, decaying organics will be incorporated into the clay build-up and other, smaller material such as microscopic organisms like diatoms may also find their way into the clay, particularly if it is formed from lake sediments. The silica skeletons of these diatoms survive firing and since they are often sensitive to such things as temperature, the rate of flow of water, acidity and salinity, they may be extracted from the

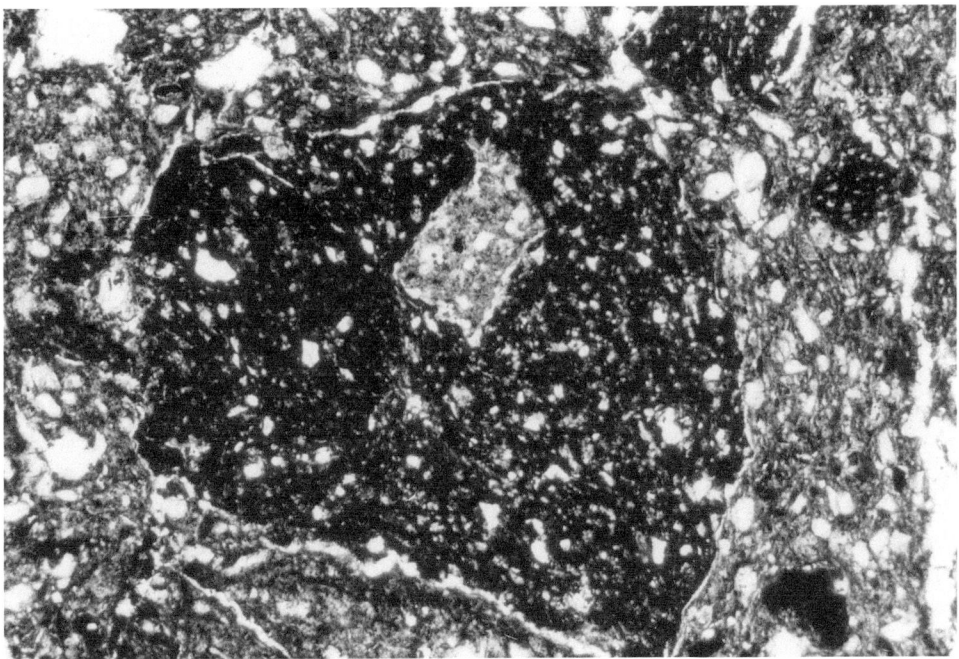

12 Bronze Age recycling. This photomicrograph of a fragment of Bronze Age pottery from Skendleby (Lincolnshire) shows a large, dark grog fragment within which is a smaller, lighter coloured piece. Photo courtesy of Ann Woods

pot and studied to provide a climatic picture of the clay source as well as a diatom 'fingerprint' for the clay. This fingerprint can sometimes be used to match pottery to a clay source. Materials such as grass or chaff may also be deliberately added to the clay to open the clay and bind it. However this material often has a high moisture content which may cause problems in the firing. Occasionally, carbonised seeds or grain may be found within the fabric of pottery. These tend to occur as isolated examples and are generally interpreted as accidental inclusions resulting from the manufacture of the pot in a domestic agrarian environment. In a Food Vessel of the early Bronze Age from Wether Hill in Northumberland, however, some dozen or so grain impressions have been found both in the surfaces and within the thickness of the fabric of the pot. This suggests that in this case, grain may have been intentionally selected amongst the deliberately added inclusions (**colour plate 3**)

At first sight, these inclusions may be considered to be a mixed blessing. While they certainly can strengthen the wet clay and undoubtedly facilitate the formation of the pot, when the vessel is fired they most likely have a weakening effect on the vessel walls and cracks can often be seen emanating from inclusions in pot surfaces. In some instances, the eruption of these inclusions through a vessel's surface might be considered as having an adverse effect on the 'finish' of the pot. However the inclusions are essential for the successful firing of prehistoric ceramics. Firstly they allow the water of plasticity (the water which lubricates the clay particles allowing the clay to be compressed and stretched) to escape during drying. Secondly, during firing, they provide escape corridors at their junctions with the clay body for the water of chemical composition (see below) to escape as steam. Accordingly, Woods has recommended that these fillers be termed 'opening materials' since this best describes their function (Gibson & Woods 1990, 29-30), and that distinction be made between deliberately added and naturally occurring opening materials. Unfortunately this plea had been largely ignored by 'archaeo-ceramicists' and less specific terms such as 'temper', 'filler', 'backing' and even 'grits' continue to be used with no distinction between natural and deliberately added elements.

As mentioned above, the deliberately added opening materials, while not necessarily of much use for provenance studies, can often be interesting in their own right. Flint, for example, is frequently added to clay (**13**) particularly in southern Britain, yet is not really a best-suited substance since, like the clay, it contains water of chemical composition. This molecular water, on contact with fire, can turn to steam, expand and explode with potentially devastating results. I have personally seen a piece of heated flint spall and shoot out of the fire like a piece of shrapnel. It landed some 3m from the bonfire. If this flint had been inside a pot, the vessel would not have survived and, furthermore, the force of the explosion may have damaged the pots next to it. It is possible that calcined flint may have been used though this was not always the case. This is flint which has already been burnt to force out the water of chemical composition. It is also more easily crushed. So far so good, but it is still a wonder why this material is used at all because crushed flint, whether burnt or not, can often have razor sharp edges and must have presented prehistoric potters with painful experiences. We have not yet detected traces of blood in the clay but lacerations must have occurred when the flint was being added to the clay and when the vessel was being formed.

Quartz also contains water of chemical composition, albeit in small quantities, and can spall (or explode) when heated. It can also cause dunting, that is cracking caused when a vessel cools too quickly, because heated quartz is quick to expand and contract. Yet this also seems to have been deliberately chosen, particularly by the Peterborough Ware potters of Wales and the Marches (Gibson 1995a). However, quartz also occurs at ritual sites of the Neolithic and Bronze Age where its reflective qualities are thought to have given it some special (magical?) significance. Could this be the reason for its selection in Peterborough Ware? Perhaps in such cases the rock can be seen as giving an added symbolism to the vessel in which it is contained. This hypothesis may be supported by the observation that in many cases, no attempt has been made to 'hide' these inclusions. They break both the inner and outer surfaces to such a degree that it would appear that they were intended to be visible. From this it can be assumed that the use of quartz inclusions was a phenomenon worth broadcasting and that the significance of this act would be readily recognised and understood by both the potters and other members of the community.

A similar argument has been proposed for the selection of dolerite in the Bronze Age Cordoned Urn pottery from Glanfeinion, Powys (Gibson in Britnell *et al.* 1997). At this site in the upper Severn Valley of mid-Wales, doloritic and rhyolitic inclusions were added to the vessels made from a local clay in which dolerite they were not naturally occurring, and in an area where these two rocks could only have been

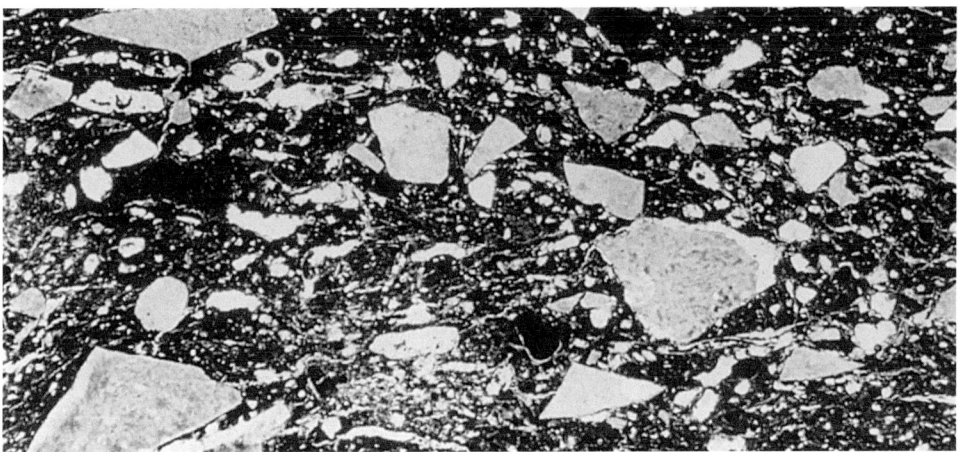

13 *Photomicrograph of flint inclusions in thin section. Note the sharp, angular profile of the fragments.* Courtesy of Ann Woods

found as rare river pebbles. This once again illustrates an element of the deliberate selection of opening materials. In this case the material selected is better known for its use in the manufacture of stone battle-axes which are broadly contemporary with this type of pottery. Are these opening materials derived from broken axes, from axe fragments or even from the waste from axe manufacture, each or all of which may have been gathered together and crushed for use in potting with the symbolism of the rock giving a greater significance (or perceived 'strength') to the ceramics? This explanation is clearly hypothetical and requires further study but the deliberate selection of specific materials for use as an opening agent is a phenomenon that is becoming increasingly recognised amongst prehistorians (Cleal *et al.* 1994; Williams & Jenkins 1999).

Manufacture

Once the clay has been prepared, the pot can be fashioned. This takes skill as observed in the opening quotation to this chapter, but it is a skill that can be easily learned through practice. There seems to be no evidence of experimentation in prehistory, no inception phase, though certainly some pots are better made than others and therefore demonstrate that some craftsmen were more skilled than others. At the beginning of the Bronze Age, the first metal artefacts, whether gold or copper, are small trinkets such as awls, simple jewellery and small blades. These artefacts are suggestive of an experimental phase at a time when the technology was new and the resource scarce. This does not happen with ceramics. There is no experimental phase at the beginning of the Neolithic. Instead, ceramics arrive in the archaeological record as a fully evolved technology comprising large and well-finished pots.

Why should this be? It could be that the necessary technology was introduced widely from Europe where it had been used for centuries. Equally likely, however, is that the resource, clay, was not such a rare commodity as was metal in the later period. Therefore larger artefacts could be made at the outset, and 'wonky' or 'sub-standard' pots, could simply be squashed up, the clay recycled, and thus the student could try again. There was no need to fire, and thus ensure the survival of, practice pieces. Firing was after all an expensive process involving the use of dry fuel. Nevertheless it would take as much fuel to fire a handful of small pots as it would to fire one and firing first attempts can be a way of encouraging beginners. Students on prehistoric ceramic courses, from school children to retired people, many of whom have had no previous potting experience, often end up with a sizeable collection of ashtrays, peanut dishes and even small figurines and animals. These constitute the repertoire of inexperience (**colour plate 4**). They represent experiment as each student literally and figuratively gets to grips with what is to them a new medium. This stage of the potting and learning process is not visible archaeologically, perhaps because these pieces were never fired. We do, however, have small pinched pots from all periods in prehistory, and while some of these are quite accomplished, others are not and may well represent the first works of a new potter.

Are we seeing (or, more correctly, *not* seeing) more taboo here? Given the transformative processes involved in making and firing pottery and the expense of the fuel needed to reach and maintain the necessary temperature, perhaps so much ritual was involved in the manufacture of pottery that substandard pieces were forbidden from the flames. Perhaps, whether due to the incorrect amount of opening agents or some other likely manufacturing flaw, apprentice pieces were left out of the fire and this practical precaution took on some ritual or traditional taboo. Likewise, many of the Jewish laws (especially those governing the preparation of food) derive from the purely practical considerations of early peoples living in a hot climate.

Once again we are dealing with hypothesis, but certainly we do not have the same extensive collection of 'ashtrays' and animals in the archaeological record that we do in basic ceramics classes. New generations of potters would have had to be trained, but we see no evidence for this. Perhaps potters only 'came of age' when they could demonstrate competence and the firing of their first work was a rite of passage.

Prehistoric pottery was hand built. This is not the same as 'hand made'. Wheel-thrown pottery is also hand made but not hand built. Hand building refers to the fact that the vessel is built up using sections or rings or coils, rather than centrifugally formed, drawn up from a lump of clay. Pinching was a technique certainly used by prehistoric potters. This is the simplest of all forms of pot building and involves the squeezing out of a small vessel from a ball of clay using the thumb and fingers. Initially small pots result (**14**), rarely deeper than the length of the potter's fingers. However, more complex forms can result from pinched pots by using secondary forming techniques such as paddle and anvil. This method involves the use of a flat paddle such as a piece of smooth wood, and a hard object such as a smooth stone. These are then used to beat the walls out into a bulbous form by hitting the outside of the pot with the paddle against the anvil which is held against the inner surface. Pinched pots may also be used as the bases for larger vessels employing a combination of two or more construction techniques. For example, a pinched pot may be used as the lower part of a vessel to which rings or straps of clay may be added to create extra height. Despite the apparent crudeness of this technique,

Aspects of manufacture and ceramic technology

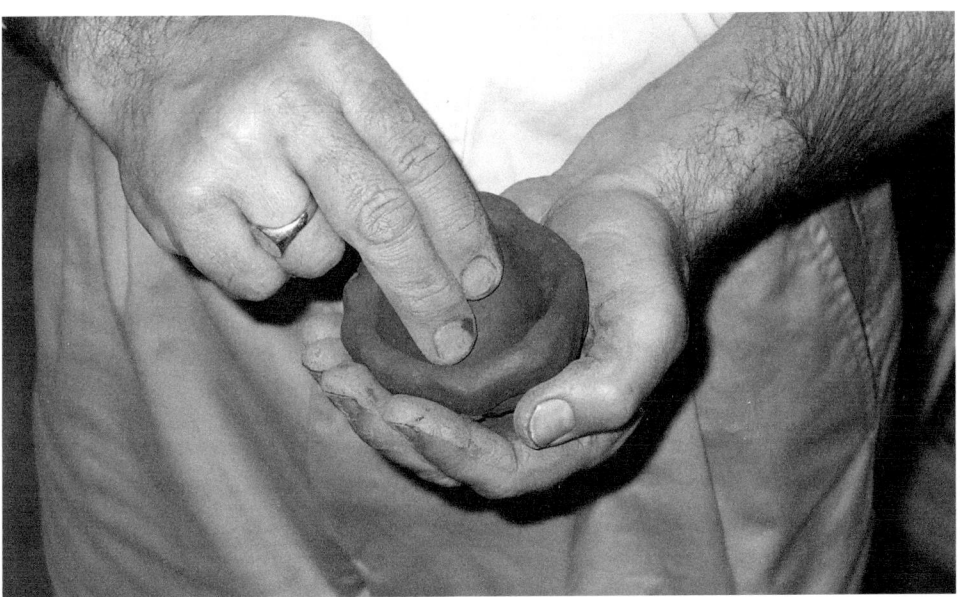

14 *Pinching out a pot. The finished 'cup' can then be used as a base for larger vessels*

pinching, when executed by a skilled and competent craftsman, can be difficult to identify and the small size of a pot alone should not be regarded as necessarily diagnostic.

The most common techniques used in British and Irish prehistory are ring building or coil building (**15**). The two techniques involve building up the pot walls in layers with elongated cylinders of clay. These are the 'snakes' of old Mitsima in Huxley's text quoted at the start of this chapter. The two techniques differ in that coil building comprises the addition of clay in a spiral arrangement while ring building consists of adding 'doughnuts' of clay in distinct layers. It is often impossible to differentiate between these two closely related techniques in archaeological material and 'ring building' is often used inaccurately to refer to either method. Strap building is a variation on this theme (**15**) and differs from ring building proper in that the cylinders of clay are flattened into straps prior to being added to the pot. This has the advantage of giving rapid height to the vessel using comparatively few layers. Strap building can sometimes be detected in prehistoric ceramics by examining the breaks within a vessel wall. Given the similarity of these techniques, ring building is used here as a shorthand term to embrace all three methods.

The joins between rings, coils or straps present obvious points of weakness in the vessel walls especially in cases where, perhaps, the rings have been too dry and have not been properly bonded. Vessels frequently break along these weak points and result in characteristically round edged sherds, often called 'false rims' because they may often look similar to simple rounded rims and, indeed, have often been mistaken for rim sherds in some of the archaeological literature (**16**). The need to ensure that rings of clay were properly bonded was a problem that was clearly understood by prehistoric potters who often went to great lengths to try and ensure

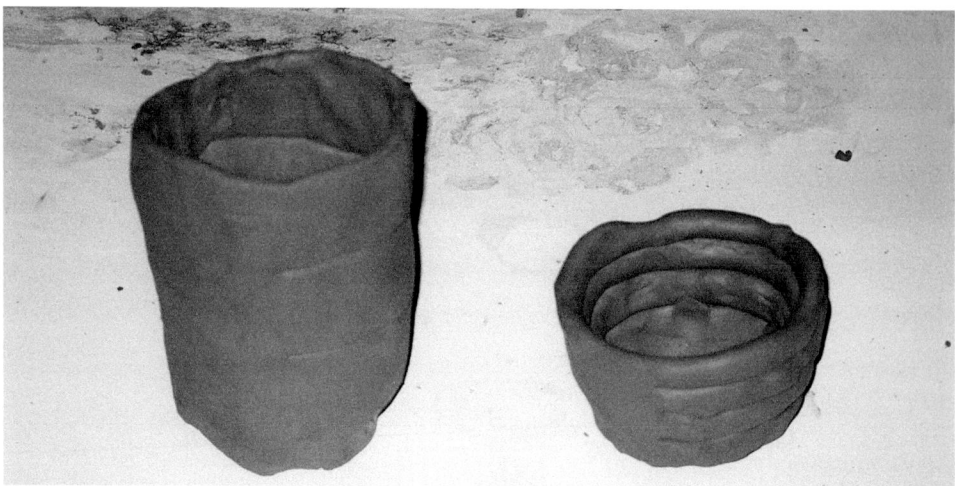

15 *The related techniques of ring building (right) and strap building (left). Notice the height difference despite only three rings being used in each vessel*

that the clay rings were properly joined. Sometimes, in order to provide a greater surface area for bonding one ring to another, they joined them at an angle – diagonal bonding – by fixing one layer to the inside edge of the other and smoothing the two together. In some instances even a form of tongue and groove jointing has been detected between coils, again to increase the surface areas to be joined. Traces of the imperfectly bonded rings can often be seen in the fabric of sherds and study of these may give insights into the method of manufacture. For example the direction of joins may change midway up the height of a vessel suggesting that it may have been made in two sections which were subsequently joined together. This has been noted, for example, in a Beaker from the settlement site at Northton on the Isle of Harris (**17**) and it has recently been assumed from the irregular shapes of some Neolithic Ronaldsway pottery from the Isle of Man (Burrow 1999).

Moulding and slab construction are other manufacturing techniques that are difficult to detect in a finished product. The former involves moulding the clay while still plastic around a template. It is not suited to vessels with abrupt changes in direction, though it may have been used for simple round-based bowls. Like pinching, however, a moulded pot may form the basis for a vessel finished in another technique. Slab building is in effect pottery prefabrication in that pre-formed slabs of clay are joined together to form a whole. Again this is difficult to identify and there is no unequivocal evidence for the use of this technique in British prehistoric pottery.

All these techniques, when practised by competent potters, may produce pots of excellent quality and so well finished that they exhibit few if any traits of their method of manufacture. They may also be supplemented by secondary forming techniques such as the use of a paddle (or beater) and anvil. Here, as described above, the vessel walls may be beaten externally with a wooden paddle against a hard object (anvil) such as a stone held on the inner surface. This further thins, expands and bonds the clay rings and can turn a straight walled vessel into a bulbous one.

Aspects of manufacture and ceramic technology

16 *Early Bronze Age Food Vessel from Northumberland clearly showing the rounded break typical of poorly bonded rings or straps*

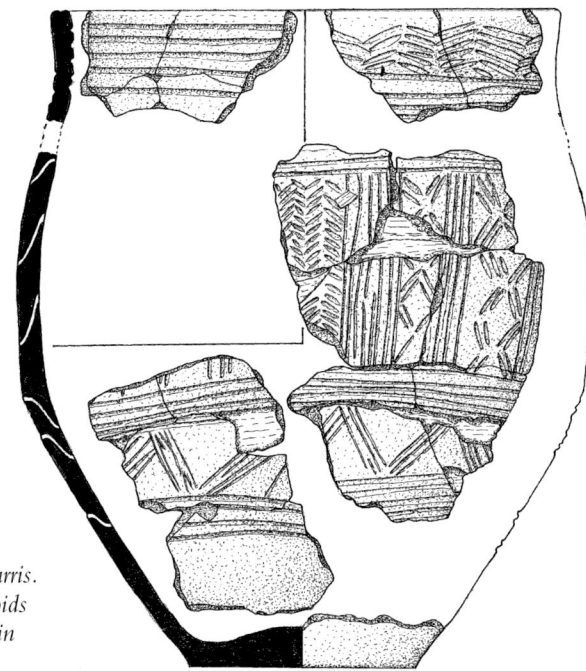

17 *Beaker vessel from Northon, Harris. The differing directions of the join voids clearly show that this pot was made in two directions*

Firing

Mention has already been made above of the two types of water found in clay: the water of plasticity and the water of chemical composition. Both have to be driven off before clay becomes ceramic and this is achieved by heating.

The water of plasticity, as the name suggests, is the water that makes clay plastic. It lubricates the clay particles, allowing them to slide over each other. It is this water that gives clay its 'squishiness' and allows it to become malleable. This water will largely evaporate if clay is left in the open air or placed near to a heat source such as a fire. This causes the clay particles to come into contact with one another and the clay appears to harden by becoming stiff and unworkable. The evaporation of this water can often be detected visually as it will generally cause the clay to lighten in colour. This will tend not to happen uniformly over the surface of the pot, but rather will be inclined to be patchy as the thinner parts of the pot such as the rim dry out first. This is called the leather hard stage of drying when the clay of the pot has dried naturally and it becomes difficult or impossible to alter the shape of the vessel. Tensions within the pot caused by the evaporation of this water may cause the pot to crack and, if dropped, it will break into fragments. However, despite appearances, this drying does not really alter the physical state of the clay since it will still absorb water and, if sufficient moisture is added, will regain its 'squishiness' or plasticity. A vessel formed and allowed to dry in this way, therefore, is not ceramic and would be useless for holding liquids or even for use in a damp environment.

The second type of water found in clay is the water of chemical composition and is the molecular water found within the chemical structure of the clay particles. H_2O, the chemical formula for water, can, for example, be seen clearly in the chemical formula for kaolinite, one of the purest clay minerals ($Al_2O_3 2SiO_2 2H_2O$). This water is chemically bound within the molecular structure of the clay and will not evaporate. It needs intense heat to break the chemical bond and convert this water to steam. Once this has been achieved, however, the clay particles have been chemically altered, they will not re-absorb water, and the pot will retain its shape, even when thoroughly wet. This stage is usually achieved when a temperature in excess of 600°C (usually 700-800°C) is reached throughout the thickness of the vessel. This stage is critical in the manufacturing process since the water of chemical composition expands, is released from the molecular structure and escapes as steam. If it is unable to escape through voids in the fabric, then it will cause the pot to spall or explode. This process may be violent and one pot may explode with such force that it damages others in the kiln or fire. It is for this reason that the opening materials are so important. Not only do they sometimes improve the plasticity of the pot during forming, but they also form microscopic voids at their junctions with the clay thus providing escape routes for this converted steam.

Despite the use in the archaeological literature of the terms 'kiln' and 'clamp', there is no evidence for the use of either structure in the Neolithic or Bronze Age. The former implies a built structure in which to control the firing environment while the latter is a temporary structure used for the firing of bricks (Peacock 1982).

Neolithic and Bronze Age pottery appears to have been open-fired in bonfires or in pits, with no or little control of the firing environment.

Once the vessel has been formed, the clay is dried to let excessive water evaporate. It is impossible in a climate such as ours to dry clay completely without the use of heat since the hygroscopic nature of clay (its ability to absorb water) will naturally be affected by the dampness of the ambient atmosphere. Instead, a low heat can be used. This will raise the temperature of the clay to 100°C and effectively boil off the water of plasticity – the water lubricant between the clay particles. This process is known as the water-smoking stage and is usually preparatory to or part of the firing process itself. It can be a crucial stage of firing for if the water is dried off too rapidly, it can turn to steam, expand and, being unable to find a sufficiently large escape corridor, can blow up and damage or destroy the vessel (see below and **colour plate 7**). Even after this water has been driven off, however, and despite the apparent dryness and hardness of the pot, the vessel will still reabsorb water and, if wetted sufficiently, the clay will revert to its plastic state since it has not passed through the ceramic change (see above). This is only achieved when the pot has been fired.

British and Irish prehistoric pottery was open-fired either in a bonfire or a pit. By their very nature, bonfires and pits leave little trace in the archaeological record, particularly if the area has been ploughed. Even where pits do survive, the excavation of an experimental pit-firing site at Leicester University showed that, despite repeated use, the heat affects on the sides of the pit were minimal (Gibson 1986) although temperatures of 800°C were recorded during the experiments (**18**). Indeed, the excavation of this pit proved interesting in other ways since the only finds recovered comprised two small sherds of pottery, charcoal, ash, some tin foil from a baked potato and the plastic top from a very cheap bottle of wine. The pot sherd bore no tell-tale characteristics to suggest that it was a casualty of the firing, only our records of the experiments documented this fact. Translating this evidence to prehistory, many Neolithic and Bronze Age pits contain just this sort of material: charcoal, a few scraps of pottery and other apparently domestic detritus. A re-examination of some of these pits may provide us with some evidence for prehistoric firing sites. Until then, the evidence for the firing of pots has to come from the vessels themselves.

Some prehistoric ceramics, when first unearthed, have a consistency that has often been described as similar to wet cardboard. The surfaces are recognisable, but the body of the fabric is often quite soft. This is indicative of imperfect firing: the surfaces of the vessel have gone through the ceramic change but the firing has not been hot or long enough to affect sufficiently the fabric core. Subsequently the outer surfaces are ceramic but the vessel core has reverted to its former plastic state. This suggests a short firing period where the maximum temperature of the fire has not been maintained. Short firing times are typical of open fires (**19**) where the firing atmosphere cannot be controlled.

Where firing has been completed successfully and the pot is completely ceramic, the fabric may, nevertheless, frequently have a black core in contrast to its pink or brown surfaces (**colour plate 5**). This colour difference is also indicative of short term firing and results from the incomplete combustion of the organic materials

Aspects of manufacture and ceramic technology

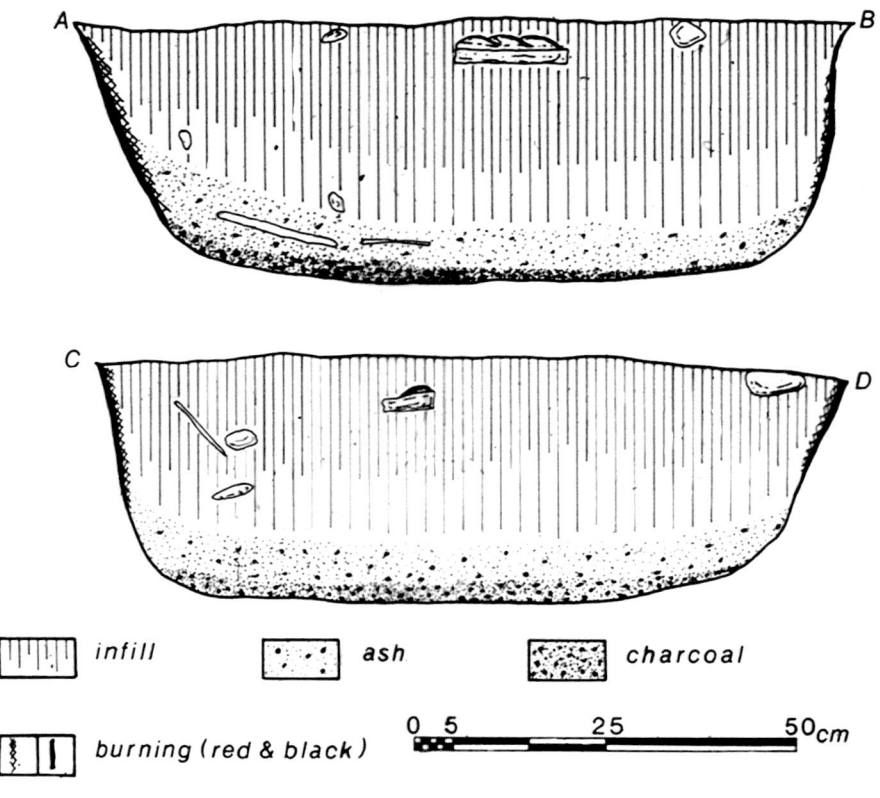

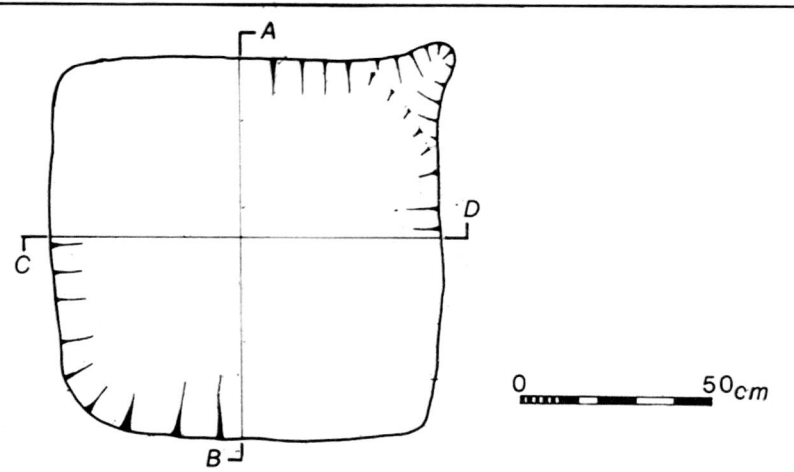

18 Sections through the experimental firing pit at Leicester

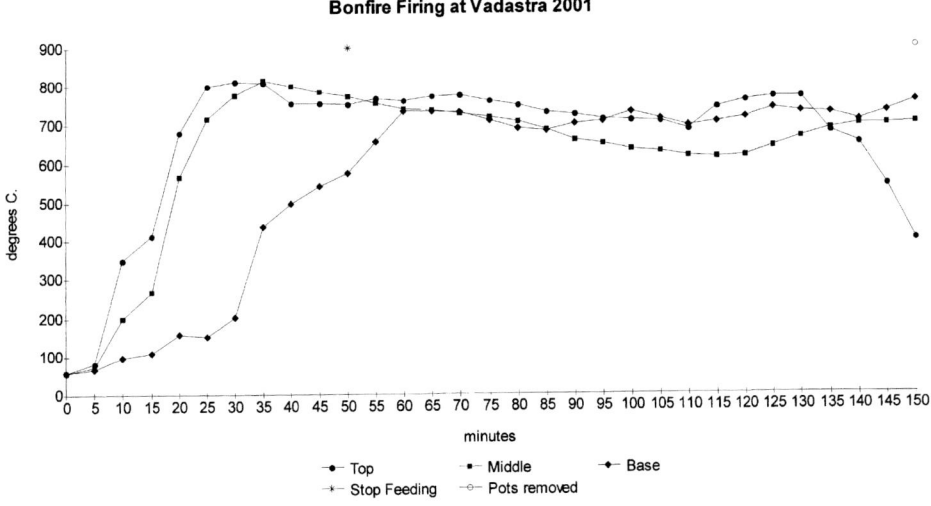

19 *Typical firing graph from an open firing at Vadastra in southern Romania. Despite the rapid temperature rise and the brevity of the fire, all pots were ceramic and there were no casualties*

naturally occurring in the clay. Were the vessel to have been heated for longer at the maximum temperature, this material would have been completely burnt out and the section of the pot would have a fairly uniform colouration. In some of the archaeological literature, this effect is frequently described as 'having a reduced core' but this is incorrect and shows an ignorance of the firing processes.

Prehistoric pottery frequently has a patchy or blotchy coloured surface and anyone who has undertaken pottery analysis knows that, when trying to match sherds to vessels, colour can be an unreliable criterion. This is due to the variability of the firing atmosphere, that is the heat and gases that together constitute the atmosphere within the fire itself (**colour plate 6**). This is difficult to control in rapid open firings and such variables as a gusty wind, the relative dryness or dampness of the fuel or even the type of fuel are all factors that will affect the firing atmosphere. An open fire such as a bonfire will draw in oxygen from the air and thus the pottery will be fired in an oxidising environment. Fully oxidised ceramics tend to be various shades of pink or brown. Some areas of the pot surface may, however, be dark or black and these black patches are known as fire clouds (**20**). Fire clouds are usually the result of sooting whereby carbonaceous matter is absorbed into the surface of the pot as a result of it being in contact with a flame or smoking ember.

Occasionally, the black area may be an area of reduction. This is caused by firing a pot in an anaerobic, or oxygen-starved, atmosphere where carbon monoxide is produced. This carbon monoxide will absorb oxygen from the ferrous oxides in the clay resulting in a darker surface colour. It is, however, virtually impossible to create a reducing environment in an open fire due to the difficulties of controlling the firing atmosphere. Even firing one vessel inside another upturned pot rarely achieves

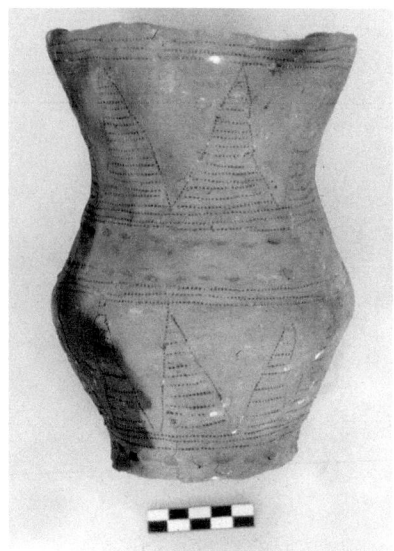

20 Black patchy surface of an experimental open-fired pot

complete reduction. Areas of pots may, however, be reduced if, for example, they have been starved of oxygen by being buried in ash or by some other locational accident within the fire.

Some prehistoric vessels exhibit spalling, which is a sign that the water content of the clay has escaped violently. These spalls frequently take the form of discs of clay that have blown off the vessel wall, often with some violence. In some experimental firings, spalls have exploded with such force that they have travelled through the air, often leaving a smoking trail, and landed several metres from the centre of the hearth. Such violent spalling can also damage other pots within the fire. Sometimes spalling can be catastrophic causing the whole vessel to collapse (**colour plate 7**). At other times spalls may only affect the surface of the pot in which case the vessel may still have been usable, almost as a 'second'. Such spalls have been noted in Neolithic assemblages as, *inter alia*, the material from Eilean Domhnuill, Uist and Allt Chrisal, Barra (Gibson 1995b) (**21**).

Dunting is also a product of an unsuccessful firing, being the cracking of a vessel wall caused when the vessel cools too quickly and resulting from the change in volume of free silica within the clay as it cools. Traces of dunting may be difficult to detect in sherd material as it is almost impossible to differentiate between breakages and true dunting cracks proper. Nevertheless, the occurrence of repair holes in prehistoric ceramics may well result from an attempt to bind together dunting cracks since, as in spalling, the damage to the vessel need not be complete and mild dunting does not necessarily render the vessel useless.

Conclusion

Technologically, the manufacture of pottery is quite a simple process once the arts of fashioning and firing the pot have been mastered. Local sedimentary clays are

Aspects of manufacture and ceramic technology

21 *Spalled early Neolithic pot from Eilean Domhnuill.* Courtesy of Alison Sheridan. Reproduced by courtesy of the Trustees of the National Museums of Scotland

usually perfectly adequate for the manufacture of prehistoric pottery and, where provenancing studies have been undertaken, the results tend to show local manufacture. In the majority of instances, particularly in the Neolithic and Bronze Age, with a few notable exceptions, there is little evidence for the industrialised manufacture of pottery; it seems rather to have been made as and when it was needed (Williams & Jenkins 1999). Indeed, with notable exceptions such as the Hembury Ware of the Neolithic and perhaps the Trevisker Wares of the Bronze Age, it is not until the Iron Age that we see pottery manufacture as in any way industrial (by industrial in this context I mean large-scale commercial manufacture). Similarly, in the Neolithic and Bronze Age, works of individual potters are difficult to identify, arguing against the suggestion that 'professional' potters may have been at work. This may be unsurprising given the relatively small amounts of pottery we have for study. Our museums and repositories must hold a mere fraction of the original output. But despite this, on rare occasions the work of a single hand can be detected surviving from this remote period. These are dealt with under decoration in chapter 3.

Evidence for the manufacture of earlier prehistoric ceramics generally comes from the vessels themselves, both as technological indicators in the fabric of vessels and as tell-tale traces of the firing process. Unfortunately many of these traces are misinterpreted in much of the archaeological literature and archaeologists should be encouraged to strive towards a better comprehension of ceramic processes and avoid the use of inappropriate terminology in their descriptions of the material. A better understanding of the manufacturing techniques, the limitations and properties of the natural resource and the processes involved in firing may all be combined to present a fuller picture of this aspect of prehistoric technology.

The above account presents the firing process in a rather detached way. It is an attempt at a factual description and hopes to outline the methods and processes involved in the manufacture of prehistoric ceramics as well as highlighting the possible pitfalls. What it does not do is convey the human aspects of pot firing. The stages involved in the manufacture of pottery are learned skills, passed on through tuition and experience. The process is a transformative one. It involves the skilled fashioning of a formless material and the transformation of that material into a new permanent state by an irreversible chemical process effected through a control of fire; a knowledge of pyro-technology.

Prehistoric populations cannot have known about the oxidisation or reduction of iron oxides or the processes involved in driving off the water of chemical composition. They would have known what to do, how to do it and how to obtain the desired effects but the chemistry could not have been understood. Consequently pottery may have had a magical facet and the potters may well have had a suitable status within the community. They may have been respected as people capable of successfully effecting the transformation. They may have been regarded as people who knew the fire, knew how to exploit and control it and as people who had powers over the clay they worked. We do not know who made pottery in prehistory. Was it restricted to a specific sex? When did apprenticeships start? Did communities have their own potters or did potters travel around communities serving local and immediate needs? A fingertip impression from a Peterborough ware vessel from London shows a small, well-formed finger and nail (**colour plate 8**). The smallness of the finger has been taken to imply that the work was that of a woman or adolescent but this is highly subjective and at any rate the impression is probably around 10% smaller than when it was made due to the shrinkage of the clay during the drying process. It must be readily admitted, however, that ethnographic parallels do tend to suggest that potting was generally a female activity, but there are sufficient instances of male dominated potting industries to preclude generalisation. We are left with abundant artefacts but only the briefest glimpses of the people responsible for them.

3 Decoration and surface treatments

The surfaces of vessels can be altered in a variety of ways and for a variety of reasons. They can be slipped, painted, polished, carry incised markings or impressed designs or have clay strips or pellets raised from or applied to the surface; this latter technique is usually labelled plastic decoration because of its moulded nature. Though these devices are generally described under the label of 'decoration' in many pottery reports, their original intention may have been functional rather than decorative. For that reason, Ann Woods has recommended that the term 'surface treatments' should really be used as this accurately describes what has happened, the surface has been treated in some way, without the prejudice towards the ornamental which the word 'decoration' implies.

However, notwithstanding this observation, prehistoric pottery need not necessarily be purely a utilitarian object. It need not simply be a plain bowl of low esteem made specifically for a mundane domestic task. Indeed, evidence from the manufacture, decoration and deposition of pottery suggests the contrary. Even today, people may have, locked away in their display cabinets, ceramics which, even if modern rather than antique, they have no intention of using in a functional sense. The purpose of these ceramics is that of display. They might communicate opulence, demonstrate an appreciation of finery, possess antique value, commemorate events or even have attained prestige from the shared histories they accumulate, that is, what we now call 'sentimental value'. How often have we heard the phrase, particularly by the unfortunate victims of burglary, 'it's not really worth much but it belonged to my grandmother'? This statement is a paradox. The hypothetical object obviously *is* worth a great deal to its current owner in terms of family history and identity. It forms a tangible link with the past, it is a token of lineage, and in an archaeological context, would be seen as providing a link to the realm of the ancestors. Therefore, despite the apparent cheapness of its manufacture and low 'wealth value' the object is clearly invaluable and irreplaceable. Its theft has taken much more from its owners than the object alone. Thus in prehistory, ostensibly poor or simple pots may have a greater significance than their appearance suggests. Equally the lengths taken to decorate some ceramics might reasonably be interpreted as evidence of their elevation above the mundane. Some Beakers, for example, decorated with complex geometric patterns impressed using the multiple and repeated applications of a toothed comb, may have taken longer to decorate than to build (**22**).

Not all decoration, however, need be purely for adornment. Rather, the patterns generated and the techniques used, or the combinations of both, may have had a deeper meaning to the users and/or craftsmen. This is difficult to prove, but the decoration we regard as indicative of 'local styles' may possibly be peculiar to local populations. They may reflect a particular group identity. This may be easier

Decoration and surface treatments

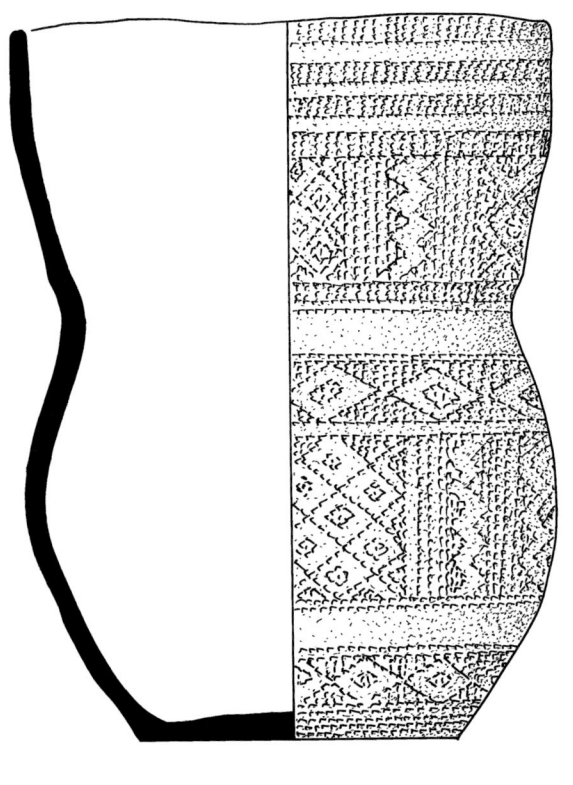

22 Highly decorated Beaker from Erriswell, Suffolk. This ornate Beaker probably took longer to decorate than it did to make. After Clarke 1970

23 *(Below)* The distribution of Durotrigian pots in relation to tribal areas. The pots are from Hengistbury Head, Dorset. *Scale 1:4.* Source: Cunliffe 1991

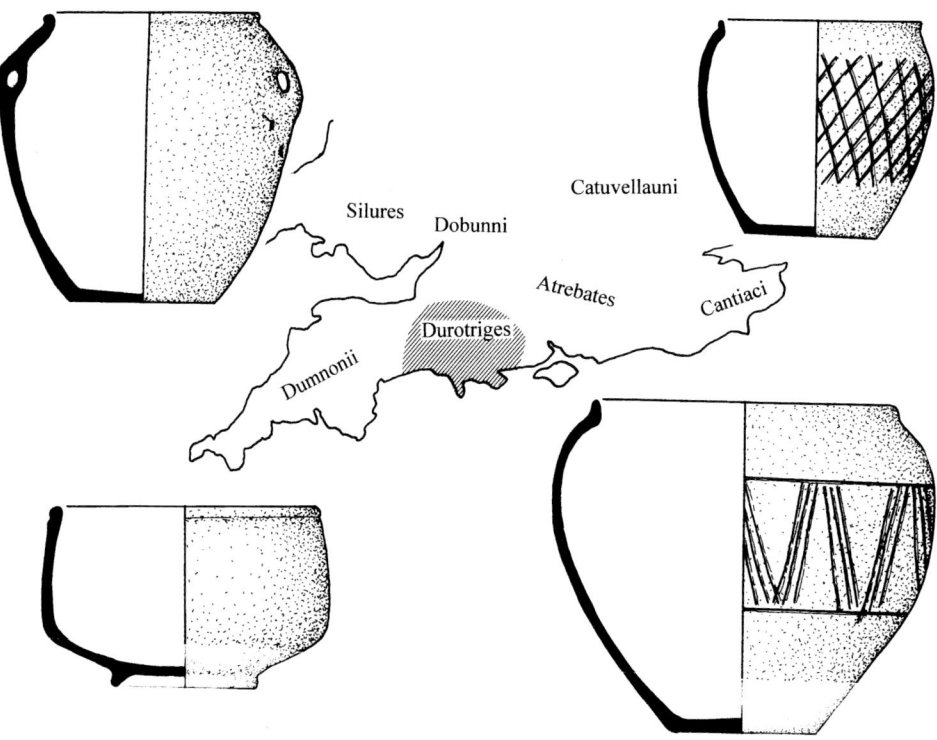

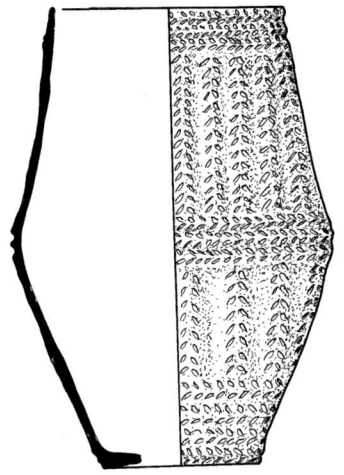 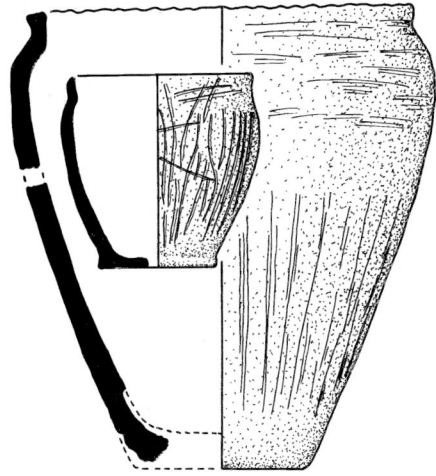

24 *Left: fingernail rusticated Beaker from Butley, Essex. After Clarke 1970. Right: Iron Age scratched pot from Breedon-on-the-Hill, Leicestershire. After Cunliffe 1991. Both techniques roughen the surfaces to facilitate handling. Scale 1:6*

to ascertain in the later Iron Age by which time a recognisable, and later documented, tribal system had been established with distinctive pottery styles peculiar to each. An example of this may be the Durotrigian Wares of Dorset (**23**). This highlights the cultural aspect of pottery whereby an artefact of a particular style and/or form is used to convey cultural identity to a specific population. College scarves, football paraphernalia and the Scottish tartans may all be modern examples of this. For example, while it is accepted that the modern tartan system is largely a nineteenth-century reinvention of tradition, nevertheless, the distinct patterns and colour combinations within a rectangular framework serve to identify clans and kinship affinities. One is 'entitled' to wear such and such a tartan and some people attach great importance to this. So distinct patterns and/or motif combinations on ceramics may identify certain segments of the population whether locally, regionally or even hierarchically.

'Decoration' may also have a functional rather than a decorative or cognitive role. For example, roughened surfaces, often referred to as rusticated surfaces, may have been designed specifically to facilitate the handling of the pot and to help reduce the risk of it slipping from grip. Rusticated sherds are often found in domestic assemblages, perhaps strengthening this interpretation. The best-known examples of this kind of pottery are the rusticated Beakers of the final Neolithic (**24**). These are often large pots and may be decorated with a variety of stabs, fingernail or fingertip impressions. Similarly, the Iron Age scratched wares of the English Midlands, for example, have their surfaces covered with multiple scratches, probably made by rubbing a handful of dry hay or straw over the surface of the wet clay (**24**). As decoration, this is quite primitive, but as a functional device to facilitate the handling of these large vessels, the technique is effective.

Decoration and surface treatments

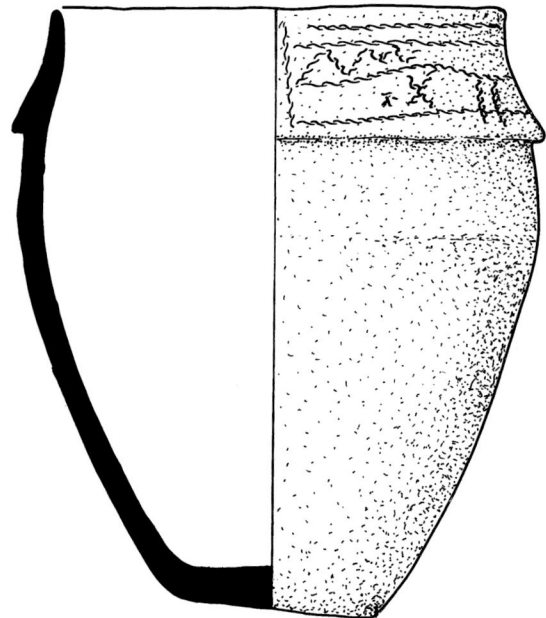

25 *Careless decoration on a Bronze Age Collared Urn from Otford in Kent. Not only is the decoration poor, but the base of this vessel is so misshapen that it could not have been very functional in an upright position.*
After Tomalin 1995

An analogy was drawn above to compare highly decorated prehistoric pottery with present-day display ceramics. This analogy can be taken further into the realm of factory 'seconds'. There are instances within prehistory of decoration having 'broken down': instances where undue care and attention appears to have been taken in the execution of the designs. The reasons for this are difficult to understand. If the decoration was intended to be seen and appreciated at whatever level, one might expect care to be taken in its execution. If, on the other hand, the decoration was unimportant, one might expect a more slap-dash approach generally. An example of this comes from a late Neolithic Beaker from Monkton-Minster in Kent. The upper portion of this vessel is decorated with a zone of comb-impressed chevrons. They appear to have been carefully done, and are well-defined and in proportion (**colour plate 9**). When the pot is turned round, however, an error in the planning of the design is encountered and two chevrons carelessly merge (**colour plate 10**). Clearly no attempt has been made to rectify this. The decoration could have been erased and re-done. The potter could have taken greater care at the outset or even in the second attempt to mark out the design. Instead, it has been left alone and un-rectified. The analogy with the factory second is, of course, a false one, as these latter pots usually result from accidental imperfections not noted until after the pots have been fired. The Monkton-Minster potter could hardly have failed to notice this glaring error but chose not to rectify it (in modern terms, a 'Friday afternoon job').

Another Kentish vessel, a Collared Urn of the early Bronze Age from Otford (**25**) also has a poorly executed decorative scheme with apparently randomly applied filling motifs between unevenly spaced horizontal lines of twisted cord impressions. There are many more examples. Does this suggest that the precision of the decoration was unimportant? Was it deemed unnecessary for the decorative scheme to be 'perfect'? Or is it a human factor, shoddy workmanship on a 'Friday afternoon'? I remember bartering for an ornate plate in the market at Marakesh. It was an intricately decorated piece and looked fantastic. But the stall-holder seemed unwilling to let me handle it. Was it too valuable? Did he not trust me to handle it with care? Neither! His thumb was skilfully hiding a glaring imperfection in the glaze and the sale negotiations collapsed. I often wonder if this happened in the case of the Monkton Beaker: was the breakdown in decoration skilfully hidden by a less than honest potter? We will probably never know the answers to these questions, particularly to the last, but Neolithic people were human too and I am convinced that similar behaviour was not unknown. It may also be stated at this point, that not all decoration is carried out to a high standard. The decoration of many other Beakers, for example, is often careless and 'poor' despite their reputation as highly decorated prestige ceramics.

Incision

Incision is one of the most common surface treatments to be used on ceramics throughout British and Irish prehistory. It is a simple technique which probably also accounts for its widespread use and longevity. At its simplest, incision involves executing linear designs and patterns by pulling a sharp point through the wet clay. This results in the compression of the clay below the point, but it also dislodges clay to the sides of the incision. This dislodged clay can be rubbed off at the leather hard stage, once the pot has dried if so wished. Incised motifs can be simple, such as the vertical lines found on some southern English decorated bowls of the earlier Neolithic (**26.1**), or complex in the case of the busy geometrical patterns and panelled decoration of Beakers (**26.2**). Incision is a technique that is present throughout Prehistory, occurring frequently on urn pottery of the Bronze Age (**26.3**), and in some Iron Age ceramics such as pots in the Saucepan tradition or on the Glastonbury Ware of the south-west of England, the decoration can be curvilinear and flowing (**26.4**). It is a simple technique capable of producing complex and aesthetically pleasing motifs.

Occasionally, the tool used to incise the pot is quite blunt, a broken twig for example, and the resulting grooves are broader than those produced by the sharp point. When these blunt implements are used, larger amounts of clay are removed from the vessel surface and this should really be termed 'excised' decoration. This term is hardly ever used with regard to prehistoric ceramics, however, and it is recognised that the techniques are essentially the same, it is only the tool that has changed. Occasionally, the tool used appears to have been freshly snapped as striations can often be seen within the grooves. These may result from the rough end of the implement but may also be caused, in the case of fabrics with large amounts of inclusions, by dislodged inclusions tracking behind the point.

Tooling is a term more commonly used with regard to post-prehistoric ceramics and within prehistoric contexts is usually applied most in relation to the pottery of the Iron Age. It doesn't actually mean anything outside the world of book-binding and stone

Decoration and surface treatments

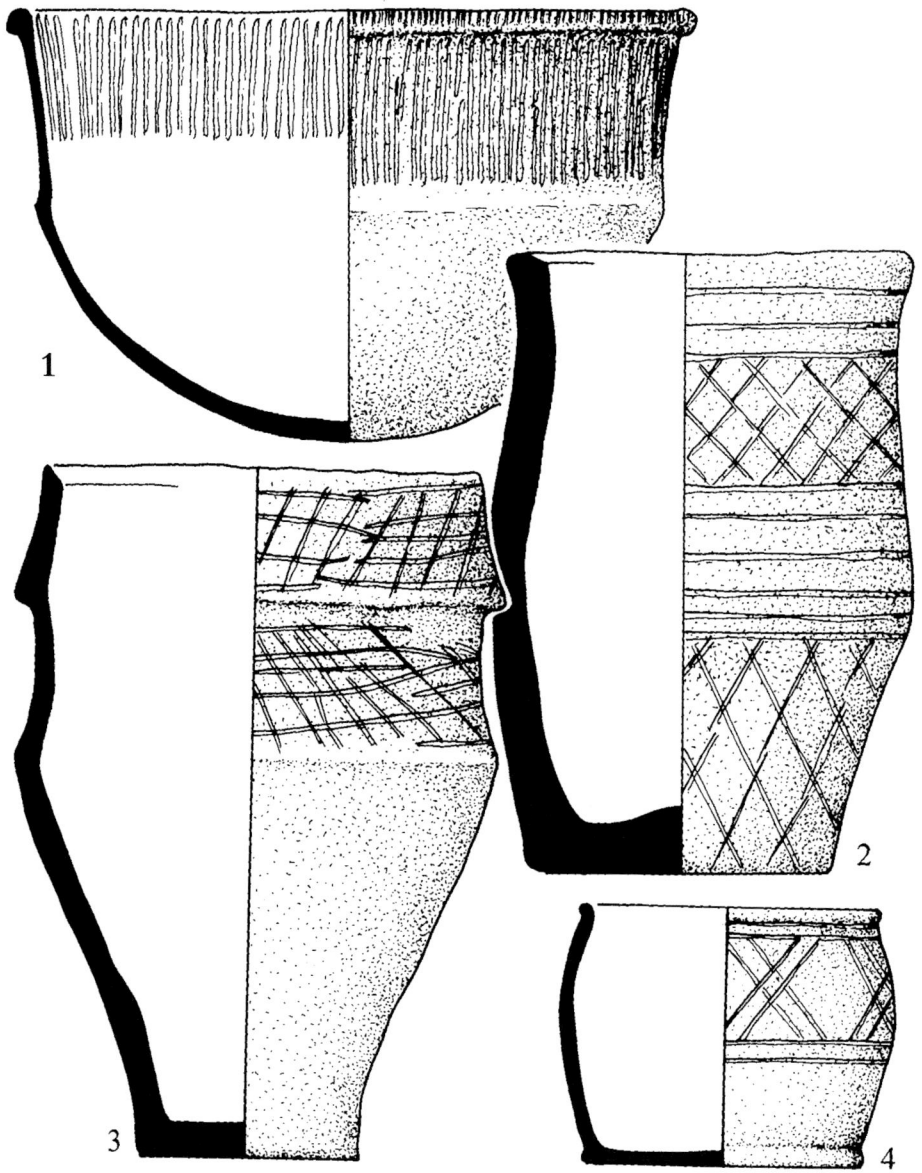

26 *Incised decoration through the ages. 1 – middle Neolithic bowl from Windmill Hill, Wilts. After Smith 1965; 2 - final Neolithic Beaker from Methilhill, Fife. After Clarke 1970; 3 – Bronze Age Collared Urn from Letterston, Dyfed. After Longworth 1984; 4 – middle Iron Age bowl from Cissbury, Sussex. After Cunliffe 1991.*
1, 2 and 4 = scale 1:4; 2 = scale 1:2

Decoration and surface treatments

27 *Some 'tooled' and incised decoration on Iron Age ceramics. A – Corfe Mullen, Dorset; B – Llanmelin, Gwent; C – Sudbrook, Gwent; D – Hambledon Hill, Dorset*

masonry where it respectively refers to ornamentation impressed onto a book cover using heated tools or the dressing of stone with a chisel. Literally, it means that a tool has been used to execute the decoration. Isn't all decoration therefore tooled, even if it is painted and the tool used is a brush or impressed when the 'tool' used is a bird bone, stick or even a fingertip or fingernail? In the context of ceramics, however, tooling is related to both incision and, in a way, to burnishing. Tooling is executed by drawing a blunt, smooth and rounded point over the clay at sometime after the manufacture of the vessel, but before it has reached the leather hard stage. The clay below the point is compressed, often slightly polished, and shallow round-profiled channels result (**27**). Tooling provides a softer result than incision. It is not as deep. It does not produce the hard shadows on the pot surface that incision frequently does, nor does it result in the 'hard', sometimes roughened, edges associated with incised decoration. The polish that may occasionally be found within the channels will be dependent on the hardness of the clay at the time of decoration and the smoothness of the point used. Where present, it indicates that the clay had been quite hard when the tooling was undertaken and in this respect it is related to burnishing. In other words it is a polish resulting from the compression of the clay particles (as opposed to the addition of a waxy or similar substance). The saucepan pots, Hunsbury Bowls and Glastonbury Ware of the Iron Age with their curvilinear designs and flowing scrollwork are frequently referred to as 'tooled'. So too might be termed the often extremely faint horizontal lines and chevrons found on the necks of Globular Urns of the Deverel-Rimbury series dating to the end of the middle of the Bronze Age. Yet this decoration is rarely described as tooled: the term 'scored' is usually more common.

If archaeologists cannot agree amongst themselves what constitutes scoring and what tooling (but does it really matter?), it serves them right for using imprecise language. The Concise Oxford Dictionary, however, does not help. To score is defined as to 'mark with notches or incisions or lines, slash, furrow, make (line etc.) with something that marks'. In short, the verb itself is imprecise. With the exception of the reference to the Deverel-Rimbury pottery mentioned above however, 'scoring' tends to be used to refer to bold and largely irregular slashes across the surface of a pot. The term is commonly used to describe the decoration on the large late Iron Age jars of the east Midlands ranging in distribution from Lincolnshire to Northamptonshire. These jars have abundant irregular multiple incisions across their surfaces. It is a moot point as to whether this surface treatment is decorative or functional. The answer is probably both, for while the scoring is bold and can clearly be seen, so too is it functional since it provides a rougher surface which affords the user a better grip (see **24** above). Frequently in these scored wares, the potter has made no attempt to remove the ridges of dislodged clay that result from these bold incisions. This suggests that aesthetics are not a high priority in these pots and reinforces the argument for functionality.

While tooling and scoring may be ambiguous terms, the same cannot be said for the 'stab and drag' variant of incision or, to be more precise, a technique which combines incision with impression. This decoration is made in exactly the way that the term describes. A stick or some other object has been stabbed into the wet clay and dragged down or across and out of the surface. The result is an impression, usually deep and 'jagged', from which a broad shallowing and irregular groove emanates. While this type of decoration may be found on Neolithic vessels, its use is not restricted to period though its appearance is very distinctive.

Impression

Stab and drag decoration is, effectively, a cross between incision and impression. As mentioned above, an implement is first stabbed (impressed) into the clay and then dragged through it (incised). Impression is the name given to any decorative technique that involves impressing an object into the clay walls while the pot is still wet and the clay plastic. Almost any object could be (and was) used, from string, wood or cord to the bones of small animals and from reeds and straw to fingernails and fingertips. Sometimes the decorative motifs and schemes are quite simple and at other times they can be highly complex. Arguably, the later Neolithic and earlier Bronze Age see the acumen of impressed decoration. It is the centuries between 3000 and 1000 BC where impressed decoration is used most inventively and abundantly. At this time, on Peterborough Ware, Grooved Ware, Beakers, Food Vessels and various urn types, the range of impressed decoration is staggering.

Twisted cord is one of the most commonly employed impressions, giving the characteristic 'cable' effect of a twisted string. Twisted cord is employed in short lengths, encircling lines or horseshoe crescents. It can appear in unidirectional lines or be arranged to form herring-bone or triangular arrangements (**colour plate 11**). The twist of the cord can be fine or coarse and often the impressions of the individual fibres can be seen in the clay. Twisted cord makes an appearance in the archaeological record sometime before 3000 BC and appears to go out of use by about 1200 BC. But during the later Neolithic and early Bronze Age, it is one of the most commonly utilised techniques.

Frequently, the twisted cord may be wrapped around something such as a stick, flint blade, or indeed itself, rather like a hangman's noose, prior to being used as a decorative tool. Where this happens, the technique is known as whipped cord (**colour plate 12**). Once more the motifs executed in this technique are varied and again the practice seems to have gone out of use by 1200 BC. Experimental work has shown that whipped impressions can vary considerably in appearance depending on variables such as the hardness of the cord and the rigidity/flexibility of the core around which the cord has been wrapped. For example, wool wrapped around itself produces a much softer impression than does sinew wrapped around a more rigid material. Occasionally, the whipped fibre can be very fine indeed and in such cases it is difficult to imagine what material might have been used: horsehair or sinew has been suggested (see **8** above).

To worry too much about this material is, however, to miss the point of this revelation. It is seldom realised that these impressions preserve the archaeological remains of organic materials that would not otherwise survive in normal conditions. They demonstrate the presence of twisted wool in the Neolithic and Bronze Age and, in the case of the finer whipped impressions, of complex and fine composite strings. Comparable composite strands may be found today in pianos, on guitars and on harps. Do these strings in prehistory demonstrate the presence of stringed musical instruments? Or can a more utilitarian explanation be offered in the form of bow strings? The argument is largely academic but these sherds give proof that Neolithic populations knew more about working with fibres and complex string technologies than is suggested by the coarse twisted wool, plant fibre and leather that has survived in some waterlogged archaeological contexts. Indeed these impressions in ceramics might be considered our greatest single resource for the study of fibres in British prehistory.

Occasionally plaited cord can also be seen (**colour plate 2**), especially, though not exclusively on the large Urns of Cornwall and the south-west of England. Plaited cord produces a particularly pleasing design resembling very fine and regular herringbone motif as the twists of the individual plaits appear to twist in opposite directions. Once again it tells us more about rope technology in the Bronze Age than has previously been appreciated.

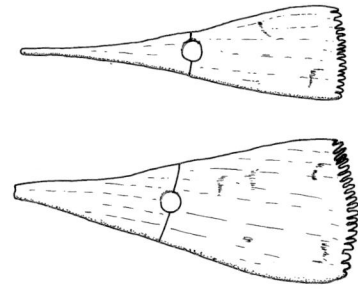

28 *Beaker period bone combs for decorating pottery from Northton Harris. The teeth are used to make dotted lines and the polished points may have been used for incision. Both combs are perforated, presumably to allow suspension or possibly to give better grip to wet, slippery, clay-covered fingers. Scale 1:2*

Birdbone impressions are also most commonly found on pottery of the Neolithic and Bronze Age, and particularly the Peterborough Ware or Impressed Wares of the third millennium BC. Once more it is a blanket term and as such is only partially correct. It is accurate to observe that the impressions are made using bones, but it is not true that all the bones used were those of birds. The term is also used to cover a variety of different impressed shapes from small, almost figure-of-eight impressions to larger teardrop-shaped forms. Clearly the type of bone used, the choice of which end of the bone to use and the animal from which it derived are all contributing factors to the variations encountered under this blanket term. As with whipped cord, often complex patterns can be created from the repeated application of these tools: decoration on Peterborough Ware, particularly on the heavy rims, can often be profuse (**colour plate 13**).

Some pioneering but largely ignored research into this topic was done by Dorothy Liddell (1929). Liddell was excavating at the Neolithic Causewayed enclosure at Windmill Hill, near Avebury in Wiltshire with Alexander Keiller and she was fascinated by the amount of profusely impressed pottery being recovered from the upper levels of the site's perimeter ditches. She also noted the variety of the impressed decoration and concluded from the large range of differences that she observed within the internal structure of each impression that different types of tool had been used to make each mark. Liddell then embarked on a series of experiments in which she tried to recreate the impressions and found that not only were birdbones used, but also the bones from other small animals. This work can be regarded as amongst the first serious experimental archaeology projects in Britain yet it is now largely forgotten. More work needs to be done on the occurrence of birdbone impressions, particularly on Peterborough Ware. It has been mentioned above that some decoration, especially on Iron Age ceramics, can be shown to be regional and/or tribal. If the bones used to decorate the pottery were from totemic or tribally significant animals, they may have varied from region to region. For the moment, however, this must remain little more than conjecture.

In the Beaker period which forms the transition between the ages of stone and bronze, impressed decoration continues to dominate the ceramic scene. The Beakers themselves may be incised or impressed with cord and/or fingernails or tips. But the decoration is comprised mainly of multiple hyphenated lines: that is lines made up of numerous small rectangular sections. This is called comb decoration, or occasionally toothed comb

Decoration and surface treatments

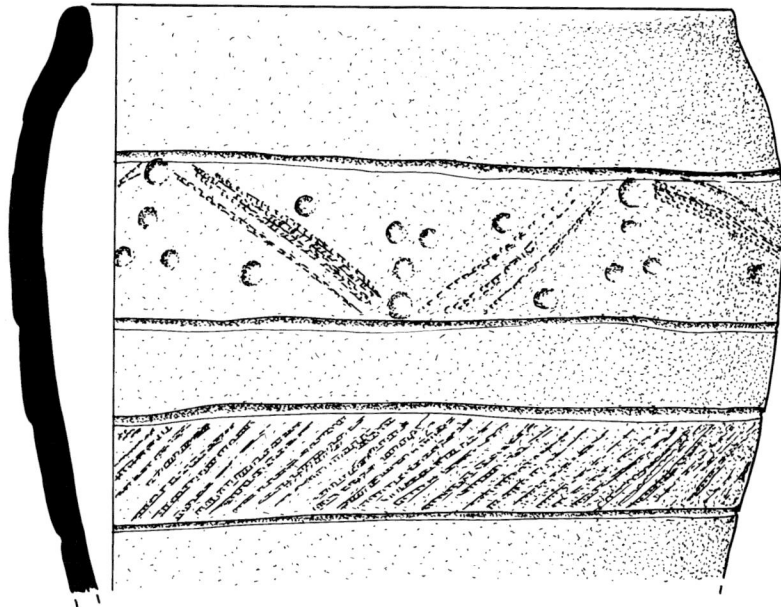

29 *Rouletted decoration on an Iron Age jar from Old Sleaford, Lincolnshire. Scale 1:2. After Elsdon 1997*

impressions. Lines such as this can be replicated using an ordinary hair comb but we are fortunate in that some of the combs used have actually survived (**28**). Two combs from the Beaker settlement at Northton on the Isle of Harris are made of thin bone. They have curved and serrated working edges and are perforated. These perforations are most probably for suspending the implements on a thong around the potter's neck, but may also have another practical function and give greater grip or purchase to the potter's fingers when wet and slippery from the clay. These combs are 'rocked' over the pot surface which allows for overlapping impressions to be arranged into continuous encircling lines. The curved nature of the serrated edge allows both short and longer lengths of impression to be made. The combs also have a pointed end which shows use-wear. These points were presumably used to incise decoration on other vessels, suggesting that here at least, where combed and incised vessels are found together, the variation in decorative techniques is not due to cultural differences. Comb decoration continues into the early Bronze Age and may be found on Food Vessels and various urn forms, but it is rare after 1200 BC. Similar impressions on some of the later La Tène pottery of the Iron Age are called rouletting (**29**). Here it is generally assumed that a small notched wheel has been used to create the impressions, though no such tools have been found.

Other commonly found forms of impressions are those made by the potter's fingernail or fingertip (or both). Fingernail/tip impressions are usually included under the blanket term of 'rustication' but, as has already been mentioned above, incision and other surface treatment techniques can also be employed to create rusticated surfaces. Fingernail/tip impressions may occur singly or in pairs. They may be scattered randomly

Decoration and surface treatments

30 *Various fingernail and fingertip impressions. The same technique can be used to create very different effects. 1-4 from Reffley Wood, Norfolk, 5-6 from Fengate, Cambridgeshire and 7-8 from Hockwold-cum-Wilton, Norfolk. All scale 1:2*

over the pot, or used to form complex designs of ribs and troughs (**30**). Paired fingernail impressions are usually termed 'crowsfoot' impressions because of their resemblance to a bird's footprint, although they resemble more the cloven hooves of cattle or sheep than anything avian. Once more 'crowsfoot' is a label given by archaeologists to refer, no matter how inaccurately, to a specific motif. It must not be confused with birdbone. Often fingernail impressions may be attended by raised crescents of clay which are often interpreted as the clay displaced by the fingernail. This is true, but the effect is not accidental but deliberate. It involves sliding the fingernail slightly across the pot and through the clay. It needs a deliberate action to raise such a crescent and the appearance of these raised pellets must be regarded as a deliberate intention on behalf of the potter.

Occasionally, fingernail/tip impressions are not immediately identified as such. For example, a Peterborough Ware bowl from the River Thames at Mortlake had deep circular impressions in the neck. Staff at the Museum of London made a latex cast of the interior of these impressions and discovered the tool used to create them (**colour plate 8**). The beautifully preserved fingertip of the potter was revealed for the first time since sometime around 3000 BC. The fingertip was impressed into the wet clay almost to the level of the first knuckle joint. It had a long and well-formed fingernail and even the fingerprint is visible. It is discoveries such as this that remind us that people lie behind these artefacts and however much we describe pots and assign them to types and typologies, we must be careful never to lose sight of the human dimension.

Other impressions are much more rarely encountered. Seed impressions, for example, are found in ceramics of all periods. These are generally considered to be accidental rather than an intentional attempt at decoration. Seeds or grains may have been lying around in the domestic context of the potting floor and so may have been incorporated into the fabric as the potter worked the clay and formed the pots. Seeds may be found in the surface of the pot or within the fabric or both, and they often preserve the complete outline of the seed in question allowing an accurate identification of the species to be made. As with twisted and whipped cord impressions, this is far more important to archaeology as a whole, for preserved in the fired clay is evidence for the past economy of the users of these pots. Seeds from Neolithic contexts, for example, are extremely rare in some parts of the country and in these areas preserved grain impressions may provide the only data regarding this aspect of the agricultural economy. Indeed, a recently excavated Food Vessel from Wether Hill in Northumberland (**colour plate 3**) has produced so many grains, all from barley, that they appear to have been deliberately added to the clay. This may have been because the potter was using the grain as an opening material. However the pot also contains abundant angular stone inclusions and so the addition of another opening agent is unlikely to have been necessary. Perhaps the inclusion of the grain was a pure and simple accident resulting from barley being around at the time of the pot's manufacture when the clay was being mixed. Equally it may have been part of some propitiatory ritual. The pot may not only have been designed to hold a food resource, but also had that food resource actually embedded within its fabric. This is a wonderful combining of the grown and manufactured economy, a merging of husbandry and industry.

In the Iron Age, incised techniques are far more commonly employed than are impressions. That is not to deny that impressions are absent however. Some of the most charming are known as 'duck stamps' (see above, **10**) and are restricted to the Malvernian pottery of the Welsh Marches in the fifth and fourth centuries BC. These stamps are, in effect, small angular S-shaped impressions, not dissimilar to some birdbone impressions and which, from a distance, resemble a row of swimming ducks. Whether this was an intentional device on the part of the potters is debatable.

False relief, despite its name, is actually also a form of impressed decoration. Once again it is more commonly found on pottery of the earlier Bronze Age and particularly on the highly decorated Food Vessels of Ireland and south-west Scotland (see below **45.8**) False relief usually appears as a raised zig-zag line standing proud from the surface of the pot. The line has been neither raised nor applied, however, but instead the effect is produced by the opposed triangular impressions above and below the line. The technique is actually impressed to create relief and hence the name.

Plastic decoration

Applied and raised decorative techniques have the effect of producing cordons or other features that stand proud of the surface of the pot. The results of the two techniques can look very similar; however, they are created in different ways. The former involves the application of strips or pellets of clay to the surface of the vessel. The latter involves raising up clay from the surface of the pot. Usually cordons such as the multiple examples on the later Iron Age ceramics from Hengistbury Head in

Decoration and surface treatments

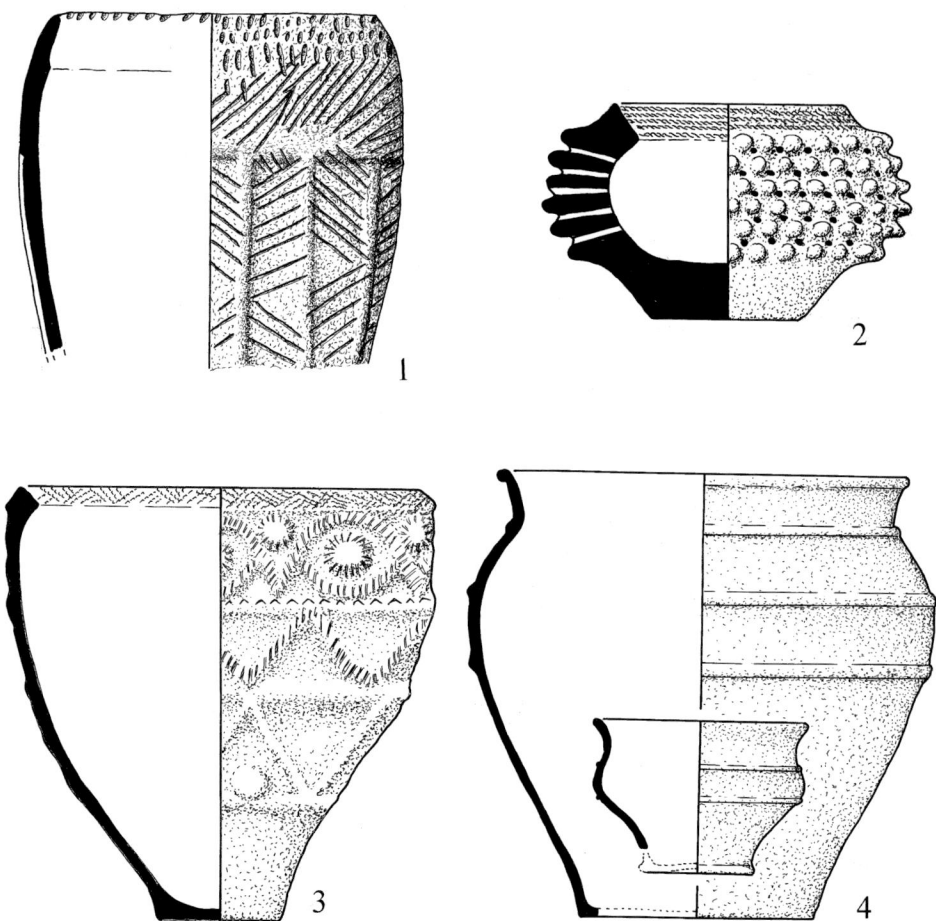

31 *Applied decoration through the ages on 1 – Neolithic Grooved Ware from Durrington Walls, Wiltshire. After Wainwright & Longworth 1971; 2 – an early Bronze Age grape cup from Wilsford, Wiltshire. After Annable & Simpson 1964; 3 – a Bronze Age 'encrusted' urn from Penllwyn, Cardiganshire. After Fox 1927; 4 – Iron Age cordoned jars from Caerloggas, Cornwall. After Threipland 1957. 1, 3 & 4 = scale 1:6; 2 = scale 1:2*

Dorset or the first-century BC Cornish cordoned jars are most commonly applied. In the Neolithic and Bronze Age, however, zig-zag cordons may be applied to Food Vessel Urns and Converging cordons may be found on Grooved Ware. Pellets of clay may also be applied to Food Vessels and small, strange cups known as Grape Cups from their pelleted appearance (**31**). Raised decoration may also be used to produce similar effects and the two techniques can often only be differentiated in sherd material where a slight void can sometimes be detected between the applied clay and the body of the pot. Applied cordons may also break off along these points of weakness and leave distinctive scars. Strips of clay may also be added to the surface of a vessel to model formal features. For example, the Collared urns of the earlier Bronze Age often use applied clay to accentuate the base of the collar.

32 Burnishing facets on an Iron Age bowl from Hambledon Hill, Dorset

In the Grooved Ware of the Neolithic, during the few centuries around 2700 BC, Richards and Thomas (1984) proposed a hierarchical ranking within the tradition. This hypothesis was largely based on the presence and treatment of cordons. This hierarchy was six-fold and comprised 1 – undecorated vessels, 2 – decorated vessels, 3 – undecorated with cordons, 4 – undecorated cordons separating zones of decoration between them, 5 – decorated cordons but undecorated panels between and 6 – decorated panels and cordons. This hierarchy seems to have been important when the pots were deposited at the timber circles of Durrington Walls, since 1-3 predominated at the north circle while 4-6 predominated at the south with 6 being particularly common outside the entrance to the south circle. It seems then that these cordons may have been more than structural or decorative but rather may have inferred special meaning to the users of the pots and have imbued the vessels themselves with different levels of prestige.

Burnishing

Burnishing is both a functional and decorative technique. It firstly gives the vessel a smooth well-finished and polished surface thus enhancing the visual appearance of the pot. However, burnishing also slightly reduces the permeability of the pot and has the effect of compacting the joins between coils or straps thus strengthening the bonding. Usually a smooth rounded object, such as a river pebble, is used as the burnisher. The effect is to compact the clay thus imparting a gloss. The facets of the burnishing tool are usually visible on the burnished surface (**32**). The technique is common on the carinated bowls of the earlier Neolithic. It is less frequently used in the later Neolithic and earlier Bronze Age (although it is present on some Beakers) but re-emerges in the first millennium BC. The most well known of the burnished wares are the haematite bowls which make an appearance in the later Bronze Age. These small bowls, restricted largely to the

Wessex area and south-east of England, represent a re-emergence of ceramic technology after the 'doldrums' of around 1000 BC. They are ceramic forms that are also found in metal and earlier debates have always seen the metal versions as prototypes, though current theories favour contemporary artefacts in different media. From their polished red surfaces, it was assumed that haematite had been burnished into the vessel walls. Research by Andrew Middleton (1987) has shown that this is certainly true on some bowls, but on others a slip was added while in yet others, the clay naturally fired to a bright red. Sometimes this is combined with incised decoration which is then inlaid with white chalk to contrast against the red background. Polish is another term sometimes used to refer to burnishing but, as Woods has pointed out, polish should really be used to describe a post-firing treatment of glazed pottery (Gibson & Woods 1990).

The haematite coated bowls mentioned above occasionally have an iron-rich slip added to ensure their red colour in firing. Slip is a suspension of clay in water into which a leather hard pot is dipped and it is usually used to change the colour of a pot and/or improve its outer surface. The use of a slip in the strict sense is unusual in prehistory. However, if during the manufacture of a pot, wet hands are rubbed over the surface of a finished but still wet vessel, the clay that is lifted from the vessel walls in suspension and then redeposited on the surface can have the appearance of a slip.

Individual potters

Occasionally, in the earlier period, works of great similarity indicative of the same hand can be recognised. In this respect two Food Vessels from Lowick and Bolton House in Northumberland are remarkable (**33**) Not only do they share form and decoration, but they are also identical in the adventurous and individualistic nature of the decorative scheme. They are decorated with deep grooves filled with reed impressions and this combination is not, to the present writer's knowledge, found on any other vessel. The spaces between the grooves are filled with herringbone incision which, in itself, is not a rare decorative motif but its employment here to highlight the ridges between the grooves is both unusual and clearly well-considered. The external rim mouldings of both vessels are also virtually identical and both pots have a foot-ring base, a comparatively rare feature amongst Food Vessels. A Food Vessel Urn from Ryton in Tyne and Wear is also skilfully decorated and uses both grooves and reed impressions in its decoration; however, a Food Vessel Urn from Bamborough, also in north Northumberland, may be better compared to these smaller vessels. This larger pot is clearly not identical to the smaller ones but is sufficiently individualistic in nature and combines similar and peculiar decorative techniques to suggest the hand of the same artist if not potter. The base, for example, has a foot-ring, the bevel is bipartite with the change in angle emphasised by a groove filled with reed impressions (identical to the vessel from Bolton House), and the combination of reed impressions with fine incisions on the rim moulding again recalls the Food Vessels. The clay pellets applied to the rim moulding and the shoulder carination, each accentuated by fine incisions, are again adventurous features in the Bronze Age decorative repertoire and have been planned with, as Canon Greenwell, the finder

Decoration and surface treatments

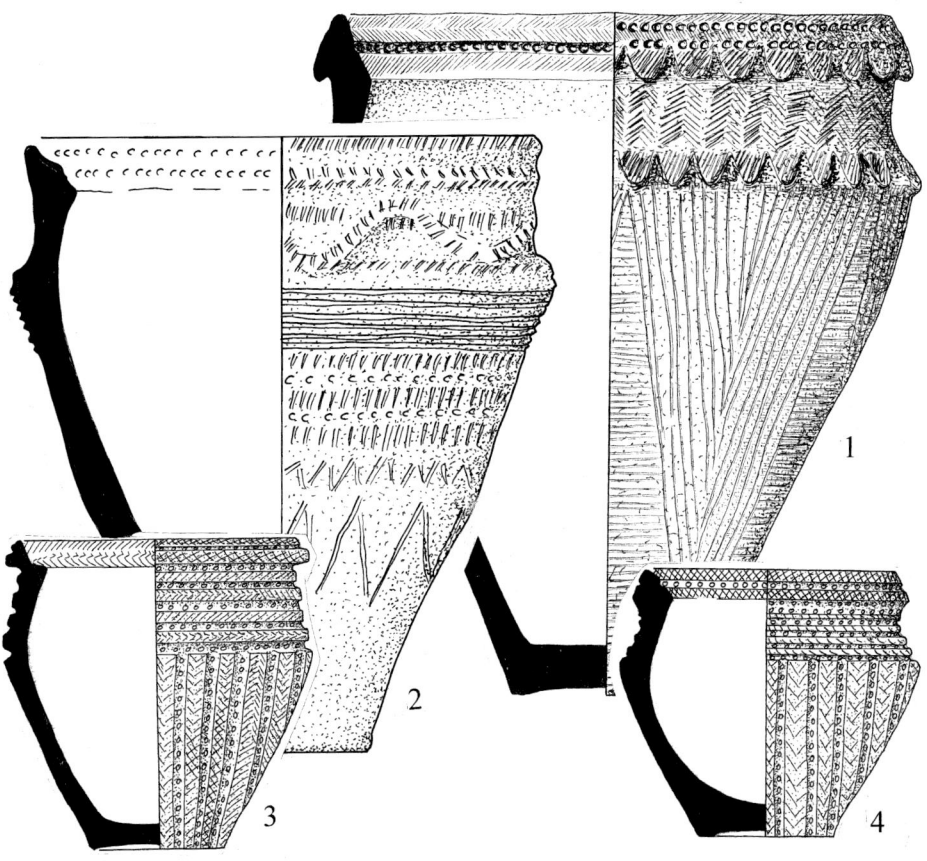

33 *The work of the same Northumbrian potter? 1 – Food Vessel Urn from Bamborough. After Kinnes & Longworth 1985; 2 – Food Vessel Urn from Ryton; 3 – Food Vessel from Lowick and 4 – Food Vessel from Beanley. All scale 1:4*

of the pot, states, 'some taste and skill' (Greenwell 1877). Were such innovation to be detected in the world of, for example, the Attic ceramics of Ancient Greece, it would be regarded as a masterpiece and attributed to an artist of genius.

David Tomalin (1995) has identified some peculiar markings on prehistoric pottery, particularly the Collared Urns of the Bronze Age. These do not appear to be part of the usual decorative repertoire. For example, a small star-shaped arrangement of fingernail impressions appears on a pot from Otford in Kent (**25** above) while a double row of similar fingernail impressions was found below the main decorative scheme on an Urn from Winterslow in Wiltshire. These and similar signs on other vessels, Tomalin interprets as potter's marks. If this is correct then the search for individual signatures on prehistoric ceramics is a hitherto unexplored avenue for research. Like the finger impression from the Thames, we are once more reminded of the human facet to ceramic studies and particularly that the potters may have had

67

a sense of pride in their work to make them want to 'sign' their pots (though the Otford pot is hardly the work of a genius).

A variety of decorative motifs and techniques are used, then, to alter the surface of prehistoric pottery. The range of techniques is quite limited but the motifs and decorative schemes show much greater variety. Even in the comb-decorated Beakers where the technique is the same and the motifs are set within a zoned and geometrical framework, there are hardly two identical pots in the whole of Clarke's (1970) corpus of some 1000 illustrated vessels. This demonstrates the diversity of decoration that can be created by human imaginations within the restricted environment of techniques and conventional schema.

4 The earlier Neolithic: 4000–3000 BC

Pottery reaches these shores at about 4000 BC. It seems to have been a rapid and widespread adoption with early and more or less identical ceramic-associated radiocarbon dates coming from England, Scotland and Ireland. This horizon, marked by the introduction not only of ceramics but also cereals and domestic animals, conventionally marks the beginning of the Neolithic or New Stone Age period. However current opinion is divided as to just how rapid was the adoption of the new economies. Early Neolithic field systems, for example the Ceide fields of Co. Mayo in the north of Ireland, suggest that here at least mixed farming was practised from early in the Neolithic. Elsewhere, other evidence such as the rarity of cereals and the perceived absence of field systems in earlier Neolithic England suggests that it may have been only after about a millennium that a truly agrarian economy was followed. In some other areas, there may be no evidence in the pollen record for forest clearance yet the presence of cereal pollen attests some small-scale arable. The question is an interesting one and it may be that we should acknowledge the co-existence of a number of regional 'Neolithics' in different parts of Britain and Ireland; after all, agricultural diversity is visible in different regions today so why not in the Neolithic. This aside, the introduction of pottery, as mentioned above, appears to be rapid, widespread and simultaneous.

The first pottery in these islands is the Carinated (or sharply-shouldered) Bowl. I use the term Carinated Bowl with capitalised initials to refer only to this primary Neolithic pottery. Other carinated types exist throughout British, Irish and even European prehistory and I refer to these and shouldered bowls generally as carinated bowls without the capitals. This Neolithic pottery was formerly called Grimston-Lyles Hill Ware after two type-sites in Yorkshire and Antrim respectively, and while this term endorses the similarity of the ceramics on both sides of the Irish Sea it fails to acknowledge the southern English or Scottish distribution of the material. The term Western Neolithic has also been used to describe this pottery since the work of Kendrick (1925), Childe (1931) and Piggott (1931) and acknowledges the widespread continental distribution of this ceramic family. The British and Irish material has particular similarities with contemporary ceramics from the Low Countries and northern France, but the widespread phenomenon of the Carinated Bowl cannot be over-emphasised. Interestingly also, the Carinated Bowl, whilst being the primary Neolithic ceramic in Britain, is far from the earliest Neolithic ceramic in western Europe. Here a distinctive round-based pottery with incised and curvilinear motifs – the Linearbandekeramik (LBK) of the Low Countries and France – had been in use for almost a millennium prior to the arrival of the Neolithic in Britain and Ireland. This LBK ceramic was distributed widely over large tracts of the European landmass from the Danube to the Rhine. However, if its users and makers did cross the English Channel then our current state of knowledge suggests that they did not leave their pots behind, nor were the local population ready to adopt this novel artefact.

It has already been mentioned that there is a great deal of uniformity in the shape and fabric of the earliest Carinated Bowls. Often characterised by a burnished or at least well-smoothed surface, the term 'leathery' has frequently been used to describe it and this subjective observation has in turn led to the invocation of leather bags and containers as potential prototypes. (Wooden hoops at the middle and top of a shallow bag might result in a carinated form with an everted rim.) While it must be admitted that absence of evidence is not synonymous with evidence of absence, this hypothesis must remain subjective, even unlikely, unless supported by organic finds. In areas where ceramics have been retrieved from waterlogged contexts, for example the lake villages of the French Jura, wooden forms of shouldered bowls have also been found, but leather examples remain absent. In other words it may be that it was the wooden artefacts that mimicked the pottery rather than the pottery being derived from organic forms.

As mentioned above, this distinctive high-quality pottery seems to have arrived in Britain and Ireland as a fully developed technology through contacts and interactions with continental groups. The pots are characterised by round-based open or hemispherical bowls superimposed by concave necks and flaring rims (**34**). The carinations usually occur low down in the overall vessel height. Rims may be simple or beaded and, as mentioned above, the fabric may be extremely finely finished. Occasionally vertical fluting may be visible within the neck and is clearly a deliberate (rather than accidental or regional) feature being distributed from southern England, to northern Scotland and Ireland. Do these flutings refer to marks that might be left by primitive flint 'gouges' in a woodworking environment? Possibly, but, like the leather analogy above, these features should not necessarily be interpreted so naïvely or so simplistically and they may have more to do with symbolic ceramic technologies than with non-ceramic (and hypothetical) prototypes. This vertical fluting may also be a practical device to facilitate pouring from these wide-flaring rims. Available radiocarbon dates put the main currency of these basic bowls between around 4000 and 3600 BC.

It is likely that these bowls, given their widespread distribution and uniformity of shape, continued to be made after this date but may be hidden amongst more developed assemblages. Sometime before 3600 BC, more diverse and perhaps emerging local forms enter the archaeological record. These were formerly used to identify regional styles and were imbued with geographical significance, but as more material has come to light, the validity of these groupings has become questioned. There are idiosyncratic pots within every large assemblage (Healy 1995), prompting the definition of a new local style every time such an assemblage is excavated. It must be remembered that, although doubtless working within set parameters, pottery is, after all, made by people. Where more than one person is involved, where different quality clay sources are exploited and where differing levels of expertise are at play, it is inevitable that there will be variations from pot to pot. Indeed, there may be variations of form on single pots.

The earlier Neolithic: 4000-3000 BC

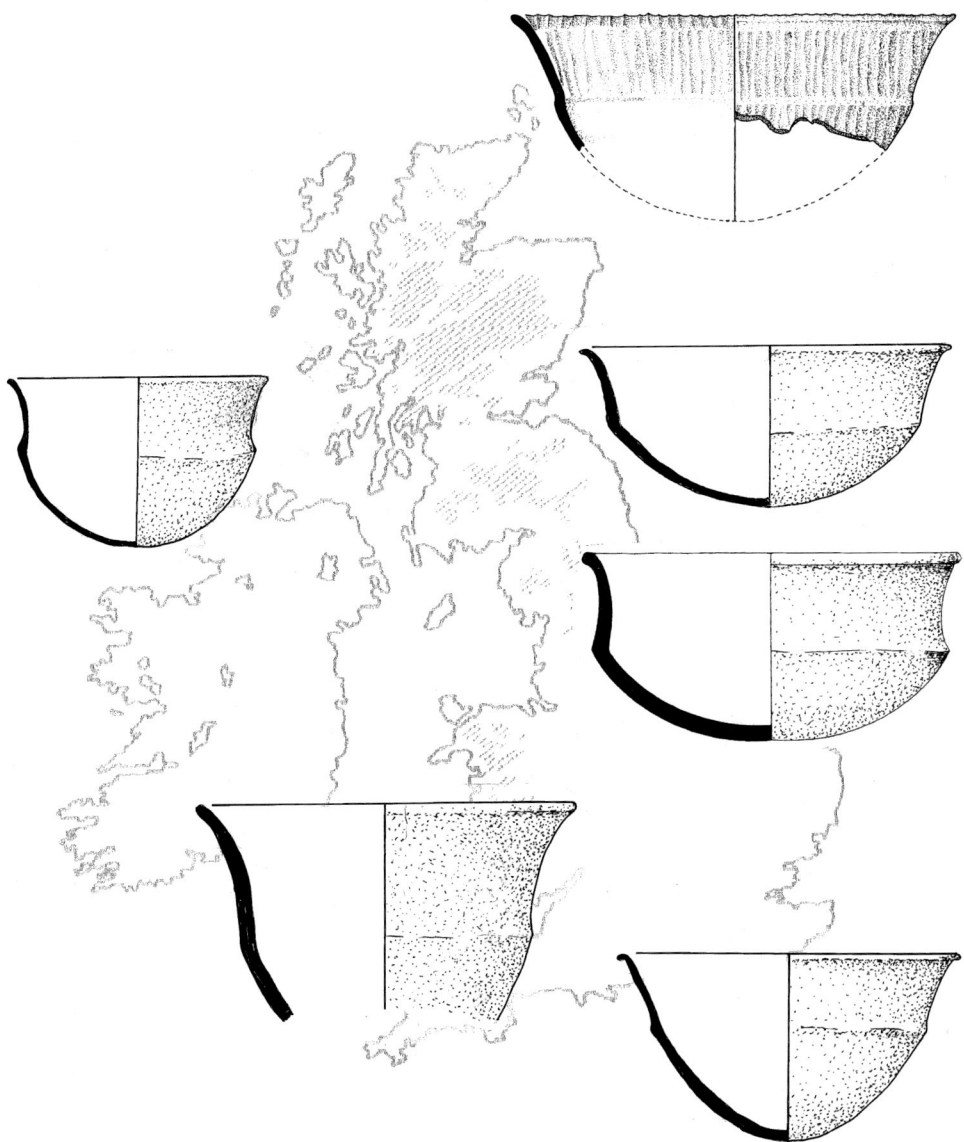

34 *Carinated Bowls from England, Scotland and Ireland. Clockwise from top left: Ballyutoag, Co. Antrim.* After Sheridan 1995; *Boghead, Moray; Balfarg, Fife.* After Barclay & Russell-White 1993; *Hanging Grimston, Yorkshire.* After Manby 1988; *Deal, Kent and Coneybury, Wiltshire.* After Richards 1990. *All scale 1:6*

For example, in this period, rim forms are notorious for changing their shape around the circumference of the vessel. This is especially so in the developed T-sectioned rim forms or other 'fancy' rim types which can often appear to have been rather carelessly formed. In these instances, too much rigour cannot be used in classifications. In addition to this, pots were doubtless made to serve specific needs and these needs or functions must have in some degree influenced the shape of the vessel.

Having made this point, around 3600 BC there emerges a distinct tradition of both simple open and shouldered bowls within south-west England that appear to demonstrate a regional style and specialist manufacture. These Hembury Wares (see above, **9**) were made from the gabbroic clay that outcrops on the Lizard peninsula in Cornwall and were distributed as far east of Cornwall as Dorset and Wiltshire. They are characterised by their extremely well-made fabric and by the presence of distinctive lugs and handles on the bodies of the pots. These latter handles, formed of strips of clay and expanded at either side, are often termed 'trumpet' lugs on account of the resemblance of the apertures to the bell of a brass instrument. Radiocarbon dates from the Neolithic defended site at Carn Brae suggest that these pots were in use by the early fourth millennium continuing towards the middle of the millennium at the causewayed enclosure on Windmill Hill in Wiltshire.

Elsewhere in southern Britain there are a series of decorated and undecorated bowls that enter the archaeological record at about this time. As well as shouldered forms, there are open and closed bowls as well as bowls with slack shoulders and S-shaped profiles. These are often seen as representing regional styles, particularly the Southeastern, Southwestern and Southern but as mentioned above the validity of these groupings is being questioned as more pottery comes to light. There would certainly appear to be a southern English decorated bowl tradition as simple decorative motifs make their appearance on pottery in this broad region at about this time, but even this label is inadequate as it omits the variety of plain wares that are also present within the assemblages. Cleal (1992) has suggested abandoning the regional labels and, following the work of Shepard (1954), has recommended that greater attention be given to vessel size and the variety of shapes that have been recognised to help define an assemblage. This plea has gone largely unheard though more consideration is certainly being given to the question of vessel size by some current researchers.

Pottery from this second, post-inception, phase of the early Neolithic has generally been recovered from the ditches of the ceremonial causewayed enclosures and pit sites. However, as well as truly carinated bowls, more globular forms have also been recovered. These include heavy rimmed vessels, vessels with sinuous profiles, vessels with very narrow necks and closed bowls with comparatively narrow rims (**35**). In Wessex, some deep, baggy vessels have been recovered from the causewayed enclosure at Windmill Hill near Avebury which are associated with decorated forms. These wares were again used to summon up visions of leather proto-types, but the problem with this hypothesis has already been discussed above. Differences in intended function may possibly account for differences in form and the increased variation at this time may well represent the expanding economic importance of ceramics and a rapidly growing population of potters. This can also be seen to have been happening elsewhere. In Scotland, a greater variety of plain wares are being increasingly encountered on Neolithic sites; these have a variety of forms including open bowls, bowls with slight carinations and forms with developed rims (see below). There are also closed forms, where the rim diameter is less than the diameter at the shoulder, and decorated vessels, particularly in the west of the country. In Ireland the 'classic' Carinated Bowl develops and also sees the emergence

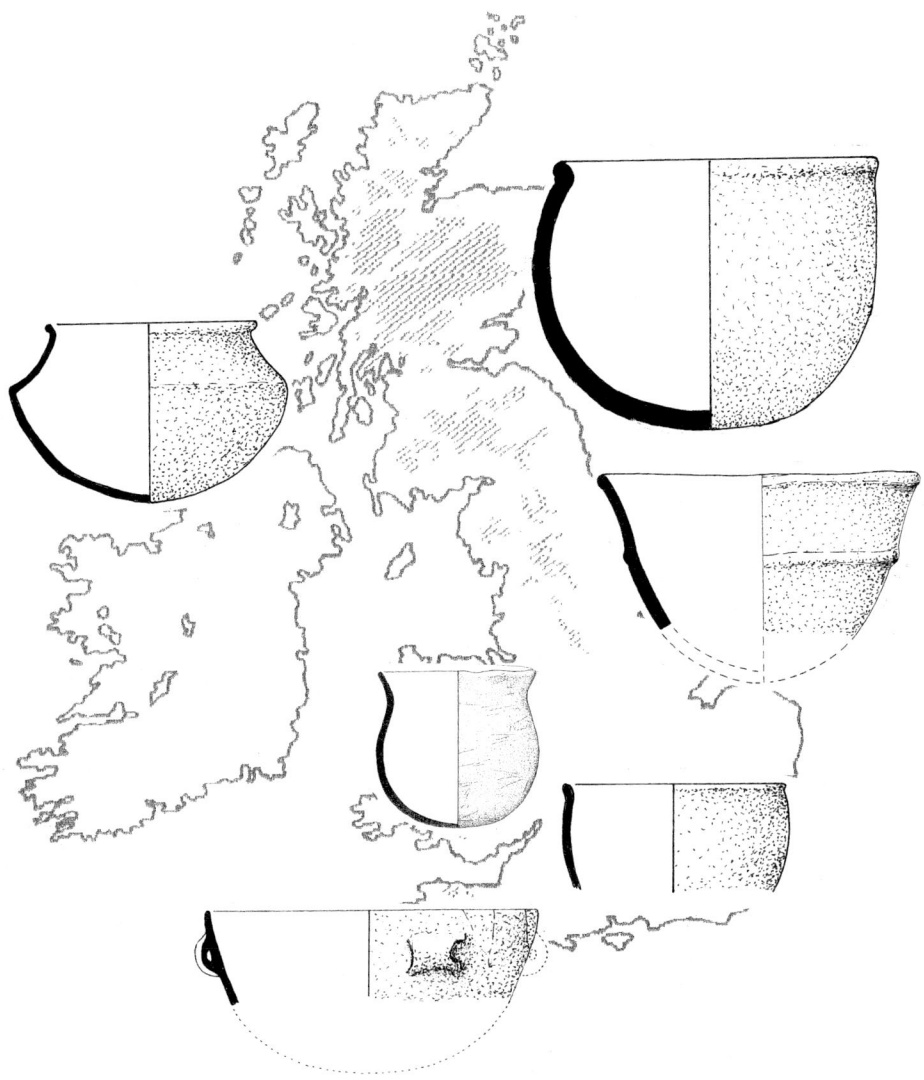

35 *Developed bowls and baggy pots of the earlier Neolithic. Clockwise from top left: Carnanbane, Co. Derry.* After Sheridan 1995; *Balfarg, Fife.* After Barclay & Russell-White 1993; *North Carnaby, Yorkshire.* After Manby 1988; *Windmill Hill, Wiltshire.* After Smith 1965; *Carn Brae, Cornwall.* After Mercer 1981; *Four Crosses, Powys. All scale 1:6*

of closed forms, 'baggy' pots like those found at Windmill Hill and simply decorated pots closely comparable to some Scottish forms.

Contemporary with these diverse plain bowls, and as mentioned above, is the introduction of decorated wares. Again, terminology has tended towards regionalising these forms. Abingdon Ware, named after the causewayed enclosure at Abingdon near Oxford, was the western variant, Mildenhall in Suffolk was the eponymous site for the eastern ceramics and Whitehawk, a causewayed enclosure in Sussex, gave its name to the central style. Once more, with the increasing number of findspots and stratified assemblages, these regional groups do not appear to be as clear cut as was previously believed. Instead, a more embracing nomenclature such as the Southern Decorated Bowl tradition may be more appropriate (Whittle 1977) although, as mentioned above, this does not acknowledge the plain wares present in these assemblages.

The decoration on these ceramics is, without exception, simple, comprising circular stabs or linear incisions, and it is most frequently (though not exclusively) restricted to the neck and rim of the vessels (**36**). There is also a tendency towards the adoption of thicker rim forms at this time and the tops of these are often decorated with linear strokes arranged radially to the circumference of the pot. In other examples, it may be the carination that is accentuated with pin-pricks or incisions. In cases where the decoration extends down below the carination, the lower third of the pot is still usually left plain and it is assumed that this is because this part of the pot would have rarely been seen. It may have been buried in the embers of the cooking fire or seated in its depression in the earth floor of the house. This contrasts with the rock art in Neolithic passage graves which is sometimes found hidden from view: for example on the back of a stone. Can this be taken to mean that the decoration on the visible areas of pottery was for human benefit? If so it represents aesthetic expression done by humans for humans. It may not have necessarily been intended to increase the status or significance of the pot. However, there are always exceptions and some pots are decorated right to their bases. Twisted and whipped cord impressions also make an appearance at this time and continue as favourite decorative techniques for the following 2000 years. Once again, when they appear, these techniques are used to form simple, linear motifs.

In Ireland, this state of affairs is somewhat similar though the variety of site names given by some archaeologists to ostensibly similar pots serves to confuse rather than elucidate the overall sequence. Rim forms develop and decoration is simple and linear though frequently more profuse than on the British material. Carinated forms persist but there is also a series of globular bowls, often named 'Goodland bowls' after the type site in Ulster, decorated only around the top of the body near the rim. The Drimnagh or Ballyalton bowls, strongly carinated bowls with a marked sharp shoulder and closed neck, are also datable to this period, around 3500-3300 BC. These bowls are often decorated with crescents on the upper portion and seem to have a wide distribution over Ireland, Scotland and Brittany though they are unknown in England. Around this time there are also thick, coarse and heavy walled bowls, sometimes with inturned rims, often named Carrowkeel Ware and a series of bowls with cavetto necks and developed but thin rims, termed Murlough Bowls. These vessels, with their profuse impressed decoration, mirror a similar development on the other side of the Irish Sea, that of Impressed Wares or Peterborough Wares (of which more later).

In Scotland, the pattern is much the same. The Carinated Bowl dominates the primary Neolithic. Once more the degree of competence exhibited in these ceramics is often considerable. The bowls from Boghead in Moray, or the chambered tomb of Tulloch of Assery, for example, have the vertical fluting and

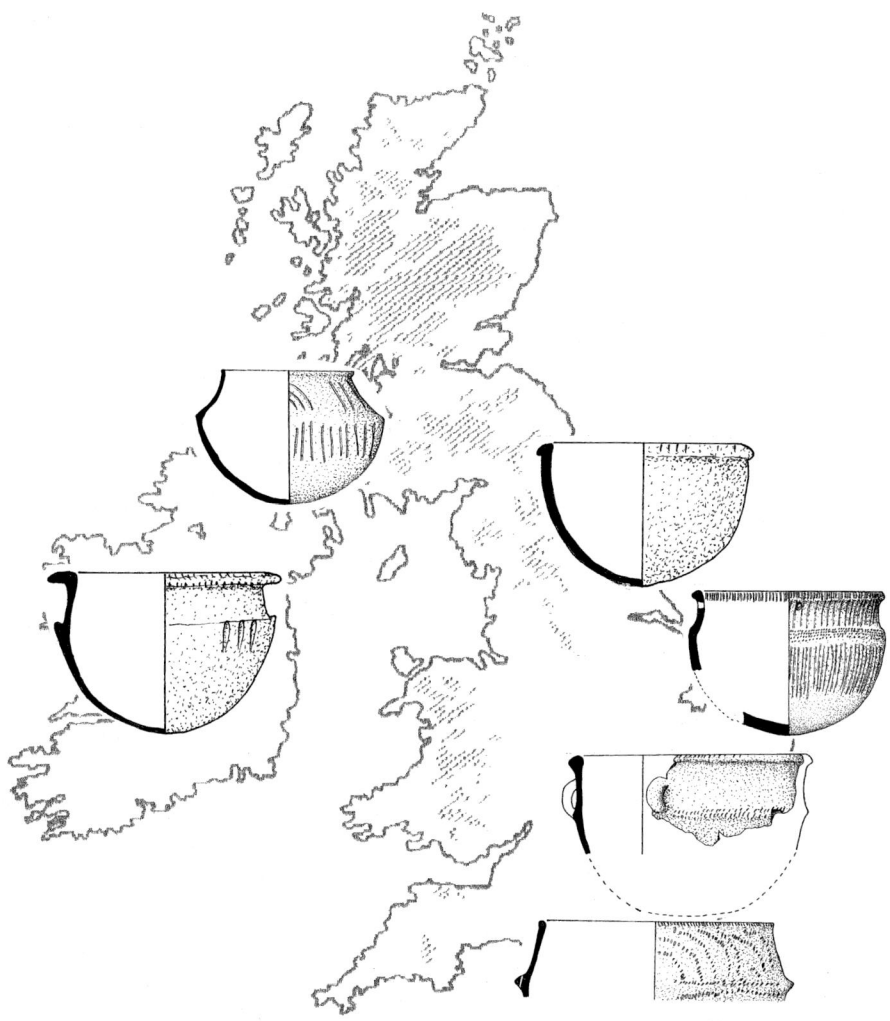

36 *Some early Neolithic decorated bowls of around 3500 BC. Clockwise from top left: Beacharra, Argyll. Scale 1:8. After Scott 1964; Rudstone, Yorkshire. Scale 1:8. After Manby 1988; Hurst Fen, Norfolk. Scale 1:8. After Clark et al. 1960; Abingdon, Oxfordshire. Scale 1:8. After Avery 1982; Whitehawk, Sussex. Scale 1:12. After Whittle, 1977; Lough Gur, Limerick. Scale 1:6. After Sheridan 1995*

burnishing seen on similarly dated ceramics from England and Ireland. Certainly by the first quarter of the fourth millennium BC, there had emerged, as in Ireland and southern Britain, a series of heavy, thick-walled globular bowls in often coarse and friable fabrics. Some, such as the material from Barbush Quarry in Dunblane, may have applied lugs while other vessels such as some from Balfarg in Fife may have applied cordons to resemble vestigial carinations. Trevor Cowie has suggested that these pots, while clearly related to and indeed derived from the earlier Neolithic plain bowls, mark the appearance of a different potting tradition in Scotland. The heavy rim forms that are often present amongst this material may also herald the expanded decorated rims of the local impressed wares. In the west of Scotland, associated with the chambered tombs, is a type of small fine bipartite bowl with a strongly inverted neck. These Beacharra bowls strongly resemble the Ballyalton bowls of Ireland and Castellic Wares of Brittany, and Alison Sheridan has used their distribution to suggest contact between Brittany and the Irish Sea province during the earlier Neolithic.

Two very distinct forms of pottery are found in the Northern and Western Isles of Scotland. They are found nowhere else and occur in both domestic and funerary contexts. These are the Unstan Bowls and the multi-carinated or ridged Hebridean bowls (**37**). The former style takes its name from the chambered tomb of Unstan on Orkney where bowls characterised by upright or slightly concave collars sitting on shallow round-based forms were found. The Unstan Ware collars are often decorated with motifs based on triangles formed by incised or stab and drag lines. Encrusted carbon deposits on some vessels, such as those from the settlement site at Northton on Harris or the chambered tomb of Isbister on Orkney might suggest that the pots had indeed been used for cooking prior to their deposition in the tomb or on the settlement's waste heap. Radiocarbon dates from the Knap of Howar in the Orkney Islands might also indicate that these pots were in use by as early as 3500 BC; however some doubts have recently been raised regarding the integrity of these dates (Ashmore 2000). The single radiocarbon date from Northton has a large calibrated age range of over 500 years (around 3400-2900 BC). However, the bulk of dates associated with Unstan Ware from the Orkney tombs suggest around 3200 BC as the start of the deposition of this ceramic within the funerary contexts, and that this practice may have continued until the middle of the third millennium.

Some added symbolism has been suggested for the decoration on Unstan Ware (Jones 2000). The form of this ceramic is unusual and difficult to parallel. Its collared rim and rounded base cannot be matched elsewhere. However, if the pot is turned upside down, we have a straight lower portion and a rounded dome. This may well be the original form of many of the round chambered tombs on Orkney with which Unstan Ware is associated. The pots may be metaphors for the monuments. In addition to this, the filled triangular motifs may be suggestive of some of the diagonal and herringbone masonry techniques noticed at some of the Orcadian tombs. There may therefore be a strong link between the shape of the pots themselves and the original form of the monuments with which they were so closely linked.

The multi-carinated Hebridean wares are again restricted in their distribution, being found only in the Northern and Western Isles and the adjacent mainland. They are also very distinctive pots. Often with elaborated rims, these round-based jars have deep baggy profiles in contrast to the shallow Unstan Ware bowls. Their rim diameters are usually narrower than the maximum belly diameter of the pots and the outside of the vessel bears multiple evenly-spaced shoulders or carinations. These ridges appear to have been raised from the fabric and rarely affect the smooth internal profile of the pots. The carinations are also fairly evenly spaced and are used to define

The earlier Neolithic: 4000-3000 BC

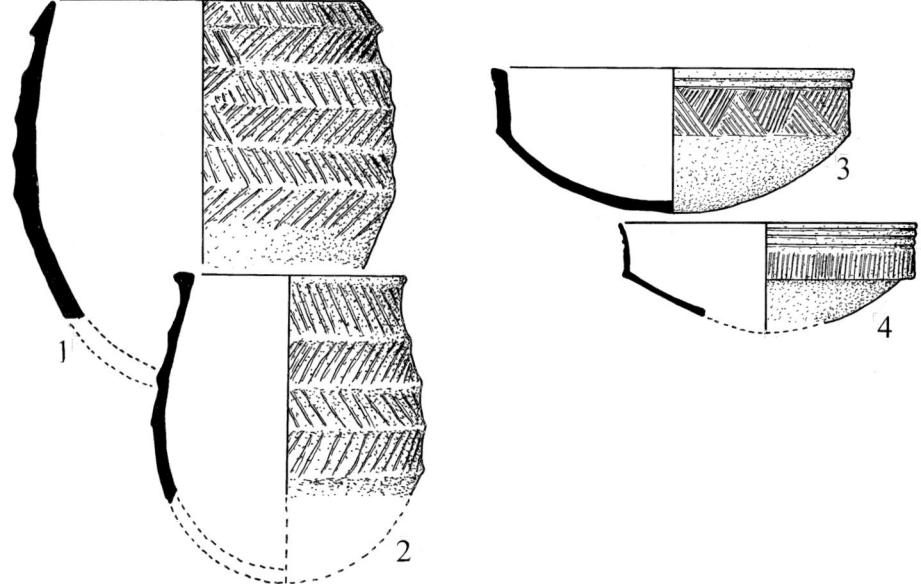

37 *Multi-carinated Hebridean jars (1 & 2) and Unstan Ware bowls (3 & 4) from the North of Scotland. 1 from Eilean an Tighe, North Uist.* After McInnes 1969; *2 from Northton, Harris.* After McInnes 1969; *3 from Unstan, Orkney.* After Henshall & Davidson 1989; *4 from Midhowe, Orkney.* After Henshall & Davidson 1989. *All scale 1:6*

zones of simple diagonal incisions arranged into horizontal herringbone motifs. They seem to vary considerably in size suggesting small, medium and large vessels making up the assemblage. The association of these bowls with Unstan Ware pots at sites such as Northton and Allt Chrisal on Barra suggests that they were in use from the few centuries before 3500 BC. It is difficult to determine when the Hebridean bowls went out of use. Recent work in the Outer Isles, however, and more carefully selected radiocarbon dates may soon serve to define better the currency of this locally distinctive style.

In a work such as this, which attempts to put prehistoric pottery into its chronological setting or framework, it is easy to forget that chronologies were probably perceived much differently in prehistory. Our dates for this chapter of 4000 and 3000 BC are artificial dates that owe their existence to the conventions of our historical mainstream religion. They are therefore little more than convenient pegs on which to hang our perceptions of the depth of the prehistoric timescale. They would have meant nothing to populations alive at the time. Ironically, the North American Indians' 'many moons' as clichéd in the Hollywood westerns may be more relevant in this context. Accordingly, and as demonstrated by the Unstan Ware and Hebridean bowls described above, it must be remembered that pottery types evolved, were adopted and displaced within a constantly fluid and dynamic system. These processes may have occurred at different times, to varying degrees and for different reasons in disparate regions; one population being slow to adopt a new style, whilst others seized upon novel forms more readily. This is certainly the case with the final type of pottery to be described in this chapter: Peterborough Ware and related pottery within the Impressed Ware tradition.

Shortly before 3300 BC, there emerged over most of Britain and Ireland a tradition of thick-rimmed round-based bowls usually decorated with profuse impressions of twisted and whipped cord, reeds, sticks and the bones of small birds and mammals. This is the Impressed Ware tradition or Peterborough Ware in England. This style of pottery was formerly considered to be later Neolithic in date, extending into the earlier Bronze Age, but a recent re-evaluation of the available radiocarbon dates shows that the style was fully developed by 3000 BC. It also seems to have gone out of vogue by the middle of the third millennium.

Forty-six years ago, Isobel Smith identified three stages in the development of southern English Peterborough Ware in her doctoral thesis, which she refined in 1974 in the light of more finds and an increasing number of radiocarbon dates (**38**). The earliest style, Ebbsfleet Ware, was seen as being related to the carinated bowls. The vessels in this style were sparsely and simply decorated and were clearly related to the southern decorated bowl traditions discussed above. Through time, the bowls became more elaborately decorated with impressed techniques such as twisted and whipped cord predominating. The Mortlake style was a more profusely decorated form of pottery (**colour plate 13**). Twisted and whipped cord continued in use, but there was also a greater variety of impressions being used such as fingernail and birdbone impressions. The shoulder, indicating the carinated bowl ancestry, was still present though the neck was often deep but narrow. The rims of Mortlake Ware also expanded to accommodate more decoration, and even took the form of narrow collars. Smith observed that the zoning of the decoration on some of these vessels may have been influenced by the comb zoned decoration on Beaker pottery which heralded the inception of the Bronze Age. The third phase of the Peterborough Ware tradition was the Fengate style which was characterised by narrow flat bases, splayed bodies and collared rims which influenced the Collared Urns of the second millennium.

Dealing with few and uncalibrated radiocarbon dates, Smith's stylistic development and the influence of Peterborough Ware on later ceramic types was an attractive set of hypotheses accepted and adopted by subsequent scholars. That this sequence remained at the centre of many discussions of the later Neolithic for some 40 years is testimony to its credibility and it served archaeology well. However work in the later half of the 1990s has come to question the chronology of this sequence. At the earlier end, Ros Cleal's (1995) study of Neolithic fabrics demonstrates that there are indeed clear links between Peterborough Ware and the earlier carinated bowls, particularly in their preference for flint inclusions. However, the other end of the sequence ultimately posed more problems.

It was in the mid-1990s that a Mortlake-Fengate style pot was recovered from a ring ditch at Horton in the Thames valley. The initial British Museum date on antler associated with this vessel calibrated to around 2800-2500 BC and was therefore considered to be too early, according to current wisdom. The date must be wrong, the sample, perhaps, contaminated. More dates were obtained on waterlogged wood associated

The earlier Neolithic: 4000-3000 BC

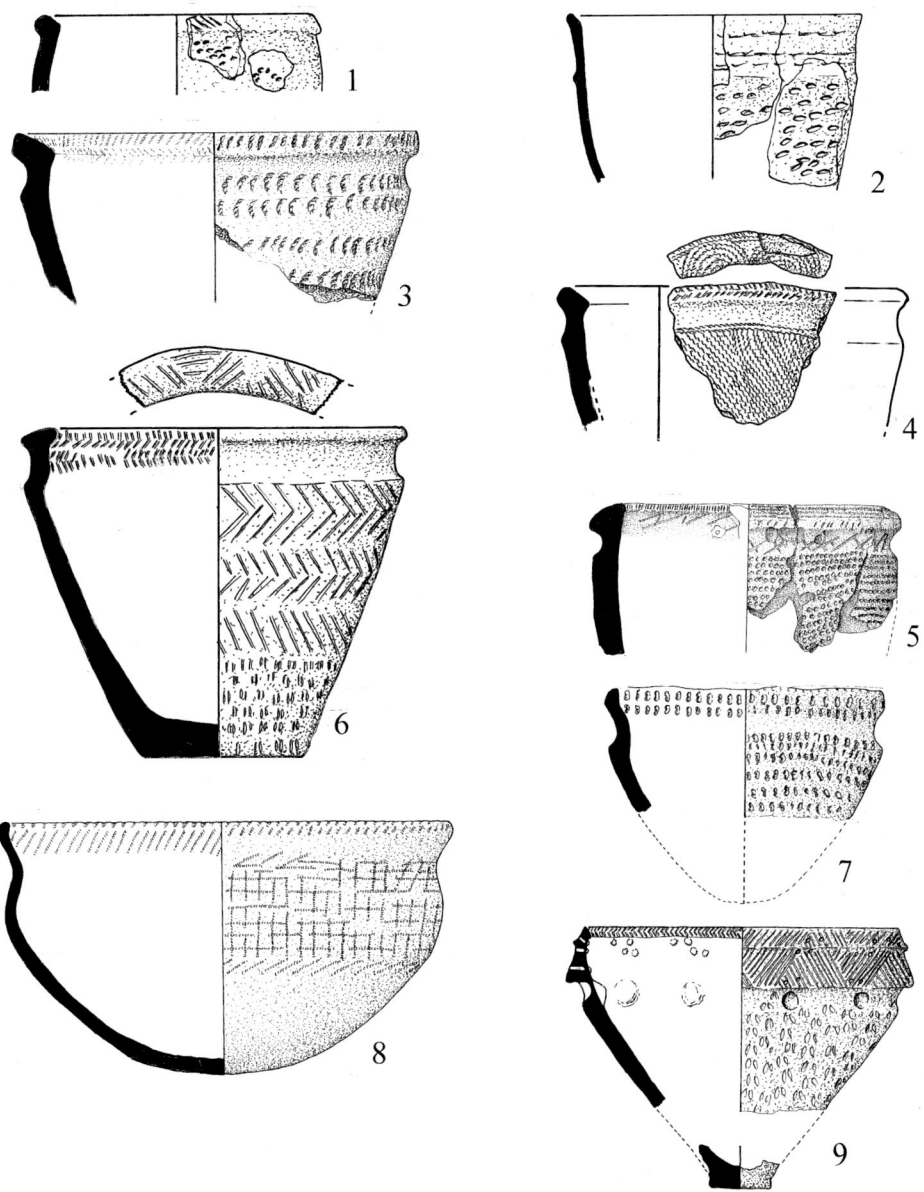

38 *Various Impressed Wares. 1 – Impressed Ware bowl from Amisfield, Dumfriess. After Strachan et al. 1998; 2 – earlier Neolithic bowl with impressed belly from Kenny's Cairn, Caithness. After Davidson & Henshall 1991; 3 – Meldon Bridge style bowl from Meldon Bridge, Peeblesshire. After Burgess 1976b; 4 – Ford style bowl from Ford, Northumberland; 5 – Welsh Mortlake style bowl from Sarn-y-bryn-caled, Powys; 6 – Rudstone style bowl from North Carnaby, Yorkshire. After Manby 1988; 7 – Mortlake style bowl from West Kennet, Wiltshire. After Piggott 1962; 8 – Ebbsfleet style bowl from Windmill Hill, Wiltshire. After Smith 1965; 9 – Fengate style bowl from West Kennet, Wiltshire. After Piggott 1962. All scale 1:6*

with the pot but these dates proved even earlier at approximately 3300-2900 BC. More disbelief followed and accordingly some small sample dates on carbon residues adhering to the pot and on fragments of two containers made out of tree bark and associated with the vessel were run at the Radiocarbon Accelerator Unit in Oxford. These turned out to date to between 3600 and 2900 BC. The seven dates on material directly associated with this vessel were now undeniable and it looked like the developed phase of Peterborough Ware was almost a millennium older than had been previously believed.

The time was right for a re-assessment of the data. In 1997 all the available radiocarbon dates for Peterborough Ware were examined (Gibson & Kinnes 1997) and some additional dates on recently discovered Fengate style vessels from Wales were obtained. All dates from dubious contexts or from wood charcoal were rejected, as securely associated material was needed to provide accurate dates and old oak wood might have already been several hundred years old when deposited. The 34 reliable dates proved very interesting indeed. The stylistic progression advocated by Smith could not be seen to have a chronological basis. That is to say that all three of Smith's styles, Ebbsfleet, Mortlake and Fengate, were in use by 3000 BC. The three dates for Ebbsleet span 3500-2900 BC. The 20 dates for Mortlake span 3600-2300 BC and the nine for Fengate Ware span 3500-2500 BC. More dates have been obtained since this initial work and these have confirmed the findings. The Scottish and Irish dates are also in broad agreement.

This research does not invalidate Isobel Smith's original sequence and typology. On the contrary, there are too few dates to allow us to be prescriptive. We also lack datable stratified deposits of Peterborough Ware on which to run statistical analyses of the dates. But what the research did show was that all styles of Peterborough Ware were fully developed by 3000 BC. This means that, if they were to have influenced the early Bronze Age pottery in the way we had always envisaged, then they must have remained unchanged in the archaeological record for almost a millennium. Only increased numbers of reliable dates from stratified contexts will resolve this problem.

The term 'Impressed Ware' has already been used above. This is a global term given to all pottery of the middle and later Neolithic which is decorated principally with impressions, and of which family Peterborough Ware is an English member. The discovery of Impressed Wares in Scotland led to the brief introduction of the term 'Northern Peterborough Ware' which served to acknowledge that this material was related to its English cousin, but that over Britain as a whole there were clear regional variations. In particular, the rim forms of the northern material can often be more angular than those in southern England and the decoration can also vary in degrees. A local borders variant of this pottery has been labelled the Meldon Bridge style after the pottery found at the Neolithic palisaded enclosure in Peeblesshire. With narrow necks, angular moulded and bevelled rims, and a preference for impressed herringbone motifs, the similarity of these vessels to the earlier Bronze Age Food Vessel forms cannot be denied. However, the radiocarbon dates from the pot-bearing pit deposits at Meldon Bridge suggest that this local variant was also in use by 3300 BC (Burgess & Speak 1999).

The term Peterborough Ware is one that has never been used in Ireland. At least in Scotland and the Borders, the links between the northern and southern Impressed Wares were acknowledged while at the same time the differences were respected. In Ireland, however, there is an abundance of richly decorated impressed ware vessels and regional styles (**39**), and a variety of labels predominate. If anything, the Irish material is much richer in terms of its expanded rims and ornate decoration than are the more conservative British ceramics of this time. This is a pattern that continues well into the earlier Bronze Age and indeed, given the richness of the Irish corpus and the early radiocarbon dates from this island, it would now appear that Irish decorated ceramics are fundamental in the influencing of British Bronze Age pottery, of which more below. The sheer variety of the forms and decorative schemes on the Irish material is largely responsible for the abundance of confusing names used for the pottery of this period in Ireland. With each site tending to produce subtly different pots, the temptation has been to name pots after the sites that produced them rather than look for overall patterns.

The Sandhills Ware, Dundrum Bowls and Goodland Bowls of the Irish Neolithic are vessels which certainly preserve a regional identity but which also bear such profuse impressed decoration and elaborate rim forms as to be unquestionably a part of the Impressed Ware tradition (**39**). As in Britain the rim forms of Irish pottery start to develop towards the end of the earlier Neolithic, so that by before 3000 BC there are a variety of elaborated forms not dissimilar to the Ebbsfleet and Mortlake types and indeed even more expanded. There are also profusely impressed coarse ware pots calling to mind the thick-walled Mortlake ware of the contemporary British Neolithic. Alison Sheridan neatly summarised the Irish scenario when she wrote:

> ... the general trend ... towards the use of decorated, uncarinated pottery offers parallel for middle Neolithic developments over much of Britain. However, whilst one can identify some specific similarities between Irish and British ... Middle and Later Neolithic pottery, it is clear that a slavish adoption of alien ceramic traditions was not involved. The Irish material contains many features which are not paralleled in Britain. ... Thus, just as the idea of a relatively homogeneous 'Peterborough' tradition is breaking down in Britain in favour of a series of regional developments, so one can envisage the Irish material as a further set of analogous developments. The similarities between Irish and British pottery can be explained by the existence of networks of contacts across the Irish Sea (1995, 15).

This is a view with which I wholeheartedly agree. The links between Britain and Ireland at this time cannot be denied. The links might be closer with Scotland and Wales, but that is to be expected given the increased geographical proximity, especially between Ulster and south-west Scotland. It may now be time to lay the term Peterborough Ware to rest. It is a label that has lasted for a century and perhaps has outlived its usefulness. It is a term that is no longer relevant outside of southern Britain. Impressed Ware has the advantage of being an umbrella term, a descriptive label that has the benefit of uniting the regional variants of a pan-British and Irish

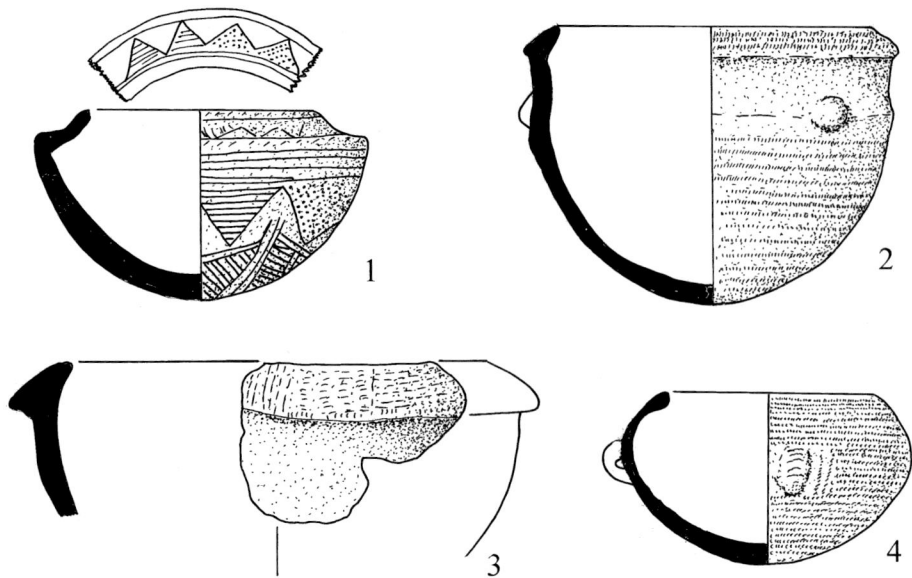

39 *Irish Middle and Late (No. 3) Neolithic Pottery (after Sheridan 1995). 1 – Shouldered bowl from Ardcrony, Co. Tipperary; 2 & 4 – Rath, Co. Wicklow; 3 – Lambay Island, Co. Dublin. The similarity of 2 and 3 to British Peterborough Wares can be clearly seen. All scale 1:4.*

phenomenon. This said, the label 'Peterborough Ware' has served ceramic studies and indeed Neolithic studies well and it will be hard to drop.

As mentioned above, the end of the Impressed Ware tradition is more difficult to determine. More radiocarbon dates from sealed contexts on which to work some statistical analyses are desperately needed. If, as current data suggests, the end of the tradition is around 2700 BC, then we are left with an embarrassing hiatus between the Impressed Wares and the Food Vessels of the early Bronze Age. These vessels have always been considered to have developed from the Peterborough tradition. They have marked shoulders, hollow necks, developed rims and impressed decoration. They would now appear to date to almost 500 years later than Peterborough Ware. This is a problem to which we will return.

The fourth millennium, therefore, sees the adoption of a new fully-formed technology. The pottery is well formed and well fired with no period of experimentation visible in the archaeological record. This adoption is widespread and rapid. Carinated Bowls remain the main stock of the millennium, with later developments stemming from, adapting and modifying this original form. By the middle of the millennium regionality has started and decoration has been introduced. The shouldered bowl is still the predominant style, though there are also globular and hemispherical bowls within the assemblages. Decoration is simple and unadventurous and rim forms have started to develop and thicken. By the end of the millennium profusely decorated vessels are the norm with abundant impressed decoration and elaborate rim forms. Many still retain echoes of their shouldered roots. Twisted and whipped cord impressions have also made their debuts and were destined to retain their popularity for the next 2000 years.

5 The later Neolithic and the earlier Bronze Age: 3000 – 1000 BC

This period is conventionally known as the later Neolithic and the early and middle Bronze Age. No period starts any more than another finishes; one merges into the other often gradually and imperceptibly. The terms Stone Age and Bronze Age would not have meant anything to people alive at the time and, in terms of human time-scales, the adoption of a metal technology was a fairly slow process. Trinkets such as earrings and hair-rings, small knives, awls and discs of gold leaf herald the arrival of metals. Copper axes may have been ingots as much as functional axes and only with a tin bronze technology did metal tools gradually establish themselves. Given such a development, one cannot say that 3000 BC marks the start of the later Neolithic or that 2000 BC marks the beginning of the Bronze Age in any way other than conventionally. Both dates are little more than convenient pegs on which to anchor our relative and absolute chronologies and they must always be regarded as such.

Such is the continuity within the later Neolithic and earlier Bronze Ages that archaeologists have for some time realised the limitations of the three-age system of Stone, Bronze and Iron and they have tried to break away from it. A pioneering work in this field was Colin Burgess' book *The Age of Stonehenge* (Burgess 1980) which described and emphasised the continuity in material culture, burial and ritual practices between the conventional late Neolithic and early Bronze Age. Burgess's approach has been applauded and occasionally copied, but the traditional labels of Stone and Bronze are proving difficult to abandon. Burgess's period has been followed here because there does seem to be a clear continuation in the pottery of this period but, as with other facets of the archaeological record, we must acknowledge considerable overlap and the failings of our need to impose a Christianity-based chronology on a pre-Christian environment.

The period chosen here is a long one, but intentionally so: it deals with the ceramic continuum between the Neolithic and Age of Bronze and can probably be regarded as encompassing the finest two millennia of ceramic production in Britain and Ireland. The point is arguable for there are some very fine Late Bronze Age and Iron Age ceramics. But in the two millennia that form the focus of this chapter, the often exquisite decoration, and the variety and quality of the pottery is universal from north of the Grampians, to Co. Cork and Kent. This compares favourably to the later periods when some parts of the country languish in a ceramic 'dark age'. Certainly this is a period of great diversity and variety. There is a range of fabrics from extremely fine and well fired to very poor and coarse. There is an abundance of impressed, applied, raised and incised decoration often forming complex geometrical patterns. Twisted and whipped cord impressions are used to make some adventurous motifs and even plaited cord can be detected on pottery from the south-west of England and elsewhere. Vessel sizes also vary considerably from large urns that may attain heights of almost 1m to small accessory vessels that may be little more than a few centimetres high. It was the pottery from this period that so excited the early antiquaries in their prolific investigations of Bronze Age barrows or burial mounds. The pots were collected avidly by the early archaeologists and some collections such as the Bateman Collection from Derbyshire, the Greenwell Collection of artefacts from northern England, the Mortimer Collection from Yorkshire and the Coalt Hoare Collection for Wessex provide much of our knowledge of these pots. They survive in great numbers and there is scarcely an archaeological museum in the country that does not possess some pottery from this period in its collections.

Our last chapter ended with a review of the pan-British and Irish Impressed Ware tradition, the origins of which, I believe, can be traced back to the earliest Neolithic ceramics. Our current chronology suggests that these wares may well have continued into the middle of the third millennium, perhaps even later in Northern Britain and Ireland. The start of the later Neolithic in Alison Sheridan's (1995) scheme for Ireland is also placed around 3100 BC. As in Britain, developed forms of carinated bowl are in use, especially closed forms, often called Ballyalton Bowls, and related forms (**39.3**). In addition there are Dundrum Bowls or open bowls with heavy T-sectioned rims and abundant impressed or incised decoration. As mentioned in the last chapter, these are clearly related to the Impressed Wares of Britain though with much expected regional diversity, and are developed from similarly impressed ceramics dating to the middle Neolithic prior to 3000 BC (see chapter 4 above).

Despite this stress on continuity, it is difficult to see Grooved Ware as anything but later Neolithic in date, at least in England. Our current chronology would suggest the appearance of Grooved Ware in southern England at about 2800 BC (Garwood 1999), but as being emergent in northern Scotland (Barnhouse and Skara Brae) possibly as early as 3400 BC and certainly by 3100 BC (Ashmore 1998). In both Scotland and England, the manufacture and deposition of Grooved Ware cannot be envisaged after 2000 BC. The same may be true for Ireland. Certainly Grooved Ware is current around 3000 BC, but the end of the Irish tradition is yet to be determined given its comparatively recent identification in Ireland and the paucity of available dates (Brindley 1999). This ceramic, therefore, was being made and deposited in these islands for over a thousand years.

Grooved Ware comprises a tradition of fairly restricted tub, bucket or barrel-shaped pots, all of which have, for the first time, truly flat bases (**40**). It marks very much the end of the round-based tradition in Britain and Ireland and, unlike the narrow and unstable 'flat' bases of Fengate Ware, the bases of Grooved Ware vessels appear to have been designed to be practical in that they would have been stable on flat surfaces. Bucket and barrel-shaped pots differ in that the latter are closed forms meaning that the rim diameter is less than the maximum diameter which is normally located in or near to the upper third of the vessel (e.g. **40.4**).

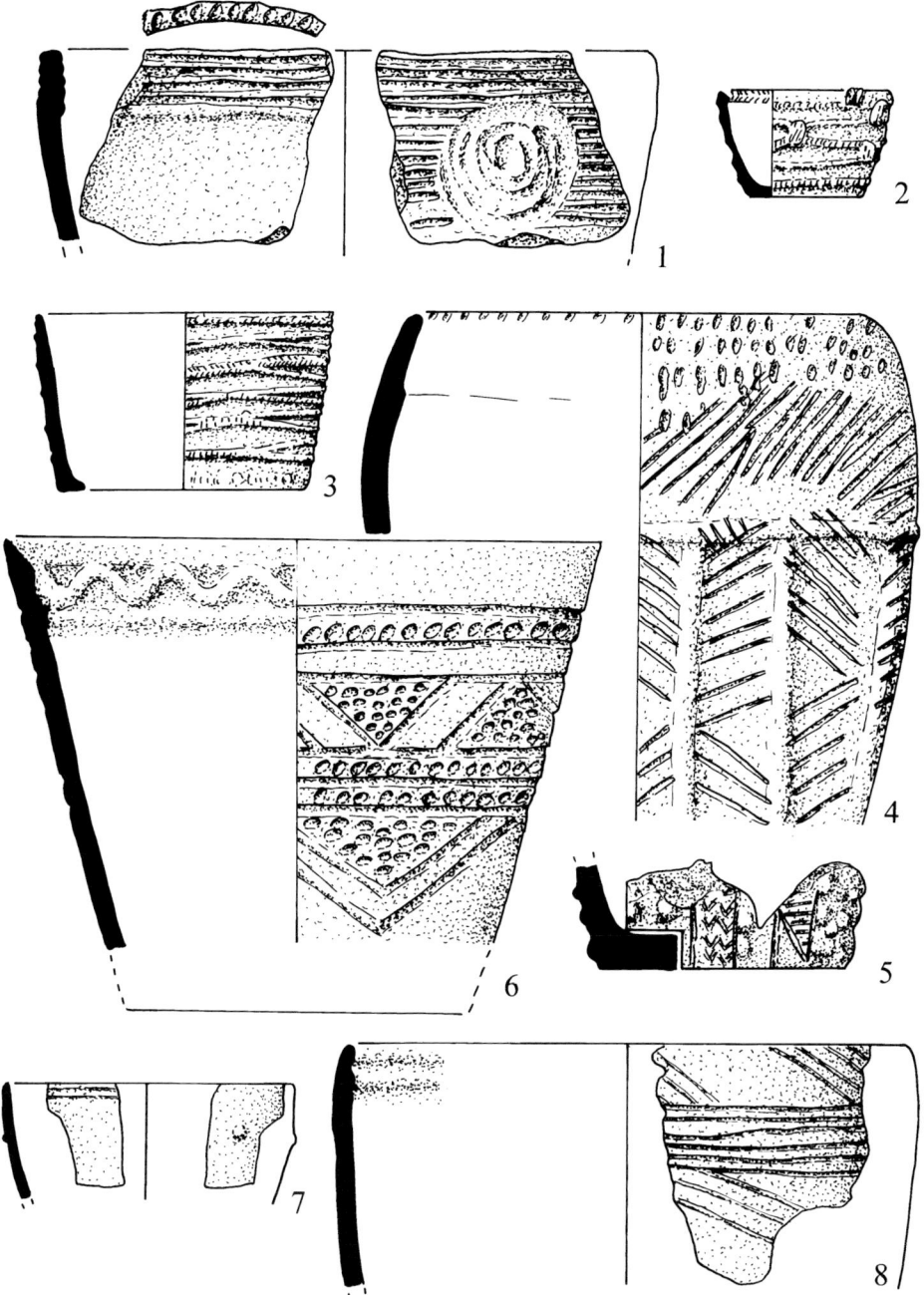

40 *Grooved Ware from Britain and Ireland. 1 – Durrington Walls, Wiltshire.* After Wainwight & Longworth 1971; *2 – Woodlands, Wiltshire.* After Stone 1949; *3 – Balfarg, Fife.* After Barclay & Russell-White 1993; *4 – Durrington Walls, Wiltshire.* After Wainwight & Longworth 1971; *5 – Skara Brae, Orkney.* After Childe 1931b; *6 – Clacton, Essex.* After Wainwight & Longworth 1971; *7 – Newgrange, Co. Meath; 8 – Knowth, Co. Meath. All scale 1:4*

Grooved Ware was identified as a type by Stuart Piggott (in Warren *et al* 1936) who was working on a collection of Neolithic and Bronze Age pottery from the buried land surfaces on the Essex coast. He was struck by some unusual flat-based pottery associated with Neolithic flintwork and decorated principally by broad incisions. The pottery bore some similarities to the sherds from the excavations at the henge and timber circle at Woodhenge in Wiltshire and to material from the Orkney stone villages such as Skara Brae and Rinyo. Accordingly in 1954 Piggott recommended abandoning the term 'Grooved Ware' in favour of Rinyo-Clacton Ware. This name was more satisfactory in describing the then known distribution of the type from Rinyo in the Orkney Islands to Clacton in Essex. While this term became used extensively, 'Grooved Ware' was never really dropped from the literature. It re-emerged as the preferred term in 1971 when Ian Longworth re-defined Grooved Ware (in Wainwright & Longworth 1971) when writing up the large quantities of such material from Wainwright's excavations at the large ceremonial henge monument and timber circles at Durrington Walls near Amesbury.

Longworth identified four main styles of Grooved Ware, which he termed the Clacton style, the Woodlands style, the Durrington Walls style and the Rinyo style. The Clacton style, seen as having a generally south-easterly distribution, comprised vessels with simple or internally grooved rims, rims with internal plastic decoration, chevrons and lozenges defined by multiple incised lines and filled with dots or oval impressions. The Woodlands style was Wessex centred and was made up of small tub-like cups with converging external cordons sometimes 'knotted' together with applied pellets of clay. The Durrington Walls style was the most widespread and consisted of large, richly decorated barrel and bucket forms. Many pots carried vertical and horizontal cordons and as well as deep incised decoration, twisted cord and whipped cord impressions were also used. A motif occurring on the style is the spiral, also found at this time in other environments such as on the rock art of passage graves and on antler and stone maceheads, all of which are generally regarded as sharing at least part of this broad temporal horizon. Longworth's Rinyo style was restricted to northern Scotland and the Northern Isles and was characterised by applied cordons and clay pellets and cordons with impressed dot decoration.

In 1984, Colin Richards and Julian Thomas suggested a hierarchical scheme for the decoration of Grooved Ware, particularly from the type site at Durrington Walls (see above p.65). This ranged from undecorated vessels at the lower end of the hierarchy, rising as the decoration increased in intensity and variability, to the upper end where the vessels are often large, with decorated cordons separating highly decorated panels. Later still, Paul Garwood (1999) has suggested, on the basis of the similarities of the converging decoration and on the available radiocarbon evidence, that the Woodlands style may be a later development of the Clacton style. This leaves us with only two distinct traditions in southern England; the Clacton-Woodlands sequence of tub-shaped vessels and the Durrington Walls style of larger pots.

The Rinyo style has tended to dominate the discussion of Grooved Ware in Scotland; however when this material was reviewed (Cowie & MacSween 1999) the pottery could be seen to be more varied than previously thought (for example

40.3 & **40.5**). Nevertheless, incised chevrons, applied dotted cordons and applied lozenges seem to be present throughout Scotland, with no regional patterning as yet apparent. As mentioned above, the dates for Scottish Grooved Ware indicate that it developed before the southern English material, and it cannot be denied that Scottish and English Grooved Ware are related. It has been suggested that the Scottish Grooved Ware derives from the earlier Unstan Ware, on which geometric decoration is common. The radiocarbon dates suggest that this is possible though by no means certain and the mechanics by which this pottery spread over Britain, and indeed Ireland, are as yet unclear.

Until 1979, Grooved Ware was unknown in Ireland. It was first recognised amongst material from the passage grave complex at Knowth (Gibson 1982) though this was slow to be acknowledged by Irish archaeologists. Since then it has been increasingly identified at various locations on the island, especially at the ceremonial complexes of Ballynahatty in County Down and the Bend of the Boyne complex in County Meath, but also during re-assessments of earlier excavated material. Doubtless more find spots will be quick to emerge now that Grooved Ware has been recognised and accepted. To date, and given the relatively small body of material available for study, there would appear to be no regionality to the Irish material with the exception, perhaps, of small curved wall tubs with single or multiple horizontal incised lines inside the rim. These have been found at the passage tomb complex of Newgrange and the timber circles at Knowth and Ballynahatty. Even these vessels are not restricted to Ireland, but have parallels in Scotland (Balfarg, Fife) and Wales (Walton Basin, Powys).

Grooved Ware, like Impressed Ware in its broadest sense, is now a pan-British and Irish phenomenon. It tends to be found on ritual sites such as the banked and ditched henge enclosures, pit complexes or the communal passage graves of Orkney and Ireland. Indeed some of the decorative motifs found on some Grooved Ware can be paralleled in the rock art associated with some passage graves. The pottery may also have been domestic, though settlement evidence is rare outside of the Orkney Neolithic villages such as Skara Brae, Barnhouse and Rinyo.

The Grooved Ware tradition was already half a millennium old, particularly in Scotland, when, around the middle of the third millenium BC, another universal tradition appeared in the archaeological record. This was Beaker pottery, part of a European-wide phenomenon. The pots are usually well made and decorated with geometric patterns arranged into zones. These motifs are usually executed with a toothed comb or are incised. Some Beakers are decorated all over with encircling lines of twisted cord impressions. Beakers occur frequently in individual burials often associated with other distinctive artefacts such as tanged copper knives, awls, archers' wristguard fastenings, and barbed and tanged arrowheads (**41**).

The rapid spread of Beakers over Europe and their introduction into Britain and Ireland was formerly attributed to a race of round-headed warriors who, as well as the pots, introduced individual burial under round barrows into the archaeological record and heralded the advent of metalworking. The picture is now seen to be far less clear and far more complicated. For example the round barrows and individual

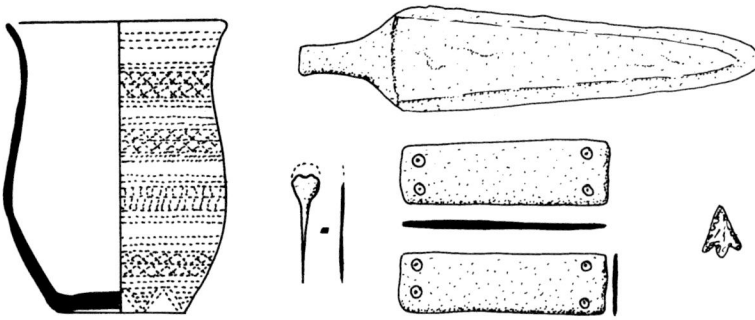

41 *A Beaker grave group from Roundway, Wiltshire. Associated with the Beaker was a collection of artefacts including a copper dagger and pin, an archer's wristguard fastening, and a barbed and tanged arrowhead. Scale 1:4. After Clarke 1970*

burials of the Bronze Age are now known to have had a respectable native Neolithic ancestry and other indigenous monument traditions continue to develop throughout this period. The only introduction at this time seems to have been the pottery itself and the distinctive artefact types with which it is associated. There are other explanations for the rapid spread of the phenomenon, such as the apparent domestication of the horse at this time leading to greater mobility of people (just as it's introduction did amongst the native American populations). There may also have been a cult involving set paraphernalia (the associated artefacts), or the pots (and contents?) may have been attractive 'must haves' for members of leaderships, warriors or those having priesthood status. In other words they may have been symbols of authority, opulence or status. Much has been written on this subject and it is fair to say that we are still uncertain as to the 'hows' and 'whys' of the introduction of Beakers. To go further into the question is beyond the scope of this book but what cannot be denied is that Beakers spread quickly and they certainly demonstrate the close links between Britain, Ireland and continental Europe at this time.

Beakers are in the main well-made, usually well-fired, pots, with S-shaped profiles and often complex decoration (**42**. See also **18, 22, colour plates 9** & **10**). Some have handles resembling present-day beer tankards and this feature has strengthened their interpretation as drinking vessels. They are visually attractive and demonstrate the high degree of ceramic and artistic competence that existed at this time. This has led some writers to elevate Beakers to extraordinary heights invoking the use of special clays, to extol the exceptional expertise of the potters and even to suggest the use of cord frameworks in the pots' construction. Most of this inflated explanation shows a lack of understanding of ceramic technology. Beakers are just pots. Yes, they are often (but not always) well made, but so are some Carinated Bowls, Grooved Ware vessels, Unstan Ware pots and Peterborough bowls and later Food Vessels and Collared Urns continue to demonstrate the skill of prehistoric potters. Beakers are not exceptional, and some are rather poor (**colour plate 12**). They do not need extra-special skills in their manufacture. They are well within the capabilities of competent potters. No special clays are needed. Thin section analysis has

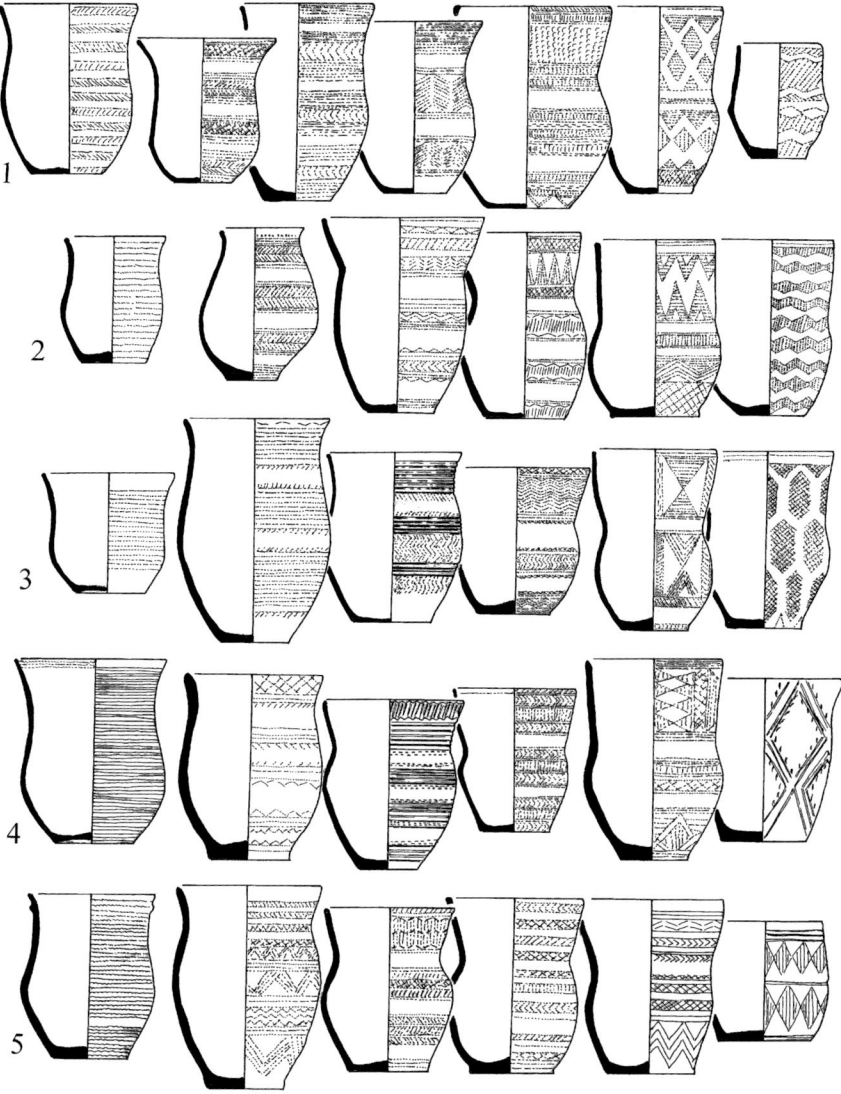

42 *Beaker sequences from 1 – Wessex, 2 – East Anglia, 3 – Yorkshire, 4 – Borders and 5 – northern Scotland. Not to scale.* Beakers after Clarke 1970

only been sporadically applied to Beakers but where it has been undertaken, it has tended to demonstrate that these pots were made from locally available clays. The prehistoric potters may have taken more care in removing larger naturally occurring inclusions from the clay, in the grinding of the deliberately added inclusions, and some iron-rich clays may have been preferred to ensure a reddish colour, but any tried and trusted clay source would have been suitable. Some beakers are very thin-walled but again this is perfectly achievable by a competent potter: so long as the clay is of the correct consistency and the building process is not rushed the thinness of the vessels denotes care rather than exceptional expertise. It is also often ignored that some Beakers are in fact poorly made of coarse clay, are thick-walled, poorly fired and have somewhat haphazardly executed decoration (**colour plate 14**). In short the description of Beakers as quality vessels is somewhat of an over-generalisation.

If, then, the technology of Beakers is not as complex as some writers would have us believe, the decoration may be another matter. The geometric patterns require repeated applications of a comb in a planned scheme of decoration. It may have taken at least as long to decorate a Beaker as to build it. Added to this, some vessels may have had contrasting inlay in the impressions (see chapter 3) and this material would have to have been prepared and then applied perhaps by dipping the comb and effectively 'tattooing' the pot. This geometric art is not unique to Beakers and indeed there can be said to be geometry in the herringbone motifs of Peterborough Ware or Grooved Ware: the chevrons of Unstan Ware have already been described. It is fair to say, however, that these patterns reach their climax with Beakers and other broadly contemporary artefacts, particularly those of gold and of copper alloy. Geometric motifs continued into the earlier Bronze Age on Food Vessels and the various types of urn.

The dating of Beakers has been largely dependent on relative chronology based on the contexts of the find, associated artefacts and the perceived development and ultimate breakdown of the shape and decoration. Generally Bell Beakers, with sinuous profiles and narrow zoned decoration, were considered primary. They developed into Beakers with a more accentuated distinction between the body and neck and the decoration then contracted into two or three broad zones. Finally, the neck lengthened and the decoration contracted into one or two zones. Occasionally the decoration broke down completely. This bell, short-necked to long-necked progression was refined in a new corpus published by David Clarke (1970) who, still firmly believing in the invasion hypothesis, envisaged successive waves of Beaker users alighting on these shores from various parts of the adjacent continent. Two native traditions then evolved in the North and South but despite the complexities of Clarke's computer-generated scheme, the bell, short-necked, long-necked sequence broadly still held good. Clarke's work was reviewed by two Dutch archaeologists Jan Lanting and Diderik van der Waals (1972) who proposed their own scheme of development for these pots based on seven stages or steps. These steps had more of a regional focus though they found it impossible to devise such a scheme for northern Scotland. This was later rectified by Ian Shepherd (1986) (**42.5**).

With very few radiocarbon dates then available, these schemes were still largely based on relative dating. Lanting & van der Waals's step development was especially attractive and did seem to work on a broad level taking into account the expected regional differences. However it was largely based on sepulchral pottery and paid scant regard to the settlement material. It was also considered by some to be over-rigorous and somewhat more relevant to factory products than to hand-built individual pots.

In the late 1980s a programme of radiocarbon dating was inaugurated and designed to consolidate existing Beaker-associated dates and provide new dates for skeletal material derived from Beaker graves (Kinnes *et al.* 1991). It appeared to show that the typological schemes of Clarke and Lanting and van der Waals had no chronological validity but that all styles were broadly contemporary in the few centuries either side of 2000 BC. This programme, however, failed to take regional trends into account and was too ambitious in its national coverage, failings exacerbated by a particularly 'wiggly' part of the radiocarbon calibration curve between 2300 and 1950 BC. What is now needed are carefully constructed regional chronologies based on equally carefully selected samples from secure and sequential stratigraphic sequences.

Humphrey Case (1993) in part tackled this when he reviewed Beakers in the light of the British Museum dating programme. Without embarking on extra dates, Case did take the non-burial pots into account and succeeded in identifying distinct regional styles and early, middle and late vessels within these groups. His important work on the volume of these vessels (1995) also demonstrated that there appeared to be evidence for the deliberate selection of small and medium-sized pots for burial taken from amongst a large range of vessel size. He further argued that Beakers were made to serve a variety of functions and uses as might befit everyday pots in a domestic repertoire. This leads us back to our initial observations that, technologically at least, there is nothing special about a Beaker.

Case's argument for a domestic component (or at least a range of pots intended for a variety of functions) within the Beaker repertoire is not new. Clarke (1970) suggested a three-tiered system of fine ware, everyday ware and coarse wares, though based largely on subjective criteria such as 'quality' and types of fabric and decoration. Case's argument based on size is less subjective and more easily demonstrable. One of the largest collections of Beaker from an apparent domestic context is the material from Northton on the Isle of Harris. This assemblage supports much of Case's argument for large and small pots, with small cups with an estimated capacity of 33cl to large vessels with a volume of some 7l (**43**). The fabric thickness and coarseness also exhibit considerable variation, as does the decoration. The latter comprises fine comb impressions carefully executed in complex though often carelessly incised motifs, incised pottery, fingernail rustication; there are also completely undecorated pots.

For over a century, archaeologists have been fixated with the idea that Beakers were drinking vessels associated with ritual drinking to induce altered states of consciousness either through alcohol or other plant-derived substances. Even if this was a function of Beakers (and handled pots suggest that at least some were drinking vessels irrespective of content), it cannot have been the only one, as their size range demonstrates. Indeed, from a purely practical point of view and apart from the handled examples, Beakers themselves are not the best designed of drinking vessels. Their wide flaring necks would lead the drinker to dribble. The bulbous bodies would trap liquid necessitating the further raising of the vessel and in turn increase the risk of spillage. In terms of ritual drinking, however, this design may have been deliberate. We know that yards of ale are not ideally designed drinking vessels, nor is the German *Stieffel* (shaped like a riding boot) nor the classical Greek two-handled *kylix* (shaped like an open, shallow pedestalled fruit bowl). Yet all of these 'impractical' vessels imbued their users with a certain

43 *Beakers from the settlement site at Northton, Isle of Harris, showing the range of sizes. All scale 1:4. Drawings by and courtesy of Derek Simpson*

amount of kudos should they manage to drain the vessel without spilling any of its contents. An intentional by-product of these drinking challenges is, of course, an increased rate of intoxication. It is therefore obvious that function and design may not always be logically linked.

Because of their distribution over almost all parts of Britain and Ireland, their aesthetic value and the invasion they were believed to represent, Beakers have received a great deal of attention from archaeologists – so much so that it has often been forgotten that there were other types of pottery in contemporary use. Grooved Ware has already been described and, assuming the demise of Grooved Ware at about 2000 BC and the arrival of Beakers at about 2400, there was almost half a millennium during which the styles of pottery co-existed. This is also true in other areas. In Scotland, for example, at Kilellan Farm on Islay and at Northton, Harris, is a type of short-necked, high-shouldered vessel known as a Kilellan Jar (**44**). The distribution of these pots seems to be restricted to the Western Isles. They are decorated with geometric zoned motifs similar to Beakers but also have impressed (cord and shell) and incised decoration more in keeping with later Food Vessels. Indeed, they may well form the link between the impressed wares of the middle Neolithic and the Food Vessels of the earlier Bronze Age. As to whether these pots were flat based or round based, the question is difficult to answer as no complete pots have been found. If the latter, then they must have been very unstable given their generally long bodies.

In Shetland, a series of roughly oval, thick-walled houses with attached yards and field systems has been dated to the later Neolithic. These have produced pottery with bold incised decoration and geometric motifs. These pots, known

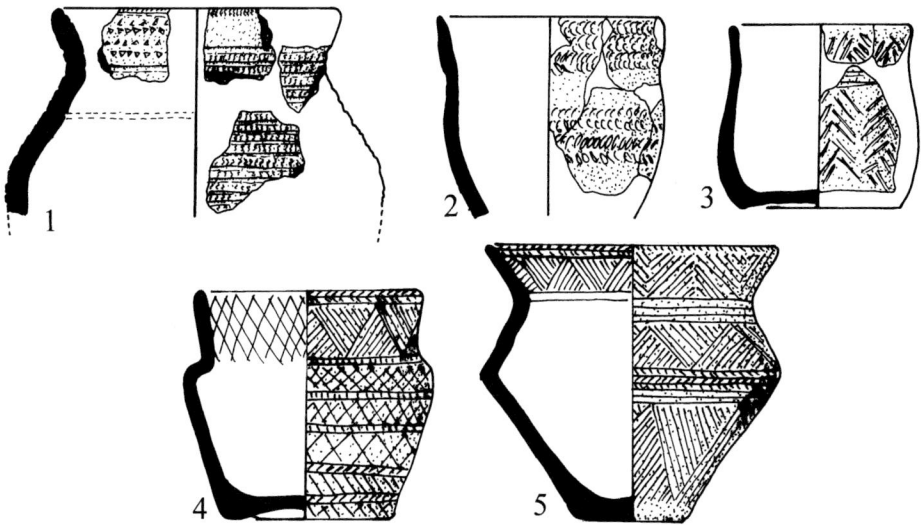

44 *Beakers on the periphery? 1 – Kilellan Jar from Islay. After Burgess 1976a; 2 & 3 – Shetland stone house pottery from Ness of Gruting. After Calder 1956; 4 & 5 – Irish Vases from Tykillen, Wexford and Kilmuckridge, Wexford. After O'Riordain & Wadell 1993. All scale 1:4*

as Shetland Stone House Wares, may well have been originally influenced by the Unstan Wares of Orkney and the Western Isles, but the presence of necked variants also suggests a Beaker influence on a native tradition. Once more the radiocarbon dates, certainly for the later phases of these houses, suggest considerable overlap with Beakers.

In Ireland, while Beakers are by no means absent, they do not seem to have been so widely adopted as in Britain. The role of Beakers seems to have been played by highly ornate earlier Bronze Age pottery types which are widely distributed over Ireland and extend to south-west Scotland and Wales. These fall under the general heading of Food Vessels but are more specifically known as Irish Bowls and Vases. The latter in particular have short-necked variants which resemble the Kilellan Jars but in a more developed form. These pots will be discussed in more detail below. Suffice it to say here that they appear to be derived, under Beaker influence, from the impressed wares of the middle and later Neolithic and radiocarbon dates suggest that they were in use from at least as early as 2400 BC. Their contemporaneity with the Beaker presence in Britain, then, cannot be denied.

Once more the question of overlap cannot be over-emphasised. The earlier Bronze Age, conventionally seen as starting shortly before 2000BC, is characterised over Britain and Ireland by Food Vessels and a variety of urn forms. Foremost amongst these are Food Vessel Urns, Cordoned Urns, Wessex Handled Urns and, more commonly, Collared Urns. While such earlier Bronze Age forms certainly outlasted Beakers, the latter pots were still current when the earliest of these Bronze Age forms emerged.

Food Vessels are not necessarily vessels for holding food. The name is derived from the early antiquarians who frequently found two distinct types of pottery in

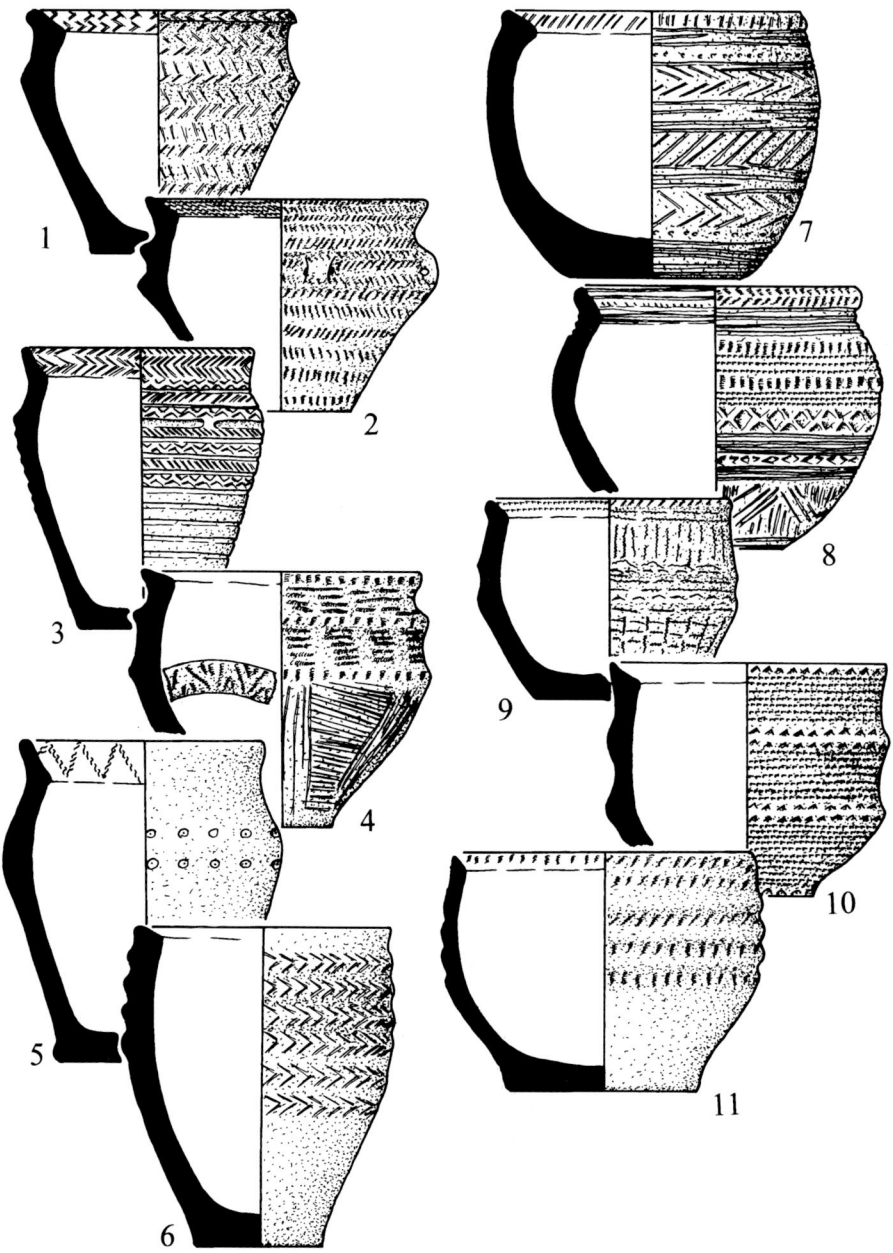

45 *Food Vessel vases (1-6) and bowls (7-11). 1 – Bipartite vase from Great Tosson, Northumberland; 2 – Yorkshire vase from Denton Hall, Northumberland; 3 – Irish vase from Craigbirnoch, Wigtownshire; 4 – Tripartite vase from Haugh Head, Northumberland; 5 – Southern bipartite vase from Belle Toute, Sussex; 6 – Ridged vase from Knocken, Lanarkshire; 7 – Globular British bowl from Ford, Northumberland; 8 – Hiberno-Scottish bowl from Jesmond, Tyne and Wear; 9 – Waisted bowl from Portpatrick, Wigtownshire; 10 – Tripartite bowl from Lochinch, Wigtownshire; 11 – Ridged bowl fom Cambuslang, Lanarkshire.
All scale 1:4. 3, 6, 9-11 after Simpson 1965; 5 after Musson 1954*

graves below round barrows. The first was a fine ware which they called Beakers or 'drinking cups'. The other pots often had heavy rims and were therefore considered to be impractical for use as drinking vessels. The term Food Vessel was therefore used to distinguish these heavy pots from the more elegant Beakers. There are two main types of Food Vessel known as bowls and vases (**45, colour plate 15**). Bowls are small vessels with their individual height being less than or equal to their greatest diameter. Vases, on the other hand, are taller than their maximum diameter. Food Vessels are generally less than 20cm tall. They are decorated with a variety of techniques such as cord impressions, comb impressions, stab, stab and drag and false relief where a triangular point is impressed into the clay from alternate and opposed directions to result in a raised zigzag. As with Beakers, the quality of the fabric varies tremendously from fine and grog-filled to very coarse with large angular stone inclusions, and the decorative schemes range from the very ornate to crudely executed: even undecorated examples are found. Beaker influence is clearly visible in the geometric zoned nature of some decoration.

Within both the vase and bowl forms there are simple, bipartite and tripartite forms (**43**). Bipartite is where the pot has two distinct sections, usually a body leading to a carination and then a neck. This basic shape has been present in the archaeological record since the carinated bowls of the early and middle Neolithic, but now the body is flat-based rather than rounded. This, combined with the heavy, moulded rim forms of Food Vessels, has often been taken to indicate that these pots are derived from the Impressed Wares, particularly those from Scotland and Ireland. The development was easy to see whilst Peterborough Ware and its regional variants were regarded as later Neolithic. Now that it is known that Impressed Ware is a middle Neolithic phenomenon, the links between this ceramic and Food Vessels are more difficult to ascertain. While there is still room for a slight overlap within the new chronology, the early date of Irish Bowls may be pivotal to this process. Ireland may provide the melting pot from which these hybrid vessels emerge. Added to this is the preponderance of Food Vessels in Ireland and the west and north of Britain in comparison to the rest of the country.

As bipartite forms are in two parts, so tripartite are, like Caesar's Gaul, divided into three. These usually comprise vessels with a broad concavity midway up. The form is present in both the vases and bowls. The derivation of this peculiar form is uncertain though some Irish material may again provide the answer: some Irish Bowls have a dramatic waist and it is not difficult to see this waist expanding to result in a tripartite vessel.

In a ceramic form spread so widely over the country it is little wonder that there are regional trends within the material. Irish Bowls have already been mentioned and are characterised by their profuse, often elaborate decoration frequently extending over the base of the pot. Irish Vases are similarly often profusely decorated with zoned geometric motifs. They frequently have very distinct necks and are relatively tall. Both forms reach Scotland and Wales. In the north-east of England, though also extending to Scotland as well as further south, Yorkshire Vases have one or more cavetto zones at the shoulder and these concave grooves have vertical knobs or ridges within. Occasionally these stops may be perforated leading to the suggestion that some at least of these pots may have been suspended.

The Food Vessel tradition, though present, is less strong in south-east England. This is strange if one is to accept the origins of Food Vessels lying within the Impressed Ware tradition for it is in south and eastern England that Peterborough Ware is most abundant. This may strengthen the argument for Irish influence at a time when contacts between the two islands were doubtless increasing thanks to the abundance of Irish copper sources. Therefore, despite the growing chronological disparity between Peterborough Ware and Food Vessels, it may still be possible to see the Bronze Age ceramics developing from the Impressed Wares. However less influence might be placed on Peterborough Ware and instead more emphasis might be given to the northern and Irish variants under Beaker influence. This is supported by the early radiocarbon dates for vase and bowl pottery in Ireland.

Collared urns pose more of a problem. These distinctive pots, originally called 'Overhanging Rim Urns', are also distributed widely over Britain and Ireland and vary considerably in size from under 10cm to over 50cm high (**46**; **colour plate 16**). Most seem to cluster around the 15-30cm range (Longworth 1984). They are characterised by heavy collared rims sitting on top of straight or slightly convex-sided pots, the bodies of which taper to a flat base. Frequently, the collar will be separated from the body by a concave neck or cavetto zone thus giving the urn a tripartite form. The collars are usually decorated with impressed or incised patterns such as filled triangles or hurdling and twisted cord, whipped cord and comb are common techniques. Until comparatively recently it was easy to see Collared Urns developing from the heavy rimmed Fengate style of the Peterborough tradition. Not only is Fengate Ware collared, but it also possesses a cavetto beneath the collar and a body tapering to a flat base. As mentioned above, Fengate Ware was always considered to be the final stage in the Peterborough sequence, originally believed to be later Neolithic, and was thus believed to have overlapped chronologically with Collared Urns. Once more Beaker influence was invoked in the form of some decorative motifs and the use of comb impressions. Now that an increasing number of radiocarbon dates are demonstrating that Fengate Ware was fully developed by 3000 BC and that Collared Urns appear in the archaeological record shortly before 2000 BC it is difficult to see how this process may have worked. It means that Fengate Ware must have lasted virtually unchanged for as much as 800 years or some 30 generations. Only a greater suite of secure radiocarbon dates from both Fengate and Collared Urn contexts might help solve the problem.

Collared Urns, with Food Vessels, very much typify the insular early Bronze Age and, as mentioned above, are widely distributed over Britain and Ireland. The name 'urn' denotes that they are frequently from burial contexts and that they were used to hold cremated bone; but this really reflects the bias of archaeology over the last two centuries towards the excavation of burial monuments. Collared Urns certainly have been found in what appear to be domestic contexts, for example around the fen edge of East Anglia. Others from graves may be incomplete or have traces of carbonaceous residues adhering to their surfaces suggesting that they have been used, probably also in a domestic context, before being removed from circulation and deposited in the grave.

1 *Excavation of a pottery cache in a pit in the Walton Basin, Radnorshire.*
Reproduced by courtesy of the Clwyd-Powys Archaeological Trust

2 *Plaited cord impressions on a Bronze Age Food Vessel from Northumberland*

3 *Grain impressions in a Bronze Age Food Vessel from Wether Hill, Northumberland.*
Photo by and reproduced courtesy of Peter Topping

4 *A selection of pots and other experimental pieces made by Romanian school children. These are the visible representations of inexperience and experiment*

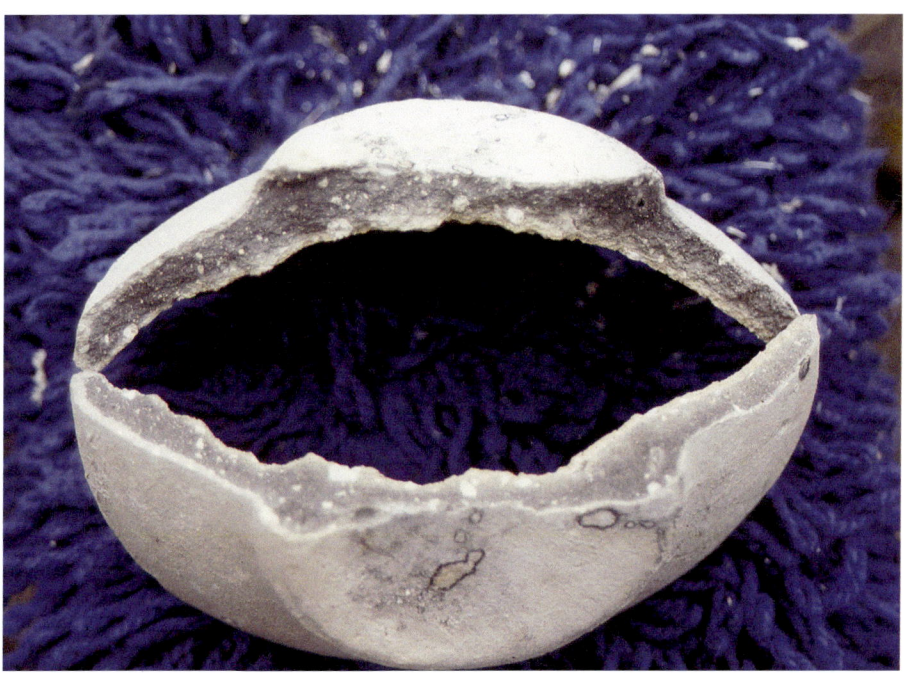

5 *Black core and oxidised surfaces in an experimental open-fired vase. The black core is the result of the incomplete combustion of organic material in the clay and this light-black-light cross-section is indicative of a brief firing period*

6 *Pots in an experimental open fire. The firing is almost over and the fire and pots are being allowed to cool down*

7 *Experimental pot with characteristic spalling and distortion resulting from the explosive expansion of the water of chemical composition as it turns to steam. This has been due to an expeditious rise in temperature within the kiln. This is a fine fabric. Coarser wares can withstand this conversion*

8 *Fingernail and tip impression from the neck dimples of a Neolithic Peterborough Ware vessel from the River Thames at London.*
Courtesy of Jon Cotton. © The Museum of London

9 *Well-executed comb impressed decoration on a late Neolithic Beaker from Monkton-Minster in Kent*

10 Breakdown in the decoration of the same vessel

11 Twisted cord impressions on a Food Vessel Urn from Goatscrag, Northumberland. Scale in cm

12 *Whipped cord 'maggots' on a Food Vessel Urn from Goatscrag, Northumberland. Scale in cm*

13 *'Birdbone' impressions on a Peterborough bowl from Sarn-y-Bryn-Caled near Welshpool, Powys.* Reproduced by courtesy of the Clwyd-Powys Archaeological Trust

14 *A Beaker from Manston, Kent demonstrating that not all Beakers are fine, well-made and carefully decorated vessels*

15 *A Food Vessel from Haugh Head, Northumberland*

16 *Collared Urn removed from its pit at Carneddau, Powys. Unusually, this urn had been placed upright in the pit. Reproduced by courtesy of the Clwyd-Powys Archaeological Trust*

17 *Food Vessel Urn from Goatscrag, Northumberland*

18 *The upper portion of a Trevisker urn from Monkton, Kent. The main distribution of this type of pottery is in the south-west of England*

19 *Later Bronze Age bowls from Runnymede, Berkshire.*
Courtesy of Stuart Needham and © The British Museum

20 *Later Bronze Age shouldered bowl from Runnymede, Berkshire.*
Courtesy of Stuart Needham and © The British Museum

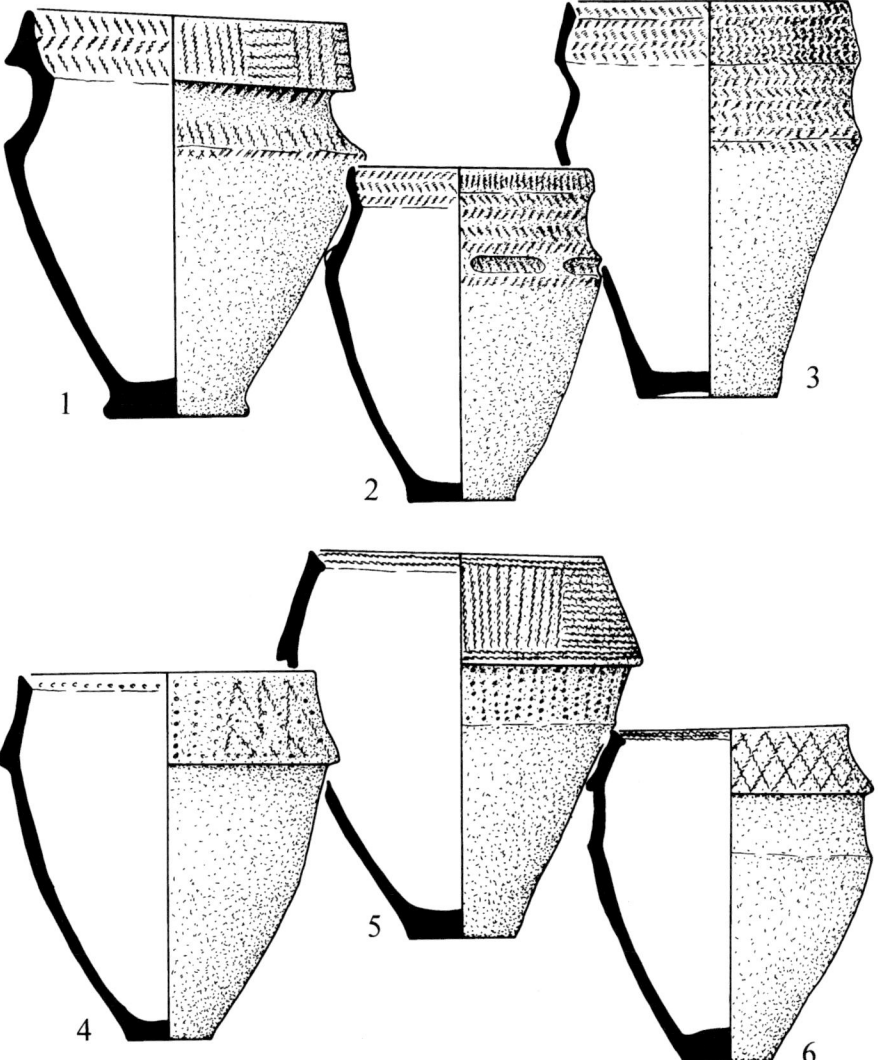

46 *Collared Urns of the primary (1-3) and secondary series. 1 – Thixendale, North Yorkshire; 2 – Pentraeth, Gwynedd; 3 – Sutton, Suffolk; 4 – Guisborough, Cleveland; 5 – Cold Kirby, North Yorkshire; 6 – Milngavie, Strathclyde. All scale 1:8.* After Longworth 1984

As with Case's analysis of Beakers, the volume range of Collared Urns suggests that they were vessels made to fulfil a variety of purposes in keeping with a domestic repertoire (**47**). Based on simple cylindrical volume (that is assuming that the pot is a cylinder rather than tapering and thus narrowing the rim diameter by 25% to compensate), Collared Urns vary from around 0.1l to 30l with the majority lying between 0.5 and 1.5l. (This is a very inaccurate way of calculating capacity but is used for illustrative purposes only.) Where they are used for burials, the cremated bones are normally found inside the pot and the urn is usually found upside down. This has prompted some researchers to suggest that the urns must have had some sort of cover to keep the bones inside whilst the pot

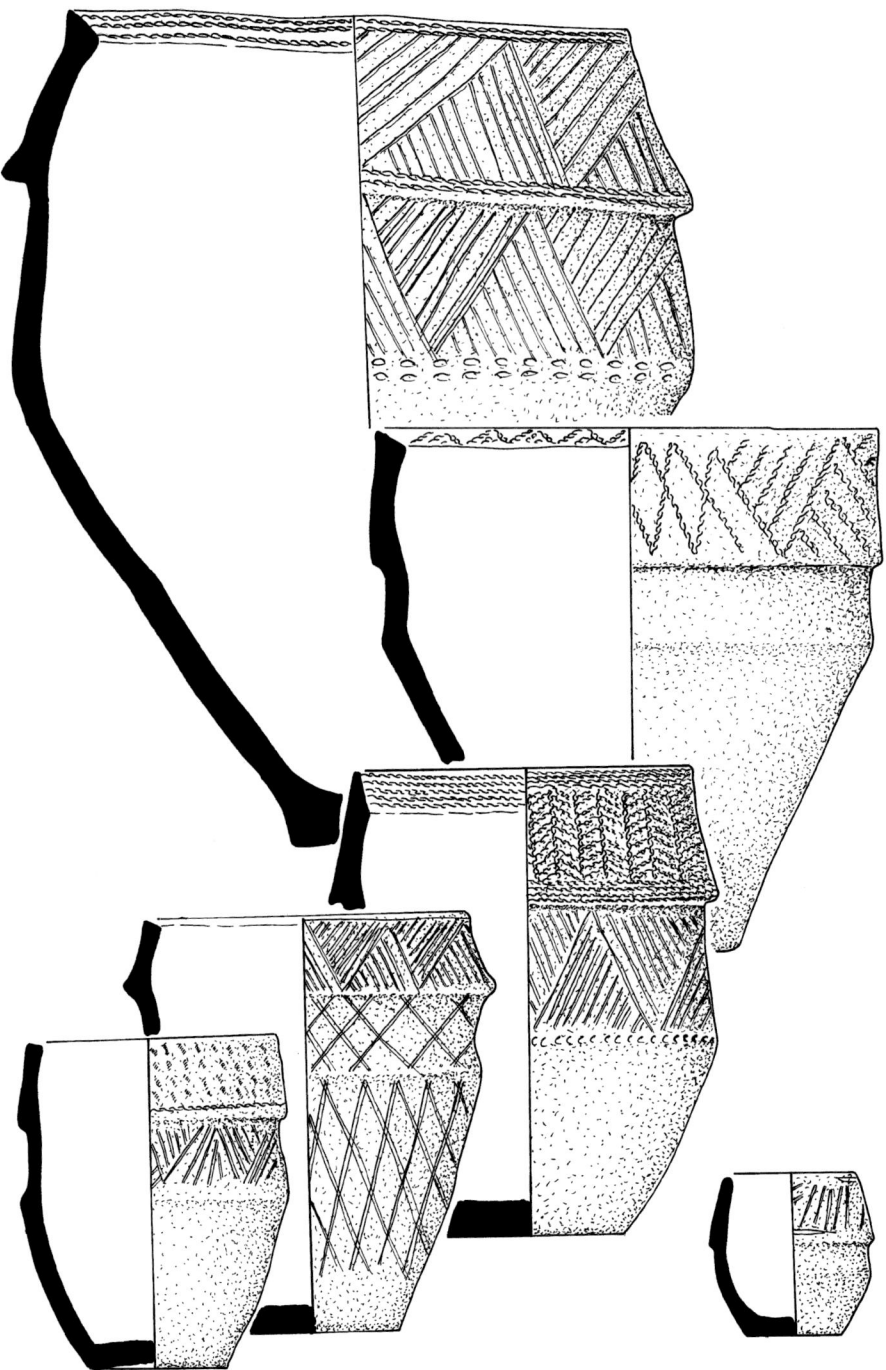

47 *Size ranges of Collared Urns. 1 – Kirby Underdale, Humberside; 2 – Scarawalsh, Co. Wexford; 3 – Bleackburn, Lancashire; 4 – Scarawalsh, Co. Wexford; 5 – Machynlleth, Powys; 6 – Witton, Norfolk. Scale 1:4*

was turned over. However it is also possible that the bones were first contained in a bag, basket or wrap of some description before the urn was placed over them. Some other, larger, urns have been found in a collapsed state with the base lying directly on the pile of cremated bones suggesting that the pot may have been placed first, the base sliced off like the top of a boiled egg, and the bones poured in. The base was then replaced but, being substantially weakened, the pot subsequently collapsed.

Collared Urns vary considerably in fabric quality. Some are in fine, grog-filled fabrics which easily rival those of some Beakers in quality. Others contain substantial and abundant stone inclusions giving them a coarse, uneven texture. The decoration also varies from fine and carefully executed to haphazard and careless. This may again reflect their initial domestic intention. As yet little residue analyses have been undertaken on Collared Urns and this must now be regarded as a research priority. The collars may often seem to have been made separately and added to the vessel neck. On other occasions, join voids in the fabric clearly show that some pots have originally had a sinuous profile and that the collar base has been added by applying a strip of clay.

Burgess (1986), using Longworth's corpus, identified early and late Collared Urns on the basis of their contexts and associations. Early urns tend to have internal decoration below the rim, repetitive short line motifs on the collar and neck, decoration below the shoulder, whipped cord decoration, shoulder grooves, external moulding and narrow collars. The later urns, by contrast, have bold decoration, no decoration below the collar, a deep collar, twisted cord crescents on the shoulder, a pinched-out collar base and angular external profile but a smooth inside profile, a bipartite form, a narrow base (30% of the maximum diameter) and a maximum diameter equal to or greater than the vessel height. Overlap between the early and late forms is to be expected but the degree of overlap and indeed the validity of the scheme remain to be tested in terms of absolute chronologies. Radiocarbon dates for Collared Urns are still lamentably few.

We have already seen that Collared Urns can vary considerably in size from small cups to large storage vessels. This is also true with Food Vessels though unlike urns, Food Vessels over 20cm high have a different name, usually Enlarged Food Vessel or Food Vessel Urn (**48, colour plate 17**). Both terms have their advantages, the former denoting the definite links with the smaller Food Vessels and the latter adding information as to function. The terms Food Urn and Vase Urn have also been recently applied to this range of earlier Bronze Age pottery but have not been widely adopted and they are not favoured here as they tend, albeit inadvertently, to return to the notion of these pots having held food rather than drink. 'Food Vessel' is now an accepted term within the archaeological vocabulary and there seems no need to change it. These large Food Vessel variants accompany cremation burials in much the same way as the Collared Urns are normally inverted over the cremation.

It is only the vase Food Vessels that occur in their larger forms. As with the smaller pots, Food Vessel Urns occur in both bipartite and tripartite forms. Shoulder grooves may contain stops as in the Yorkshire Vases and decoration is normally, though not always, restricted to the upper portion of the vessel. This said, some vessels, particularly from northern and western Britain, may be highly decorated. A vessel from Bamborough in Northumberland is highly unusual in having a scalloped

The later Neolithic and the earlier Bronze Age: 3000 – 1000 BC

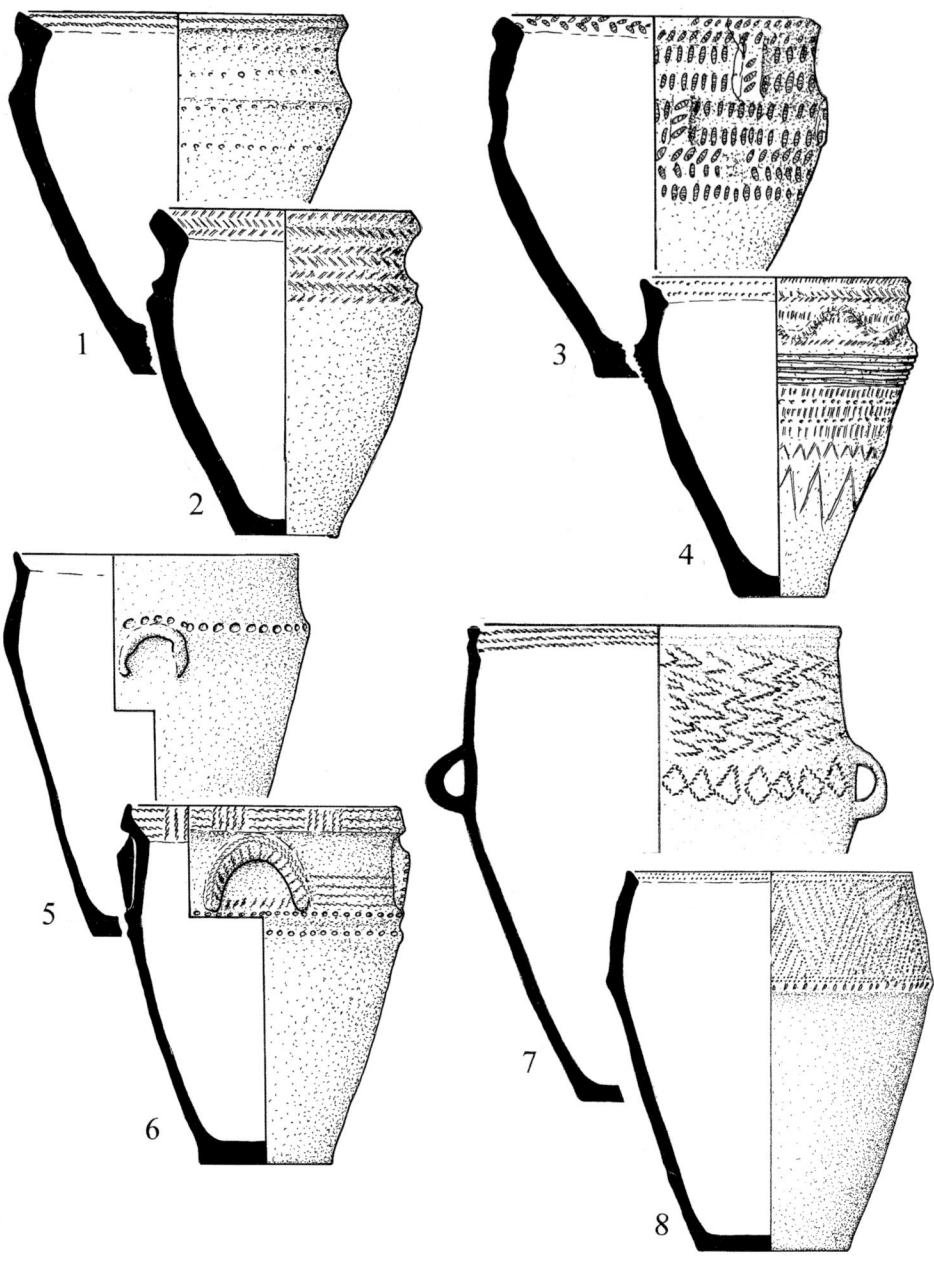

48 *Food Vessel Urns and related pots. 1 – Catcherside, Northumberland; 2 – Houghton-le-Spring, Tyne and Wear; 3 – Goatscrag, Northumberland; 4 – Ryton, Tyne and Wear; 5 – Wessex Horseshoe-handled urn from Roke Down, Dorset. After Calkin 1962; 6 – Wessex Horseshoe-handled urn from Corfe Castle, Dorset. After Longworth 1984; 7 – Cornish handled urn from Tregaseal, Cornwall. After Patchett, 1944; 8 – Wessex Biconical Urn from Cherhill, Wiltshire. After Annable and Simpson 1964. All scale 1: 8*

rim and shoulder. It was described by Greenwell (1877, 415) as 'a very remarkable specimen of the class to which it belongs . . . ' and he commented on the unusual scalloped decoration on the rim and shoulder and also referred to the extraordinary fact that the entire body was decorated (see **33** above). Indeed this urn has very strong similarities to some smaller Food Vessels from the same county and it may be that we can identify the work of a single, highly accomplished, potter.

A variant of the Food Vessel Urn carries a remarkable type of decoration in the form of raised or applied wavy cordons and, sometimes, rosettes, on the neck of the pot. These vessels are predominantly found in northern and western Britain and Ireland and may occasionally be called 'Encrusted Urns' after the distinctive plastic decoration (**48.4**). The origins of this decoration are obscure. They may be a very elaborate development of the stop ridges found in the grooves of some Food Vessels. They may derive from the plastic cordons on later Neolithic Grooved Ware, particularly the wavy cordons of the Scottish material. Some authors have also suggested that they may be references to rope-carrying frames or panniers. This argument largely rests on imagined rope artefacts and, to a certain extent, on the fact that these wavy lines are occasionally emphasised with twisted cord impressions or incised 'fringes' that resemble stitching. The rosettes, though admittedly rare, are less easy to explain but may again have Grooved Ware ancestry.

A southern variation on these urns may be the Wessex Handled Urns or Horseshoe Handled Urns of the early Bronze Age (**48.5** & **48.6**). As the first name suggests, these pots have a restricted geographical distribution and a characteristic feature is the presence of raised or applied crescentic handles in the neck or on the shoulder of the pot. These handles resemble the zigzag cordons of the northern vessels but, it must be admitted, only slightly. Once more, the shape is essentially that of a bipartite vase Food Vessel and in this case it is difficult to see these handles as anything other than functional devices to facilitate lifting. Frequently found by the early barrow diggers, these vessels date towards the middle of the second millennium and examples are also found in Continental Europe from France to the Netherlands. With the exception of the pan-European Beaker phenomenon, this is the first time that there have been close ceramic parallels between Britain and the Continent since the Western Neolithic Carinated Bowls of 4000 BC. This is almost certainly linked to the widespread trade networks established since the introduction of metals. Finds of bronzes from the seabed such as the Dover hoard prove beyond doubt the international trade in these artefacts, and sea-going vessels such as the Dover boat provide evidence for the practicalities of this trade.

The second half of the second millennium is dominated by a variety of different urn styles. Food Vessels, their relations and Collared Urns certainly continue up until the second half of the second millenium (Sheridan 2004). But there are other Urn types, both widespread and regional, that occur in the archaeological record at this time. First amongst these, and perhaps the most widespread, is the Cordoned Urn. In the field of prehistoric ceramic studies, nomenclature is rarely a difficult concept to grasp and Cordoned Urns, being urns with cordons, are no exception to this rule. These pots, generally upright or occasionally barrel-shaped, carry one or more encircling raised or applied cordon generally on the upper part of the vessel. As many as four cordons

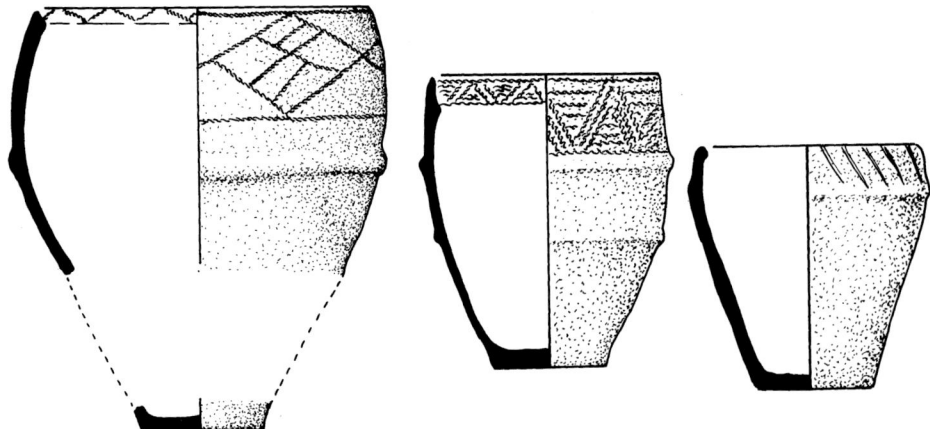

49 *Cordoned Urns. 1 – Moralee Farm, Northumberland; 2 – Laheen, Co. Donegal. After Waddell 1985; 3 – Houseledge, Northumberland. After Burgess 1985. All scale 1:8*

may be found but one or two is the norm (**49**). The cordons are often situated at the same point on the pot as the collar bases and shoulders of tripartite Collared Urns and consequently the proportions of these pots are often similar. Likewise the decoration tends, in general terms, to be restricted to the upper part of the pot and twisted cord and incised chevrons, lattices and lozenges predominate in the decorative repertoire.

The distribution of these pots is largely restricted to Ireland, Scotland, Wales and the north and west of England. They are found principally in graves but have also been found in settlement sites such as the predominantly Cordoned Urn assemblage at Downpatrick in Ulster. Cordoned Urns have been relatively little studied though there are now out-of-date corpora for Ireland (Kavanagh 1976) and south-west Scotland (Morrison 1968). Both these writers, and Longworth in his corpus of Collared Urns (1984), regard the Cordoned Urn as a separate and distinct ceramic tradition. Only further study will prove or disprove this but it must be said that, on form alone, it is often difficult to draw the distinction between Collared and Cordoned Urns. This was recognised as long ago as 1912 when Abercromby in his first great corpus of British Bronze Age pottery considered the Cordoned Urn to be a degenerate form of its Collared cousin. This theory, though now regarded as somewhat simplistic, still has some attraction and, as mentioned above, some collars on Collared Urns are accentuated by the addition of a strip (cordon) of clay. At the very least this observation and Abercromby's original theory illustrate the close cultural links between the users of these ceramic types at this time. Quite how these links functioned and what they mean in terms of sociology remains an exciting avenue for research.

The Biconical Urns can also be added to this discussion (**48.8**). These are usually barrel-shaped pots. The body splays outwards from the base then distinctly changes direction in the upper third of the vessel to close towards a narrower mouth. This gives the vessel the appearance of one truncated cone inverted and sitting on another and it is this 'biconical' shape that gives the pots their name.

These are generally restricted to southern Britain and may very well be the lowland equivalents of the Cordoned Urns already described. This is especially so as some Biconicals also have raised or applied cordons accentuating the carination or change in direction. These pots are found too on the Continent from France to the Netherlands and further demonstrate the close links between Britain and Europe at this time. The occurrence of horseshoe-shaped handles on some of these pots, the Wessex Handled Urns mentioned above, and the incised wavy lines often found on the neck of some pots reinforces their links with Food Vessels and related pottery. Twisted cord decoration is present, though it is not found as frequently as on Food Vessels or Collared Urns and lozenge and lattice motifs, particularly on the upper third of the pot, are also present. Many of these pots are undecorated, however, or occasionally the shoulder cordon may be decorated with fingertip impressions. This heralds the southern British Deverel-Rimbury ceramics which close the earlier Bronze Age.

In Cornwall, and within the Biconical Urn tradition are local variants known as Cornish Ribbon Handled Urns or Trevisker Ware and related south-west forms (**48**; **colour plate 18**). Both pottery types are similar and the latter, once again as the name suggests, have broad looped handles normally applied to the shoulder of the pot. Plaited cord impressions are a rare form of decoration on prehistoric pottery generally but are relatively common on Trevisker ware and the Urns of south-west England. The decoration is once more normally restricted to the upper part of the pot and herringbone motifs predominate. Trevisker Ware is named after the Bronze Age settlement at Trevisker Round in Cornwall. It consists of a variety of urn-shaped and tub-shaped vessels including some biconical forms. The fabric of this material is generally good and the larger vessels in particular may have cordons around the upper part of the pot, bold incised herringbone decoration and moulded rims. Typical of this type of pottery and rare outside of Trevisker Ware is the occurrence of applied crosses to the inside of the bases, presumably as a form of strengthening.

Like the earlier Neolithic Hembury Ware, Trevisker Ware is made of Gabbroic clay from the Lizard peninsula in southern Cornwall and the pottery may be traded outside of the counties of Devon and Cornwall as far afield as Hampshire and Dorset. Recently, a large, well-made pot of this type was recovered from a ring-ditch at Monkton in Kent (**colour plate 18**). This large barrel-shaped pot, over 60cm high, had a capacity of over 30l and lipid residue analysis of the inside demonstrated that it had held beef or mutton. Thin section analysis of the fabric demonstrated that it had indeed been made from Cornish clay yet this urn was discovered some 500km from the clay source. The vessel must have looked strange to the Biconical Urn users of Bronze Age Kent and its fineness and other 'exotic' features may well have imbued it with special significance. Trevisker-like pottery has been found even further afield at Île Tatihout off the Cherbourg peninsula in Normandy. This too is made of gabbroic clay but unfortunately such clays also outcrop in Normandy and therefore it may be locally made rather than an import. This point is rather academic however. The similarity of the Cornish and French pots is sufficient to further demonstrate contacts across the English Channel.

There is also a variety of miniature vessels present at this time in the archaeological record (**50**). They are often found associated with Food Vessels or with the various urn types and for that reason fall under the general heading of accessory vessels because they act as accessories to the main pot. Their diminutive size also won them the name 'Pigmy cup' though this term is becoming increasingly less common in our present politically correct environment. There are various types of small vessel, such as the perforated wall cup, the grape cup and the Aldbourne cup. These small pots are often very simple. They may be small vessels, smaller than a tennis ball, pinched up from a ball of clay. They may be poorly finished and have little or no decoration. On the other hand, they may be elaborately decorated with geometric motifs.

Some of the most elaborate are the Perforated Wall Cups. As the name suggests, these have panels cut out of the walls of the vessels. These can be oval, triangular or rectangular and were done while the clay was still wet. They were formerly known as Incense Cups for it was believed that the perforations were to allow the fumes of burning incense to escape during the burial ritual. Given that some of these small pots do exhibit signs of burning on the inner surface, the theory sounds plausible if, as yet, unproven. Residue analysis might prove productive here, though a small private study failed to find any organic traces (Gibson 2004).

Other cups are, in effect, miniature Food Vessels. They have Food Vessel decoration and normally share the shapes of the carinated bipartite vases and bowls. Some are, also like Food Vessels, undecorated or sparsely decorated. Their function is less easy to speculate and research into whether they were to accompany children's burials has usually proved fruitless. Given the quality range of these vessels, it is possible that some may be at least partly products of a learning process. Many are capable of being pinched and formed from a single ball of clay. Indeed, many are obviously pinched and simple in their decoration. Are they practice works or apprentice pieces or is there something more significant to the process of miniaturisation? The questions may, at present, be unanswerable. Accessory vessels which certainly cannot be regarded as practice pieces are the Aldbourne and Grape Cups. The former are bipartite vessels with open flaring rims and are decorated internally and externally with geometric (usually triangle-based) motifs that often resemble the internally decorated bowls of the Grooved Ware tradition. The Grape Cups are peculiar small vessels. They are usually globular in shape and take their name from the small pellets of clay applied to their outer surface which, with a slightly stretched imagination, resemble a bunch of grapes. Many may also have multiple perforations, normally in the 'valleys' between the pellets. We can only assume a purpose to their peculiar design and it is difficult to envisage such a purpose that does not involve ritual. Were they, as the Perforated Wall Cups may have been, suspended, smoking from the beams of a shaman's hut, filling the air with aromatic or even intoxicating vapour? Did their fragrance purify the air and mask the stench of death rituals? Until science can shed more light on these fascinating and often charming pots we may only speculate.

The end of the early Bronze Age and indeed of the second millennium BC is marked, at least in southern England, by a ceramic tradition known as Deverel-Rimbury after two sites in Dorset (**51**). This type of pottery is found both in cremation cemeteries and on domestic sites and is therefore truly universal. It clearly has its ancestry

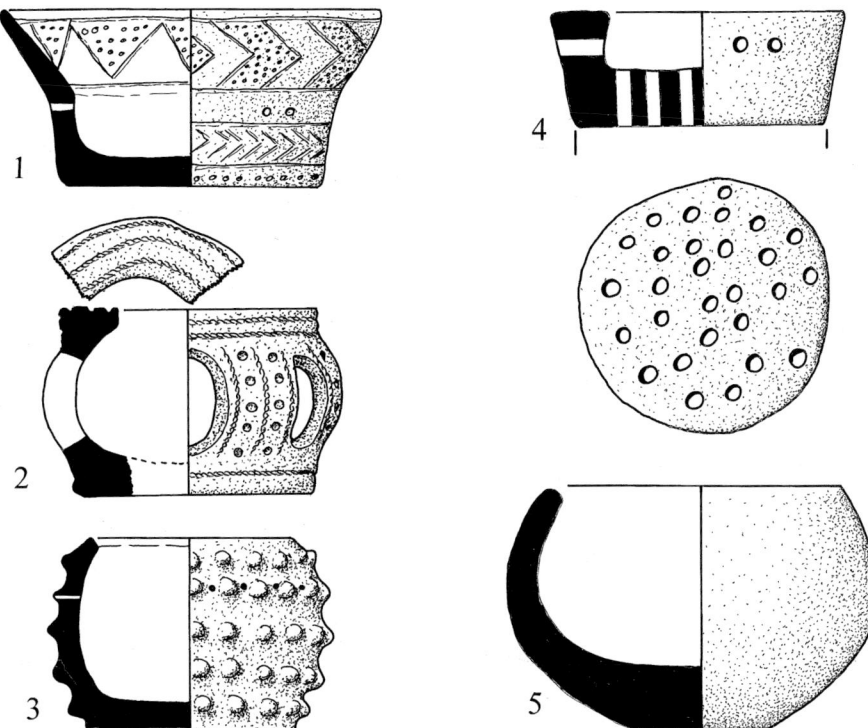

50 *Bronze Age Miniature Vessels. 1 – Aldbourne Cup from Durrington, Wilts; 2 – Perforated Wall Cup from Great Shefford, Berks; 3 – Grape Cup from Preshute, Wilts; 4 – Perforated cup from Wilsord, Wilts; 5 – small simple cup from Wilsford, Wiltshire.
All scale 1:2. 1, 3 & 4 after Annable and Simpson 1964, 3 after Longworth 1983*

in the preceding Urn traditions, especially the Cordoned Urn and the Biconical series. Vertical cordons on some pots may be a distant recollection of Grooved Ware. There are three main types of Deverel-Rimbury vessel: the bucket urn, barrel urn and globular urn. In addition there are smaller vessels, such as cups with applied pellets, which may be found mainly, though not exclusively, in domestic contexts.

The Barrel Urns, as the name suggests, are large vessels with convex sides and with mouths narrower than the maximum girth. They may be decorated with cordons around the upper third of the vessel and these cordons may be accentuated with fingertip impressions. Vertical cordons may also be so treated and there may be wavy cordons on the upper portion of the pot, between the horizontal cordon and the rim. These large urns may be termed South Lodge Urns after a settlement site which produced a number of them and where the type was recognised. Bucket Urns may also carry plastic cordons or rows of fingertip impressions in the upper third of the pot. Some may have applied knobs or even horseshoe handles and others may be decorated with profuse fingertip impressions. In East Anglia, rather squat pots with profuse all-over fingertip decoration comprise the Ardleigh regional style.

Globular Urns (**51.4** & **51.7**) are a new form to the repertoire of the earlier Bronze Age ceramic record. They are fine pots with bulbous bodies and constricted

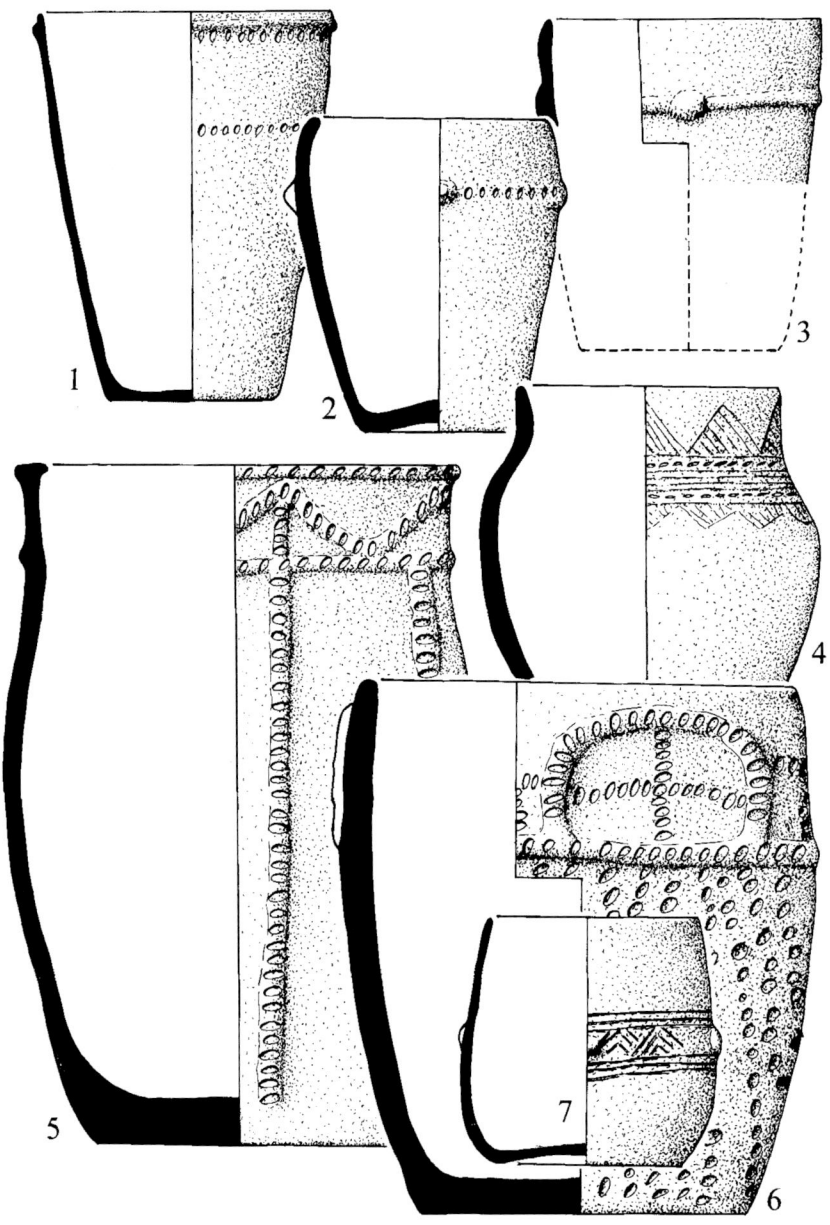

51 *Deverel-Rimbury pottery of the middle Bronze Age. 1 – Pokesdown, Dorset. After Calkin 1962; 2 – Stourfield, Hants. After Calkin 1962; 3 – Puddletown Heath, Dorset. After Calkin 1962; 4 – Salisbury, Wilts. After Langmaid 1978; 5 – Bower Chalke, Wilts. After Annable and Simpson 1964; 6 – Ardleigh, Essex. After Burgess 1980; 7 – Brow Hill, Hants. After Calkin 1962. All scale 1: 6*

necks and rims. The vessels are generally in a fine fabric contrasting with the heavily flint-tempered fabrics of the larger vessels. The surfaces of these Globular Urns are often burnished or well smoothed and the decoration is frequently also burnished into the surfaces, sometimes so faintly as to be only visible under the correct lighting conditions. The decoration is restricted to the neck and shoulder and usually comprises filled triangle motifs and horizontal lines. The ancestry of these vessels is uncertain. They do not closely resemble any of the immediately earlier ceramics and it may be that they are a distant descendent of Beakers. The S-profile does resemble Beaker and the geometric motif may also be derived from this source. There may be at least 200 years between the last Beakers and the earliest cordoned urns, perhaps 10 generations in a period where life expectancy was considerably less than it is today. If the globular urns are indeed derived from this earlier ceramic, then it suggests a remarkable survival of Beakers, perhaps as heirlooms or in the folk memory. The alternative is that these pots may be a new 'invention' designed to fulfil a specific role within the emerging homestead settlements of the period.

The cordons on these vessels may be multifunctional. While they are undoubtedly decorative, the vertical cordons may well strengthen the bodies of the larger vessels, helping to bind the straps of clay from which they were constructed. The making of the fingertip impressions on the cordons will also have the effect of further compressing the clay and improving the bond of the applied cordon to the body of the vessel. The horizontal cordons in the upper third may well be there to facilitate handling. These pots are heavy, even without their contents, and while the protruding calcined flint inclusions and, where present, fingertip impressions would have the effect of rusticating the surface and giving greater purchase to the hands, so the cordons would further reduce slippage.

The ancestry of these vessels is easy to trace. The position of the horizontal cordons is reminiscent of the Cordoned Urns and the collar bases of Collared Urns. The Barrel Urns recall the Biconical series. Horseshoe handles bear comparison with the Wessex Handled Urns of the Food Vessel tradition and the Horseshoe Handled Urns of the Biconical tradition. These pots are, therefore, a melting pot of and logical development from what went before.

Elswehere in Britain and Ireland, there is also a tradition of barrel and bucket urns. They are generally undecorated and certainly twisted cord decoration is difficult to date much after 1200 BC. As well as Barrel and Bucket urns, Biconicals and Cordoned Urns continue though they are usually undecorated or else decorated with crudely incised lines forming unelaborate and basic motifs such as chevrons and bands of diagonal lines. Some urns may have broad grooves or ridges on the upper third of the pot below the rim. These are often slightly formed by no more difficult a practice than running the fingers round through the wet clay. The practice of barrow burial seems to be dying out in the north at this time and there do not appear to be the cremation cemeteries of the Deverel-Rimbury complex further south. These vessels are better known from settlement sites such as the platform settlements of Green Knowe in Peeblesshire or Standrop Rigg in Northumberland excavated by George Jobey (**52**).

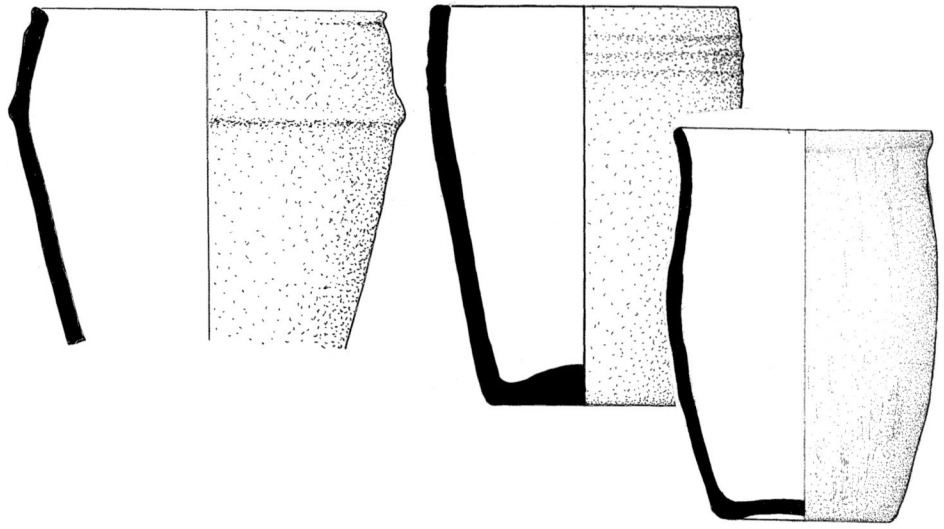

52 *Undecorated Middle Bronze Age urns. From left to right, Green Knowe, Peeblesshire. After Jobey 1978; Eggleston, Co. Durham; Roseash, Devon. After Wainwright 1980. All scale 1:6*

There are other complexities within the ceramics of this period which lie outside the scope of this work. For example why should grog appear as an opening agent at the beginning of this period and disappear from the archaeological record by its end around 1200 BC? Why is flint favoured as an inclusion by some urn traditions yet completely shunned by others, for example Collared Urns? Why is flint used at all since the razor sharp edges of this material must have proved an occupational hazard to the potters? (Will residue analysis in the future be able to detect human blood and tears?). The symbolism of inclusions has already been commented on above and this is certainly an avenue worthy of future research. There are also greater complexities of regionality which have not been discussed here and studies of this aspect of ceramics may lead to the identification of tribal units and social networks. There have been many PhDs undertaken on the pottery of this period, and there is scope for many more.

As mentioned at the beginning of this chapter, ceramically speaking this period is one of the richest in its sheer diversity. It is the earlier Bronze Age that arguably sees the greatest variety of highly decorated pots with domestic vessels being as highly decorated as those selected for sepulchro-ritual use. Yet it also sees the decline of potting technology and decoration and the vessels from the end of this period are sorry indeed compared to the richness of the ornate Beakers or Food Vessels. Why should this be? Was pottery being replaced by bronze as the main display medium? Was the magic of the potters' transforming fire being transferred to the developing and increasing metal technology; the potters' art being replaced by that of the smiths? It is a difficult question but certainly the decline in ceramics is total in some parts of the country. Later Bronze Age Ireland and Wales are almost aceramic and, in the North and West, pottery never again reaches the excellence of the earlier Bronze Age.

6 From bronze to iron 1000 – 600 BC

This, in comparison to the previous chapters, is a short period of only 400 years which spans what is conventionally known as the later Bronze Age and marks the first appearance of iron objects. For the sake of this work, the beginning of the early Iron Age proper is taken as 600 BC (the start of Cunliffe's (1991) early Iron Age) despite the fact that small iron objects start to appear in the archaeological record from around 800 BC. I have chosen this short period as previously it has been thought that the later Bronze Age was a time when pottery was scarce and that some parts of the country were aceramic. It is also a period that sees a dramatic change from the previous two millennia. Round barrows, up until now the most common type of burial monument, decline and cease to be built. The famous Neolithic ritual monuments such as the stone and timber circles and henges are also no longer constructed. Instead, artefacts are deposited in wet places such as rivers and bogs and the veneration of natural phenomena seems to be preferred to man-made monuments. This period sees bronze taking over as the main utilitarian medium, and the introduction of ironwork. It is also a time when we know much more about settlement archaeology. It sees the growth of nucleated agrarian settlements and, of course, the emergence of one of Britain's most prolific and famous types of field monument, the hillfort. It is also a period when the links with Continental Europe, already established in the preceding period, strengthen and become more visible.

In terms of ceramics, there is a distinct change in the pottery record at this time, particularly at the very start of the first millennium. The elaborately decorated vessels of the earlier Bronze Age give way, as mentioned in the last chapter, to a series of coarser and undecorated urn and jar forms. The decorative repertoire is decidedly limited and some areas of the country still appear to have been virtually aceramic. Now, however, radiocarbon dating of some sites (particularly settlements) is helping to fill these perceived gaps. A case in point, by way of an example and already alluded to in the previous chapter, happened in Northumberland in the 1980s. In the Cheviot Hills and the Scottish-Northumberland borders, stone round houses were believed to be Romano-British in date and excavations at such sites, especially when the houses lay within small enclosed settlements, tended to confirm this hypothesis. Therefore the coarse bucket-shaped pottery with which these round houses were associated was believed to be Romano-British 'native' ware. We now know that some stone houses, especially those that are unenclosed or associated with irregular field systems, are much earlier, dating to the middle and later Bronze Age, and excavation at these sites has consequently identified a series of later Bronze Age ceramics. Coincidentally these also tend towards coarse bucket, barrel or tub-shaped pots. This makes the dating of later Prehistoric settlements in northern Britain extremely difficult by any means other than radiocarbon dating.

In Northumberland, some cordoned forms persist into this period. These are bucket and barrel-shaped pots with an encircling cordon around the upper third of the vessel which are doubtless derived from the Cordoned Urns of the preceding period. There are also plain bucket forms and pots with horizontal finger-grooves around the outside of the pot immediately below the rim. As is always the case with archaeology, once a phenomenon has been recognised, it will be seen more frequently. The phenomenon in question here is the recognition and identification of early first millennium pottery. Armed with this hindsight it is possible, indeed probable, that some earlier identifications of Neolithic pottery in the north-east of England may have been erroneous and that the pottery was ascribed to the Neolithic simply because the later material was then unknown. If this is correct, then suddenly the gap in the ceramic record of the late second and early first millennia is not so gaping.

Indeed, it is a range of coarse urn forms and jar forms that characterise this period in northern and western Britain and Ireland (**53**). These pots tend to be simple, unelaborate vessels occurring in a variety of sizes, either undecorated or decorated with restricted and simple motifs and techniques. Uncomplex incised motifs dominate the repertoire. The unremarkable nature of some of this pottery has led, particularly in Scotland, to the use of the name 'flat-rimmed ware' as this seems to be the only defining formal characteristic of the ceramic. The rim is flattened on top and there is none of the rim elaboration such as the moulding or internal bevels of the preceding earlier Bronze Age. However the term is not at all satisfactory as there is also 'flat-rimmed' pottery in the Neolithic and indeed in the Iron Age and furthermore, the coarseness of the fabric and the 'lumpiness' of the surfaces mean that the rims are usually irregular. As the late George Jobey remarked during the excavations at Green Knowe 'the distinguishing feature of "flat rimmed ware" is the fact that the rim is very rarely flat'. The Covesea Ware of north-eastern Scotland is a generally fine-walled ceramic in a variety of barrel forms. This is just such an example of 'flat rimmed ware' (as the rims are rarely flat) and similar pottery was associated with late Bronze Age metalwork at the Heathery Burn cave in County Durham.

In the Outer Isles of Scotland representing a zone from the Inner Hebrides in the south-west to the Shetlands in the north-east, there is an 'Atlantic' zone of large urn-shaped pots and smaller tubs once more with simple incised and fingertip-impressed decoration. These are associated with settlements comprising substantial stone-built round houses such as at Clickhimin and Jahrlshof and it seems that in these islands pottery was a more important element of material culture than elsewhere in Scotland. Could this be due to the absence of trees in these windswept locations? Were the later Bronze Age populations of mainland Scotland better wood-workers than potters?

In Wales, a range of later Bronze Age material was recovered from the earlier phases of the hillfort at the Breiddin in Powys (Musson 1991). The fabric is generally coarse and the very abundant angular stone inclusions within the fabric also frequently

From bronze to iron 1000 – 600 BC

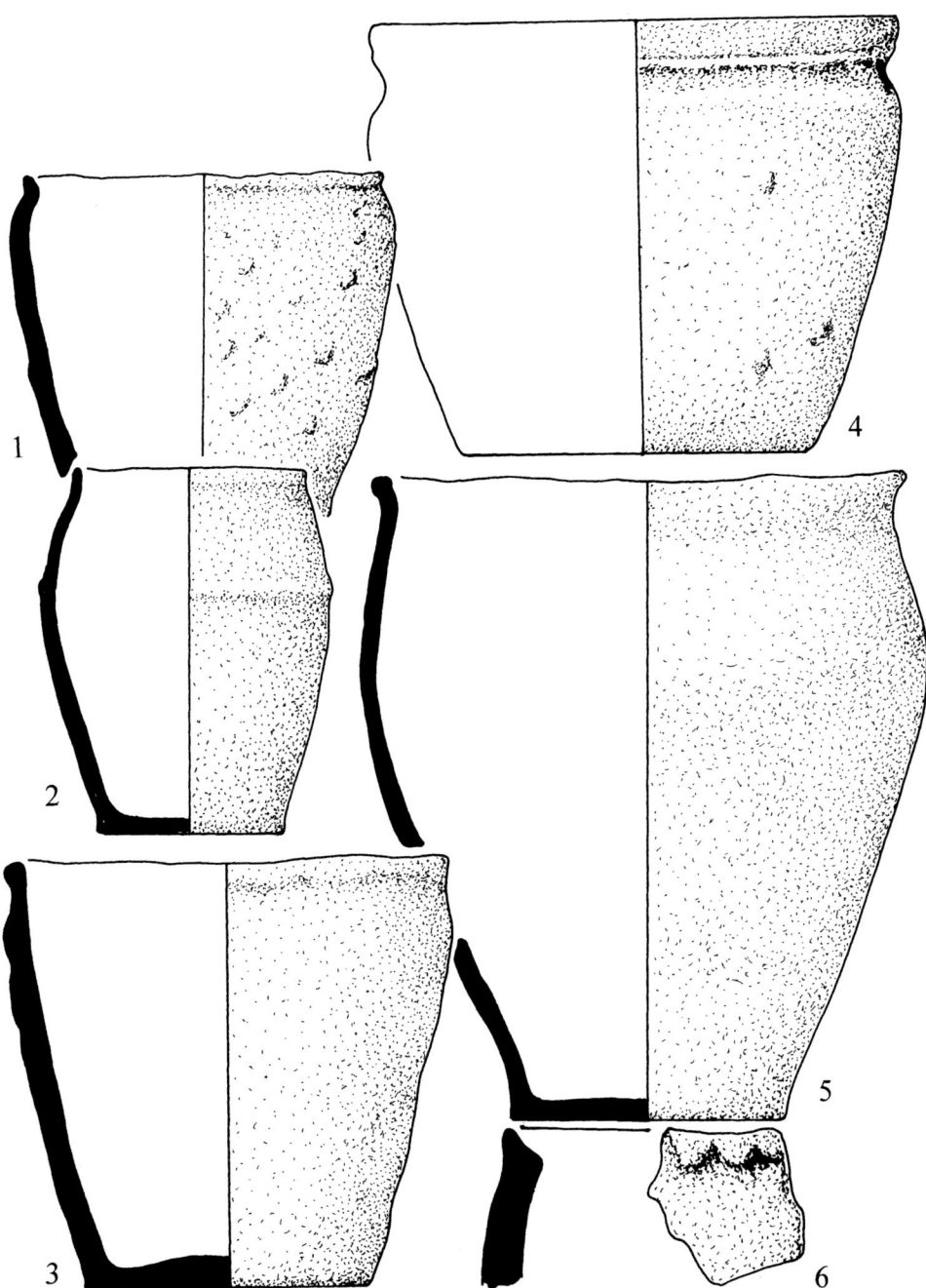

53 *Later Bronze Age pottery from western and northern Britain and Ireland. 1 & 2 – The Breiddin, Powys. After Musson 1991; 3 & 5 – Mam Tor, Derbyshire. After Challis & Harding 1975; 4 – Haughey's Fort, Co. Armagh. After Mallory 1991; 6 – Covesea Ware from Tentsmuir, Fife. After Longworth 1967. All scale 1:4*

break through the surfaces of the pots or at the very least result in some of the pots having very uneven lumpy surfaces. There are cordoned forms as well as open bowls, closed jars and sinuous-profiled pots. The assemblage is interesting as the technology of the pottery is quite poor but nevertheless there is evidence of experimentation with new forms and there appears to have been a real attempt to produce a varied assemblage. Some of the bowls and jars recall the more developed assemblages of lowland England but they are very much in the league of 'poor cousins' rather than close copies. Radiocarbon dates from the later Bronze Age phases of the Brieddin range from 1050-410 BC but centre around 800 BC.

In the Midlands and the north of England between the Wash and Tees, bucket and barrel urn types also predominate, some of them coarse and poorly made, appearing sad reflections of the earlier periods. However there are also some innovations in the form of jars and shouldered vessels with fingertip decorated cordons recalling some of the late Bronze Age Urnfield pottery of the Continent. These are particularly well-known from the hilltop palisaded site at Staple Howe in Yorkshire where the long settlement sequence starts in the later Bronze Age. By the sixth century BC at this site, strongly angular forms had become established including large closed bowls and jars. Two main types of ceramic were represented here, an imported pot with a slightly sandy texture and gravel opening agents and a finer ceramic, made from the local Speeton clay, and with often black, smooth and burnished surfaces. The pottery was fired at fairly low temperatures but was nevertheless well-made and often comparatively fine-walled. A range of fine and coarse bowls and jars as well as cups suggest a broad, varied, well-designed and functional domestic assemblage. Fingertip-impressed cordons on the neck of some of the larger jars may be strengthening cordons or handling devices as much as decorative features.

It is generally accepted that these tall, sometimes angular jars with fingertip decoration as found here at Staple Howe (and at sites further south along the east of the country such as Fengate near Peterborough, West Harling (Norfolk) and the Thames Valley) are derived from the large *situlae* of the Bronze Age/Iron Age transition on the Continent (**54**). A *situla* (from the Latin for 'bucket') is a tall, flat-based vessel made of sheets of Bronze riveted together. The straight-walled varieties widen out towards the shoulder and sometimes have everted necks. They are presumed to have played an important part in feasting activities. They date to the Hallstatt C and D phases which mark the Bronze Age/Iron Age transition in this country. The ceramic variants, or *situla* jars, are also large vessels whose beaded rims may mimic the thickening and reinforcing necessary in sheet bronze vessels and the fingertip decoration may represent the rivets of the metal originals.

In southern England, the Deverel-Rimbury tradition had been thought to represent the end of the Bronze Age until an assessment of the associated metalwork and the application of radiocarbon dating demonstrated that the tradition was much earlier than thought. This left a very real vacuum as far as pottery was concerned in the three centuries between 1000 and 700 BC. However John Barrett undertook a study of the pottery from the late Deverel-Rimbury settlements and earliest Iron Age sites (1980) and was able to identify a series of bowls and jars that seemed to

From bronze to iron 1000 – 600 BC

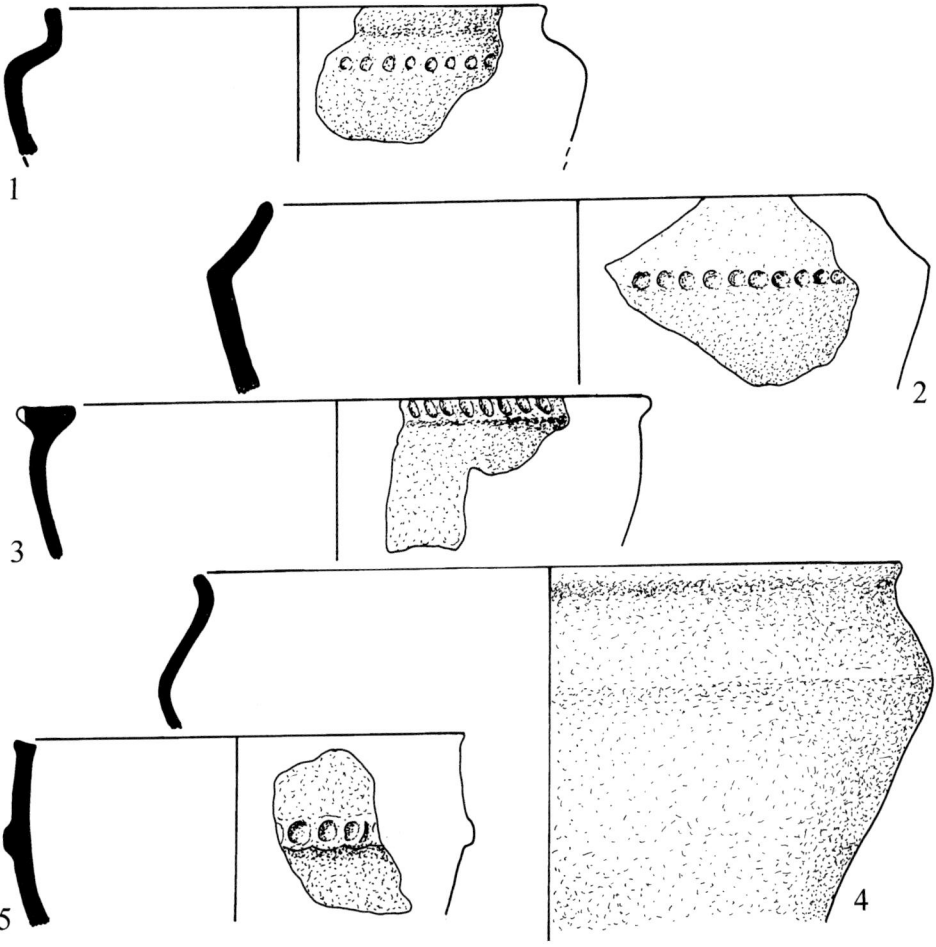

54 *Later Bronze Age jars from southern and eastern England. 1 & 2 –* Situla *jars from Staple Howe, Yorkshire. After Harding 1974; 3 – 'Cauldron' pot from Dorchester, Oxfordshire. After Harding 1974; 4 & 5 – respectively shouldered jar and cordoned jar from Eldon's Seat, Dorset. After Cunliffe 1991. All scale 1:4*

herald the potting traditions of the Iron Age. Pottery of this period also exhibits a far wider range of forms and sizes than the preceding, rather restricted, Deverel-Rimbury repertoire.

The first of these 'new' forms is the bowl. This is a form which had been virtually absent in the ceramic record since the Food Vessel assemblages of the early Bronze Age. These bowls tend to be comparatively fine in fabric and may have the application of iron-rich slips or haematite burnishing to ensure that they fire to a deep red colour. Some may have scratched or lightly incised designs and they may also be bipartite with a distinct change of direction in the vessel profile resulting in closed and angular forms. Some may have grooves on the upper part and a strong case has been made for these pots being derived from metal prototypes such as, for example,

From bronze to iron 1000 – 600 BC

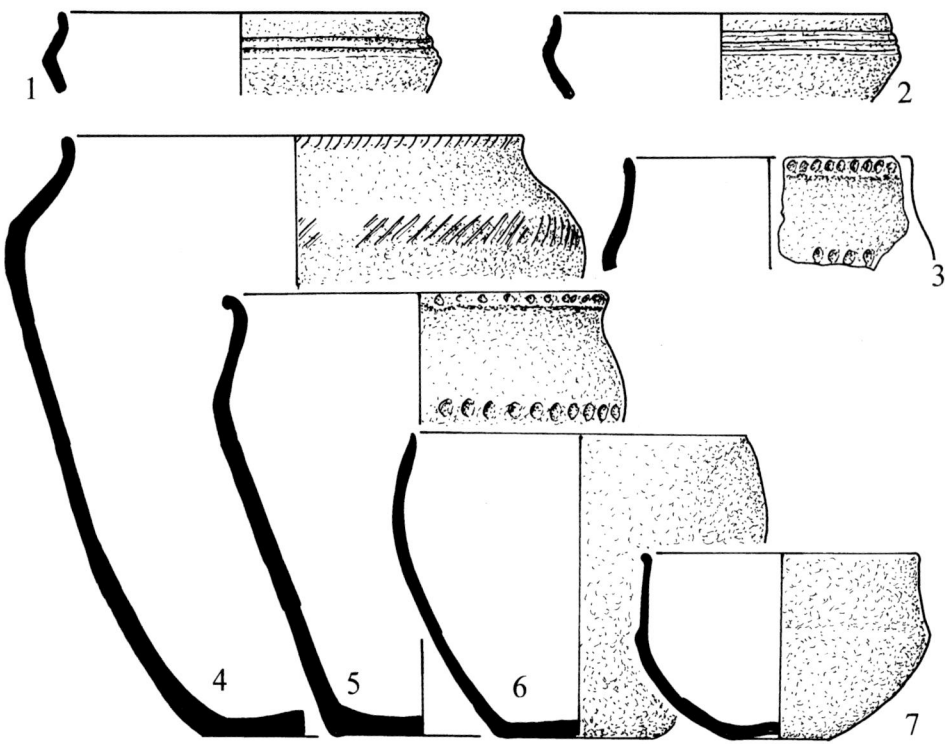

55 *Late Bronze Age pottery from the south of England. 1 & 2 – shouldered furrowed bowls from All Cannings Cross, Wiltshire.* After Cunliffe 1991; *3-7 – Reading Business Park.* After Moore & Jennings 1992. *All scale 1:4*

the bronze bowl from Welby in Leicestershire which has been dated to around the ninth century BC. Stuart Needham (1995) has pointed out the chicken and egg nature of this argument and instead of being definitive about which medium influenced the other, has preferred to see metal and ceramic forms being in contemporary use. These haematite bowls develop in the later part of this period towards more decorated examples, often with cordons, and sometimes with slightly more elaborate bases. Decoration between these cordons is often scratched on after firing and may be inlaid with whitening to make the decoration stand out. We have already seen this with Beakers of the later Neolithic.

The jars in these later Bronze Age assemblages are tall, closed forms. They flare up from the base to rounded shoulders and upright or slightly everted rims. The coarse elements are either plain or decorated with fingertip impressions or fingertip-impressed cordons clearly derived from the Deverel-Rimbury tradition. Finer elements may have a much better surface finish and may be decorated with a variety of incised motifs based on zoned arrangements, the filled triangle motif or multiple oblique lines. These jars are also shouldered. They may have sharp or rounded carinations, sometimes accentuated with decoration and upright or

From bronze to iron 1000 – 600 BC

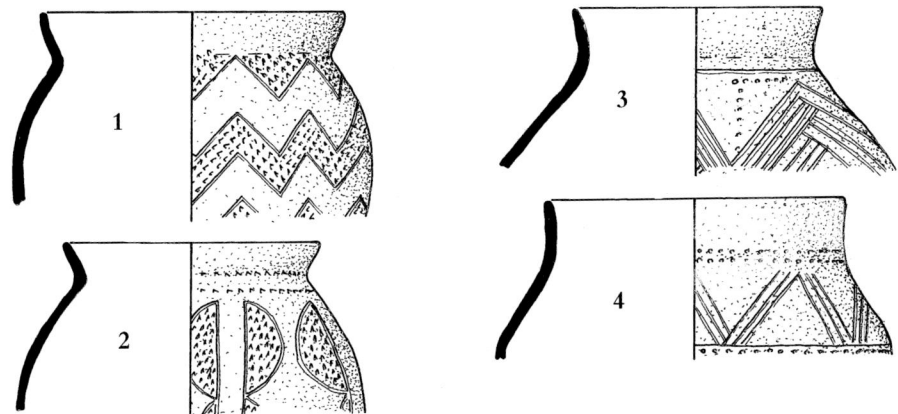

56 *Late Bronze Age bulbous jars from All Cannings Cross, Wiltshire. Scale 1:6.* After Cunliffe 1991

flaring rims (**55**). As a general rule of thumb, the decorated elements tend to increase in numbers towards the end of the Bronze Age.

Barrett's sequence has been supported by recent large-scale excavations at the Reading Business Park (Bradley & Hall in Moore & Jennings 1992) (**53**) and Runnymede (Needham 1991) (**colour plates 19 & 20**). The Bronze Age landscape at Reading produced a sequence from Deverel-Rimbury through plain wares to a decorated assemblage lasting into the earliest Iron Age. The main phase of occupation at Reading Business Park was associated with a very varied assemblage of coarse through to extremely fine pottery. There were angular bowls, angular or rounded jars, coarse straight-sided jars and straight- (or slightly convex-) sided cups. In short, some 25 different forms were identified in the type series from this site and lasted until about the eighth century BC. The later assemblage contained many of these plain ware forms but also a large element of decorated types. The decoration comprised fingertip or fingernail impressions directly on the shoulder and/or rim though they may also be found on shoulder cordons much as we have already seen in other parts of Britain. Incised decoration is present but rare. These decorated forms herald the start of the early Iron Age.

Barrett (1980) noted that it was at this time, particularly with the rise of the decorated assemblages in the south of England, that the developing regional patterning of the Iron Age ceramics could be identified. These regionally coherent groups form the basis of the early Iron Age style zones as identified by Barry Cunliffe (1991) which herald the recognition of the emerging tribal territories documented and named by the classical geographers and confirmed in the placenames of Roman Britain.

Certainly by the eighth century BC in Wessex, at All Cannings Cross, large bulbous jars with out-turned rims had appeared (**56**). They were decorated with incised geometric motifs filled with dot impressions or stabs. There were also bipartite bowls with sharp carinations and decorated on the upper part by encircling grooves (**55.2**). They are fired to a bright red colour – the haematite bowls already

115

mentioned in chapter 3. These are almost certainly related to contemporary metal examples. Along the south and east coasts, by the end of the early seventh century a series of bipartite bowls and angular tripartite jars constitute what Cunliffe refers to as the Kimmeridge-Caburn group. A third regional and contemporary group identified around the Chilterns and the south-east Midlands is recognised by round-, or slightly angular-, shouldered bipartite jars and bowls, sometimes with fingertip impressed shoulders and rims. These pots link the north and central English material with the more adventurous and less conservative assemblages of Wessex. As Cunliffe succinctly observes 'these ninth-eighth century innovations heralded the development of an inventive and dynamic ceramic industry in the south and east of the country which can properly be considered to be Iron Age' (1991, 54).

7 The Iron Age: from 600 BC to the Roman Conquest

Six hundred BC is taken here as representing the beginning of the Iron Age proper. As mentioned in the last chapter, iron objects had already appeared in the archaeological record by the eighth century BC and while bronze artefacts certainly did continue in use beyond 600, it is now that iron starts to be more widely used and more readily available. As with the later Bronze Age, the traditional focus has been on settlement archaeology, especially on small agricultural farmsteads with their so-called 'Celtic' field systems and, of course, the famous hillforts and defended settlements that so seem to typify later prehistory and its warrior tribes.

As far as ceramics are concerned, the earlier part of this period in Britain sees a continuation and development of the trends emerging at the end of the Bronze Age, thus once again illustrating the continuum that is prehistory and the inadequacy of our chronological divisions. It also reinforces the very real break in traditions that occurs just after 1000 BC. The jars and carinated bowls of southern Britain continue to dominate many assemblages and the regional diversity noted in the earlier material becomes more visible. In Northern Britain, coarse bucket forms predominate but these are largely indistinguishable from those of the later Bronze Age and Romano-British periods and, as will be seen below, it is not possible to create a relative chronology for the Iron Age in the north of England and mainland Scotland based on ceramics. In Ireland, the country appears to be aceramic. It is not surprising therefore, that Iron Age ceramic studies have largely centred on southern Britain where, in contrast to the North, there is an abundance of richly decorated pottery and large assemblages of fine and coarse wares. For this reason it is necessary to look at broad regions rather than at pottery types as assemblages often display great regionality and may contain a variety of different pottery types. A work such as this must be introductory rather than definitive and so it is the aim here, as in previous chapters, to give a broad-brush overview of the trends and diversities.

Southern England

Earlier Iron Age: to c.350 BC
In Wessex, the haematite-coated bowls continue and increase in numbers. The furrowed necks are still present but the rims tend to flare and the pots almost resemble the Carinated Bowl of the early Neolithic in profile save for their flat,

The Iron Age: from 600 BC to the Roman Conquest

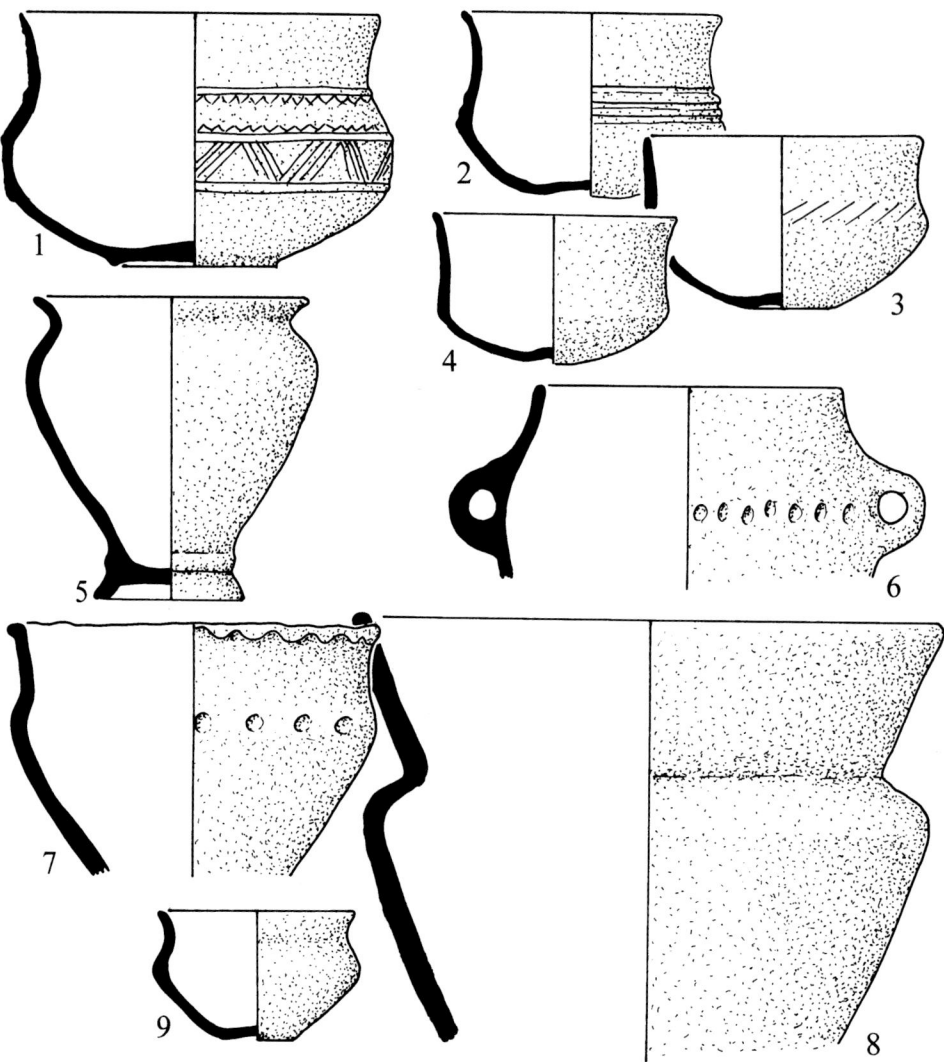

57 *Early Iron Age pottery from southern England. 1-3 – haematite bowls from All Cannings Cross, Wiltshire; 4 – heamatite bowl from Eldon's Seat, Dorset; 5 – pedestalled jar from Swallowcliffe, Wilts; 6 – handled jar from Pagan's Hill, Somerset; 7 – shouldered jar from Wimbledon, Surrey; 8 – shouldered jar from Park Brow, Sussex; 9 – shouldered bowl from Weybridge, Surrey. All scale 1:4. After Cunliffe 1991*

sometimes omphalos, bases. Other bowls and jars may be decorated with simple geometric designs in narrow bands around the neck or shoulder and there appears in Wessex a distinctive haematite-coated bowl with decorated zones defined by cordons (**57**). The decoration is scratched onto the pot after firing and is then inlaid with white material to contrast with the dark background. Barry Cunliffe (1991) has suggested that these bowls emanate from a single workshop in the Salisbury area and if this is the case then it demonstrates the rise of specialist workshops and the emergence of industrial manufacture. There are also coarser undecorated jars within the assemblage and the appearance of pedestalled bases towards the middle of the fifth century is indicative of continental La Tène influence, of which more later.

Further south, along the Dorset coast, haematite bowls continue but are not as elaborate as those in central Wessex (**57**). This area also sees the introduction of a distinctive, slightly bulbous jar with large shoulder handles which becomes so distinctive of the Durotrigian Ware of the later Iron Age, which in turn develops into the Black Burnished ware so popular with the Roman Army.

In south-eastern England, black bowls and jars predominate, often with footrings or, later, pedestalled bases (**57.5**). Once more the fabric is often burnished and of a high quality. The pots are rarely decorated save for some fingertip impressions, but nevertheless, the fabric can be fine and well polished. Distinctive amongst the assemblage are vessels with flaring necks and high shoulders (**57.11**) not dissimilar to the Kilellan Jars of Bronze Age Scotland.

Middle and Later Iron Age: c.350-the Roman incursions

Within this broad continuum, it is difficult to subdivide the period into meaningful phases in terms of the ceramic evidence, but broadly speaking the fifth to third centuries BC see the beginnings of another ceramic phase, particularly in southern Britain. These are ceramics that are strongly influenced by so-called La Tène pottery. La Tène is the name conventionally used to refer to the second part of the European Iron Age. It takes its name from the site at La Tène on Lake Neuchâtel in Switzerland. This was an incredibly well-preserved lakeside complex with remains of wooden buildings and organic artefacts preserved in the silts below the icy waters. Some of the pottery and metalwork was decorated with curvilinear motifs, often quite complex, and these swirls and curves, executed within a geometrical framework, characterise much of the 'Celtic' Art of Europe including Britain and Ireland. I put 'Celtic' in inverted commas because the classical writers refer to the Celts as a distinct group of Iron Age people living in central and western Europe but the adjective Celtic has come to be used to refer to all Iron Age peoples over the whole of the Continent and western islands. Thus western England, Scotland, Wales and Ireland have become known as the Celtic fringe, despite being separated by many miles from the home of the Celts or 'Keltoi' as the classical Greek geographers appeared to know them. It is largely the pan-European nature of La Tène art that has been responsible for this perceived European unification some two and a half thousand years before the EC. There were certainly pan-European links at this time whether through culture contact, migration or a combination of different processes. Some La Tène art also has decorative elements that show links with what we would now term the Middle East and Black Sea areas.

La Tène art can reach high levels of sophistication, especially in the metalwork record. Intricate designs may be engraved, incised or embossed on metal objects as diverse as sword scabbards, pins, or buckets. These are based on circles and in-filled arcs and certainly suggest that the craftsmen had a knowledge of the use of compasses. Representational art is also common. Animals and humans may be portrayed in both stylised and realistic forms. This animal representation reaches Britain particularly in the metalwork of the period. A bronze-mounted wooden bucket from Aylesford (Kent) bears a human head with an elaborate helmet or headdress. The Witham Shield from Lincolnshire has a stylised boar draped over the central boss. Swords and daggers occasionally have small figures on the hilt (anthropomorphic hilted weapons). In Continental Europe this figurative art spills over into the ceramic repertoire.

However in Britain (and the distribution of this decorated pottery is generally restricted to Southern Britain), it is only the swirls and curves so absolutely typical of La Tène art that can be seen in the pottery record. The representational art does not seem to have been transferred across the media. It raises the question 'why?' We posed this question in earlier chapters and have commented on the fact that there is a complete absence of figurative art in the British native ceramic traditions. Is it taboo? Is there a lack of imaginative innovation on the part of British potters? While in mainland Europe we have depictions of people, animals and even architecture from the Neolithic onwards, this never reaches Britain where ceramic art is always non-representational. The reason for this is unlikely to be due to a lack of imagination. Some Beaker and earlier Bronze Age ceramics are richly and skilfully decorated with carefully executed geometric designs. Artisans were clearly capable of creating these images in metalwork, wood and, later, stone; therefore contemporary potters would have been perfectly capable of drawing images on pots. The fact is that they never did, not even when representations became increasingly common on other artefacts. Perhaps there were very good reasons why pottery and representational images could not go together. We might think, for example, of the avoidance of figurative art in Islamic cultures, although here the avoidance is common to all media and not just ceramic. Such a direct parallel, however, is clearly anachronistic. I personally find it fascinating that this rarely commented upon phenomenon lasts in the British ceramic repertoire for over 4000 years.

Middle and later Iron Age pottery, like the material before it, is still hand-built until the introduction of the wheel immediately before the Roman conquest. We have already seen that hand-built need not mean coarse and some of this Iron Age material is indeed fine and of an extremely high standard. In the Thames Valley and southern England, angular-profiled bowls continuing from the preceding period may be decorated with simple, incised designs around the shoulder of the pot or occasionally cordons running around the upper portion of the vessels. Angular vessels with wide flaring rims and pedestal bases are also encountered. Some omphalos-based pots also appear in these assemblages. The fabric of the fine ware is usually black and burnished and the fabric can be incredibly thin. Coarser wares with shell inclusions may also form part of the assemblages.

By 300 BC a distinct, squat form known as the 'saucepan pot' can be found over large areas of southern central England. Particularly prolific in Wessex (**58**), they also extend into Somerset and the Welsh Marches. This is a long-lived tradition surviving up until the Roman occupation in some areas. These vessels may be straight-sided and tub-shaped or have more convex walls giving them a slightly closed or barrel form. They show a remarkable uniformity in form and decora-

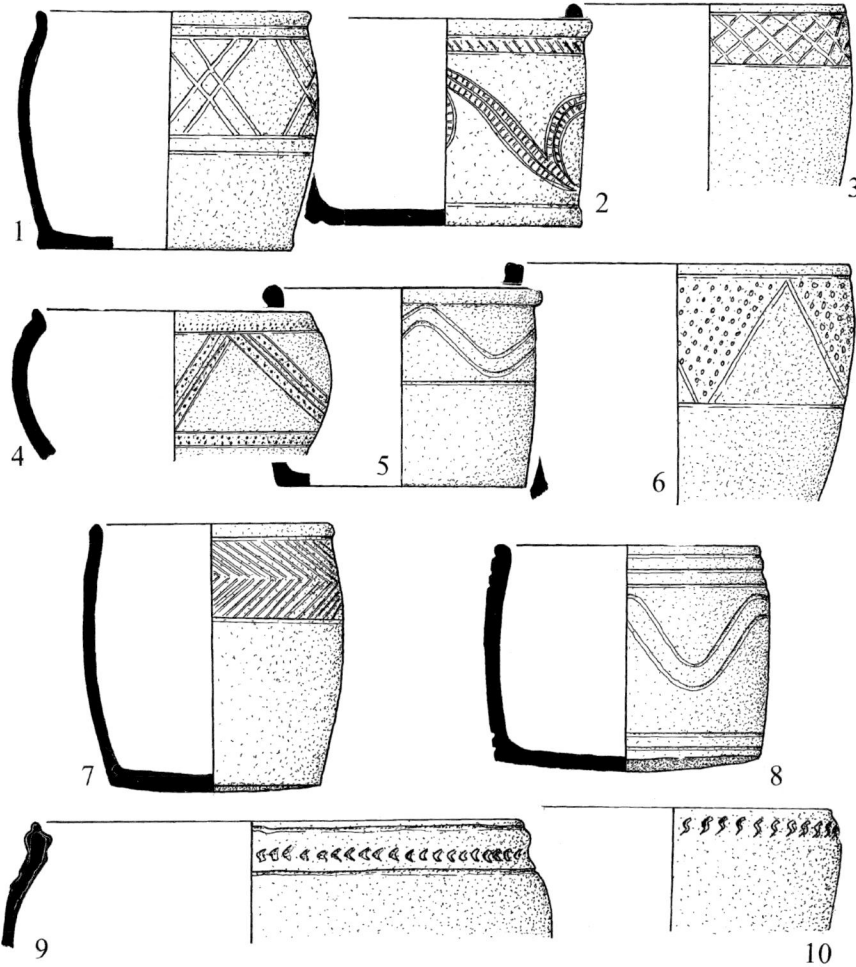

58 *Iron Age pottery in the Sucepan Pot tradition of southern England and the Marches.*
1 – Cissbury, Sussex; 2 – The Caburn, Sussex; 3 & 4 – Blewburon Hill, Oxon.; 5 – Hawk's Hill, Surrey; 6 – Knighton Hill, Berkshire; 7 – St Catherine's Hill, Hants; 8 – Worthy Down, Hants.; 9 – Sutton Walls, Hereford; 10 – Cleeve Hill, Glos.
All scale 1:4. After Cunliffe 1991

tion though Cunliffe (1991) has identified some subtle regional variations beyond the scope of this book. The rims are generally simple or slightly everted and the rim diameters are comparable to or only slightly larger than the base diameters. Decoration is usually incised though dots may be used to fill in areas between two parallel, incised lines. Either straight geometric decoration such as a narrow band of oblique lines between two parallel lines or more complex curvilinear patterns may be employed. The former, linear, decoration is usually restricted to the upper third of the vessel while the latter, resembling some of the motifs found on the La Tène art already described, tends to cover more of the vessel body. In the excavations

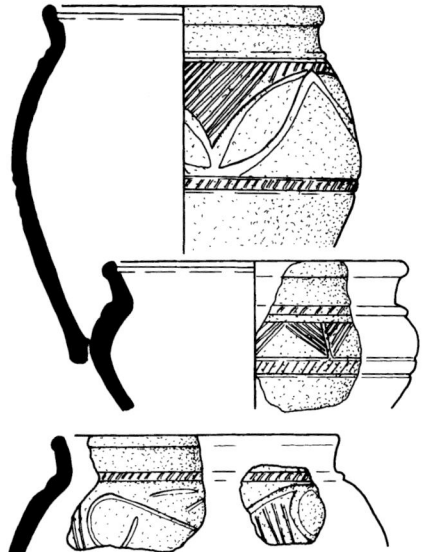

59 Glastonbury style pottery. Top and bottom – Castle Dore, Cornwall; centre – Caerloggas, Cornwall. Scale 1:4. After Cunliffe 1991

by Arthur Bullied and Harold St George Gray at the Glastonbury Lake Villages, wooden saucepan bowls were found in the waterlogged deposits, which gives us an interesting and rare insight into the forms of some of the contemporary organic containers (Bullied & Gray 1911).

In the Malvern region and the Welsh Marches, peculiar 'duck-stamped' pottery is typical of this overall tradition, so-called because of the presence, in a narrow zone around the rim, of small impressed zig-zags superficially resembling swimming ducks (**58.9** & **58.10**). Petrological examination of this material by David Peacock (1968) has identified three clay sources (and therefore three centres of manufacture) in the Malvern area from which this pottery was distributed over the whole region. It suggests specialised craft industries and centres of local manufacture and distribution within an overall and wide ranging cultural background.

In Somerset, towards the south-western limit of the pottery's distribution, more ambitious decorative schemes tend to be used and there appears to be a fusion between the form of the saucepan pot and the decorated bowls and jars from the south west. Also in the south west, a variety of necked jars and bowls, often with bead rims, and decorated with complex incised curvilinear motifs, have been designated the Glastonbury style (**59**) though their distribution ranges far wider than the site-specific name suggests. There were several centres of manufacture from Avon to Cornwall and much of this pottery was traded widely over south-west England and even the south Wales coast. The fabric of these pots can be incredibly fine and the decoration skilfully executed. These decorated styles seem to give way in Cornwall to a series of undecorated cordoned wares but in other regions they persist until the end of the Iron Age.

By the end of the pre-Roman Iron Age, in the first century BC, scholars feel confident enough to start ascribing tribal names to some pottery traditions in the

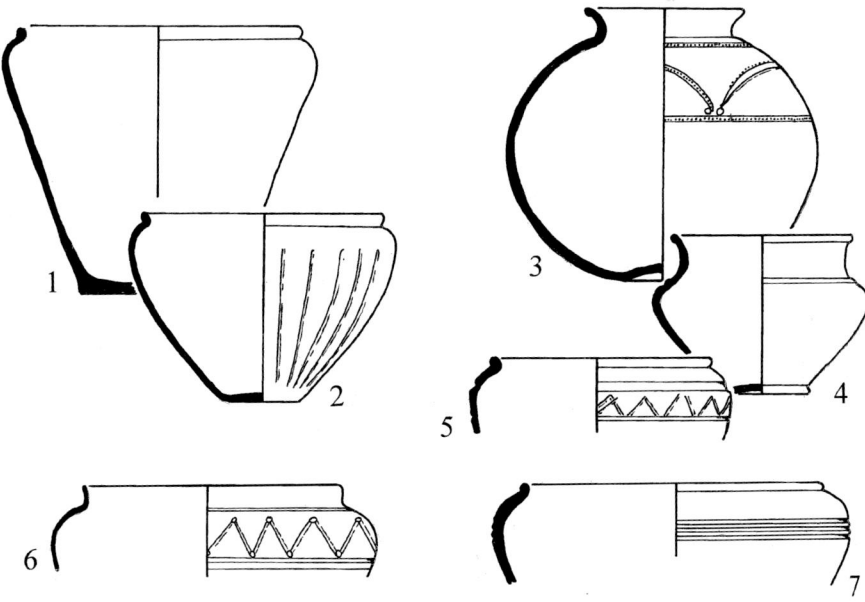

60 *Atrebatic pottery. 1 & 2 – Horndean, Hants.; 3 – Saltdean, Sussex; 4 – Worthy Down, Hants.; 5 – Boscombe Down, Wiltshire; 6 – Charleston Brow, Sussex; 7 – Oare, Wiltshire. Scale 1:6. After Cunliffe 1991*

south of England. Thus Atrebatic and Durotrigian wares may be identified in the areas now known broadly as Wiltshire, Hampshire and Sussex and Dorset. The Atrebatic pottery (**60**) is characterised by bulbous vases with severely constricted necks. There are also bead-rim jars where the rim is formed by a single cylinder of clay, tripartite bowls and jars with high rounded shoulders. The decoration is simple and usually geometric though the use of some circular stamps may be derived from the saucepan pot complex and related La Tène ceramics. As well as tooled and incised decoration, some is painted. Some pedestalled bases show links with the Belgic pottery to the east.

The Durotrigian pottery of the first century BC (see **23** above) owes much of its development to earlier local styles but was also influenced by pottery traditions from Armorica. There seems to have been a major production centre around Poole Harbour and traces of this have been found. The Durotrigian assemblage comprises high-shouldered bead-rimmed jars, necked jars, globular jars with countersunk handles and a variety of open and shouldered bowls. Handled tankards represent a form that had been absent in the ceramic record since the handled Beakers of about 2000 years earlier. The decoration is simple but the appearance of scored lattice panels around the belly of some pots is a motif that is well known from Roman military sites because this high quality pottery was later adopted by the Roman army. It becomes known as Black Burnished Ware type 1 (BB1) and is one of the major types of coarse pottery used for the dating of Roman military sites, particularly in the North. Durotrigian Wares of the later phase show that the potters had some knowledge of the wheel:

61 *Scratched jar from Breedon-on-the-Hill, Leicestershire.*
Photo Leicestershire Museums and Art Galleries

although much of the pottery is hand-built, the wheel seems to have been used extensively to burnish, finish and, where appropriate, decorate the vessels

The Midlands

The Early Iron Age
The earlier Iron Age pottery of the Midlands is characterised by Scratched Wares (**61**). These often comprise large storage jars as well as smaller bowl-shape vases, occasionally quite bulbous in profile, the surface of which is covered with linear scratches, sometimes vertical, diagonal or arched. These scratchings are presumed to be practical in their purpose rather than simply decorative and the roughened surface is assumed to have been a device to facilitate the handling of these large jars. Scratched wares continue in the third to first centuries and are associated with various undecorated shouldered jar forms and globular bowls.

Further south, in the Thames Valley, carinated forms, like those of the south-west with acute shoulders and flaring rims, continue from the early Iron Age. They may still have incised and simple geometric decoration and, as with the Wessex material, large handled storage jars are found. Similar vessels are found in the area of the Home Counties, extending in their distribution up to the Fenland. Once again simple

The Iron Age: from 600 BC to the Roman Conquest

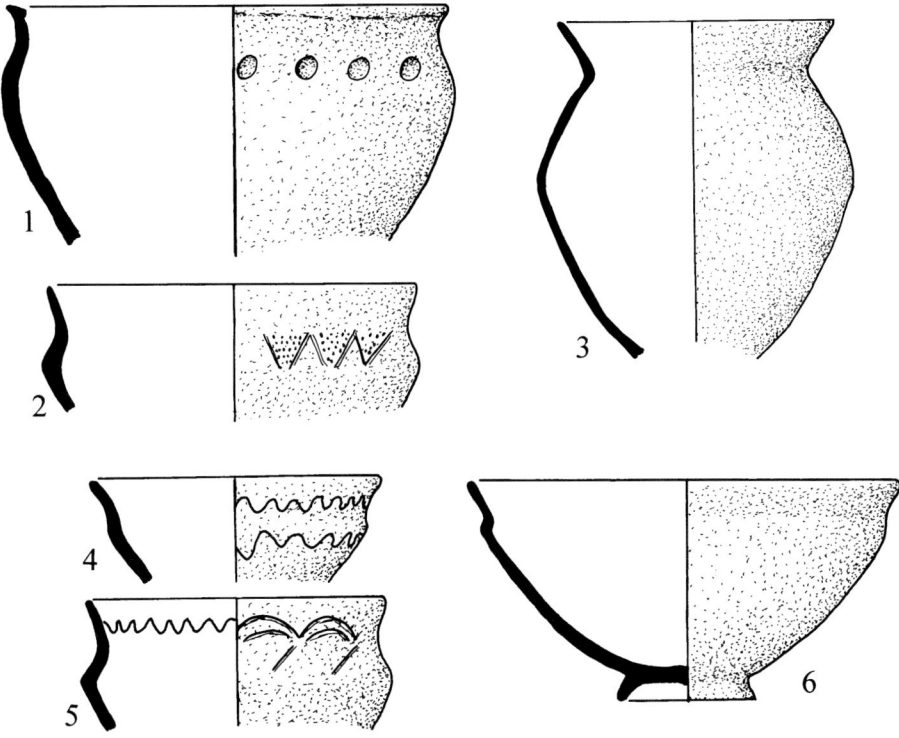

62 *Early Iron Age pottery from the Thames Valley area. 1, 2 & 5 – Chinnor, Oxon.; 3 – Long Wittenham, Berkshire; 4 – Great Wymondley, Herts.; 6 – Wandlebury, Cambridgeshire. 1, 2, 4-6 scale 1:4; 3 scale 1:6. After Cunliffe*

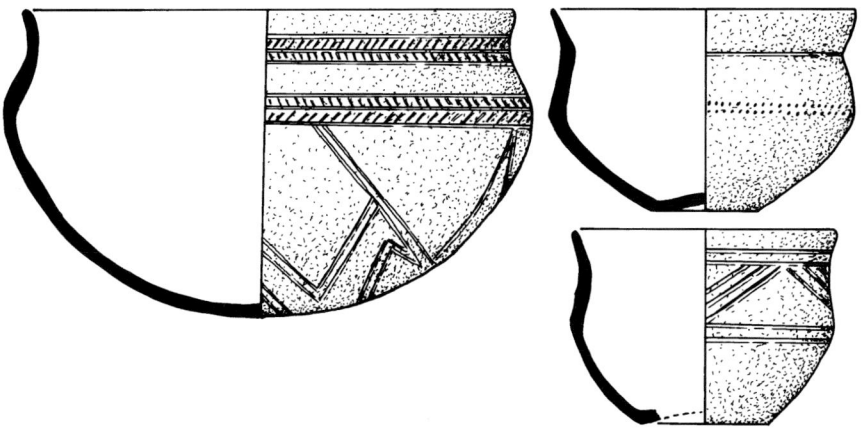

63 *Early Iron Age pottery from East Anglia. 1 – Cromer, Norfolk; 2 & 3 – Fengate, Peterborough. Scale 1:4. After Cunliffe 1991*

decorated motifs are executed using dots and incision; sometimes the decoration is scratched onto the surface of the pots after they had been fired. The fine angular bowls from Chinnor in Oxfordshire may also represent the work of a specialist potter or group of potters since they too display a remarkable uniformity in shape as well as in the high quality of their burnished fabric (**62**). They are also decorated with incised arcs. These have sometimes been considered to refer to former handles but are now purely decorative and earlier handled varieties are not easy to find. White inlay may also have been used to highlight this incised or dotted decoration.

The carinated forms are also common in East Anglia at this time. The shoulders may be decorated with grooves and there may be omphalos and pedestal bases. In Norfolk and the Fen edge some more highly-decorated rounded bowls have been identified (**63**), particularly in the extensive excavations at Fengate outside Peterborough. Incised geometric designs may accentuate the shoulder but may also extend below this onto the body of the pot. Once again the fabric of these vessels is fine and well-finished.

The middle and later Iron Age

The middle and later Iron Age of the Midlands, from Thames to Trent, is also represented by globular bowls that are decorated with swathes, arcs or zones of geometric incision or tooling (**64**). Sometimes called Frilford or Hunsbury bowls after two find sites in Berkshire and Northamptonshire respectively, these are round-profiled bowls with short upright or slightly everted rounded rims and in a good quality, often burnished fabric. The decoration is rarely as complex as the Glastonbury style, but nevertheless comprises well-formed and carefully executed integrated designs. Dot rosettes are common on the northern Hunsbury bowls while in the southern variants, the Frilford Bowls, pendant arc designs are typical. Another subtle difference between the two styles is that the decoration on the Hunsbury bowls is usually set within horizontal zones, while in the Frilford type the decoration tends not to be bounded. The distribution of these bowls complements that of the saucepan pots in the counties to the south and west.

The later Iron Age sequence for the north-eastern midlands of England is best exemplified at the large complex site at Dragonby in northern Lincolnshire (May 1996). The site was excavated mainly in the late 1960s and early 1970s and revealed a palimpsest of rectilinear enclosures and associated ring-gullies and other domestic features. A large pottery assemblage was recovered and placed into a relative chronology, based on the stratigraphy of the features; however it proved difficult to anchor this relative chronology into an absolute chronological framework despite using dating methods such as thermoluminescence and radiocarbon. All that can be said is that the sequence almost certainly began *before* the first century BC and possibly before the middle of the third. This clearly exemplifies the problems relating to the chronology of Iron Age pottery generally. Six ceramic stages were identified up until the Roman conquest but many of these groups merge into each other and so assigning a precise date range for any single ceramic group is difficult (Elsdon in May 1996).

This is to be expected. We have seen in earlier chapters that ceramic styles gradually develop and change over time and space. Good, practical designs may last

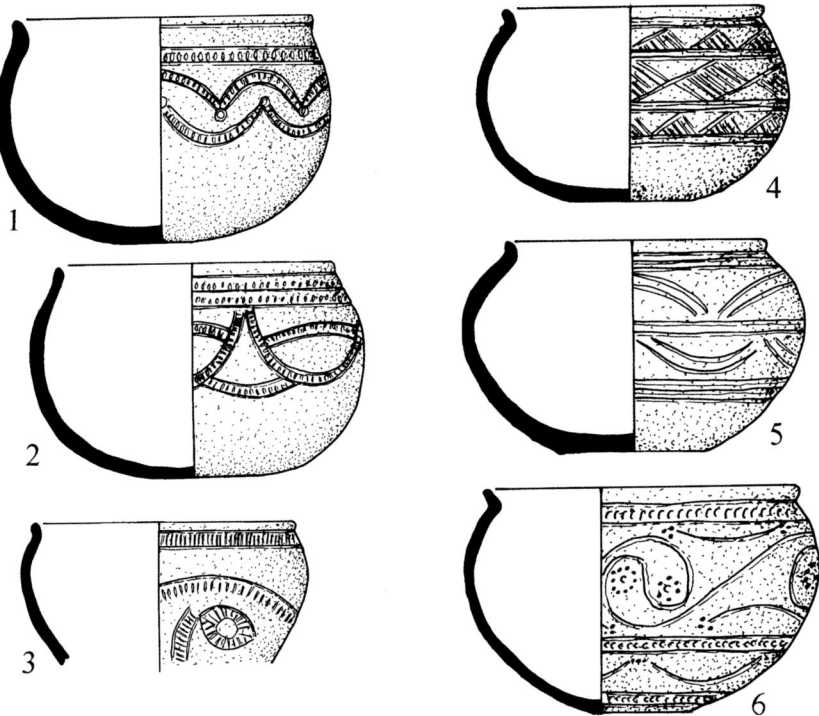

64 *Frilsford and Hunsbury Bowls from the Thames Valley and the Midlands. 1 & 2 – Frilsford, Berkshire; 3 – Ifley, Oxon.; 4-6 – Hunsbury, Northants. Scale 1:4. After Cunliffe 1991*

longer than less suitable forms and their chronological development may be slow and gradual. After all, when we have guests my wife and I sometimes use my grandmother's dinner service dating from the end of the nineteenth century. Any future archaeologist dating our residency at this house by this crockery would be out by 100 years (though coincidentally it would match the *construction* of the house quite nicely). However, in our private ceramic assemblage, all in contemporary use, we have various souvenir mugs and a range of 'everyday' ware as well as limited edition modern ceramics, unglazed earthenwares, foreign imports and ethnographic pieces. In short we have a mixed and long-lived assemblage in contemporary use and this would make precise dating by ceramics alone quite difficult. This is no different in prehistory although the range of ceramics is obviously less varied. The pottery record at Dragonby is long and intricate and the simplification offered here does not do justice to the complexity of the sequence.

All the pottery from Dargonby is hand-built with wheel-thrown wares being introduced late in the sequence. The earliest pottery (Stage 1) comprises some pedestal-based urns as well as jars with cordons or multiple ridges. There are also some less well-finished coarser jars and bowls as might be expected in a domestic assemblage. Some fabrics are burnished and some are pitted where shell and calcitic inclusions

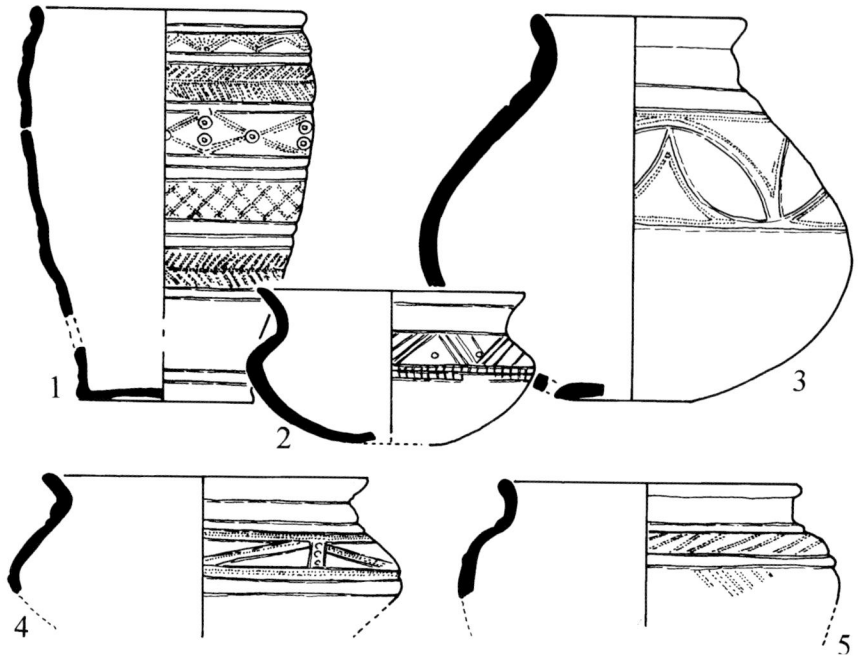

65 *Iron Age pottery from Lincolnshire. 1, 2 & 4 – Dragonby; 3 – Ingoldmells; 5 – Ancaster. Scale 1:4. After Elsdon 1975*

have leached out of the fabric. The decoration may consist of circular stamps and rouletted impressions (**65**), occasionally in intricate designs. Many of these types continue through subsequent stages. Stage 2 pottery comprises small, shouldered jars with marked necks and a range of S-profiled coarse ware jars. Some of the fine ware is again burnished. Some coarse ware jars may be quite angular. In Stage 3, the presence of angular jars persists and there are also omphalos-based pots and scratched wares. In Stage 4 there are square-rimmed and S-profiled coarse ware jars and large, multiple cordoned vessels with bulbous profiles termed 'cauldrons' in the report. These vessels are decorated between the encircling cordons. Such features may have two main functions; firstly they may strengthen the pot, bearing in mind that they are large, bulbous and comparatively fine-walled, and secondly they may be devices to aid handling as the pots must have been heavy when full. Stage 5, once again a continuation from earlier stages, sees the appearance of decorated bases on the jars. Jar decoration tends to be incised (or tooled) rather than rouletted. Stage 6 sees the introduction of wheel-thrown pottery and some Gallo-Belgic imports. These imported wares mark a great innovation in the ceramic record but appear in this stage in very small quantities. There are also jars with lattice decoration and with 'large shoulder bulges' which give them an appearance similar to corrugated iron. Large, handled jars also make an appearance in this stage. Unfortunately, as mentioned above and as with many other Iron Age sites, it is difficult to put these stages into a precise chronological framework.

Elsewhere in the east of the country, bulbous jars with La Tène decoration are

The Iron Age: from 600 BC to the Roman Conquest

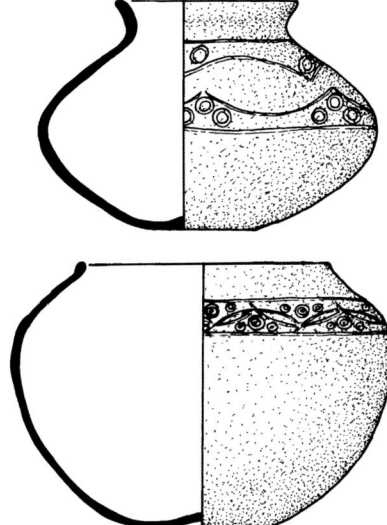

66 *Bulbous jars from the Thames estuary. Upper – Mucking, Essex; Lower – Canewdon, Essex. Scale 1:6. After Elsdon 1975*

found from the south coast to the Wash. They are invariably closed forms with rims narrow in comparison to the large diameter of the bellies' girths. The bases are also narrow, sometimes little more than an omphalos. They are incredibly well-made pots, often burnished, and with well-designed curvilinear motifs (**66**).

The North of England and mainland Scotland

North of the Trent, the pottery tends to display neither the technological standards nor the decorative qualities of the southern material. Instead, some coarser wares deriving from the later Bronze Age urns and bowls predominate. These display a marked conservatism and differentiation between later Bronze Age and Iron Age ceramics in the north of Britain can be very difficult. Frequent references to 'coarse pottery' and 'flat-rimmed pottery' occur in the literature and archaeologists generally rely on other artefact types and/or radiocarbon dating to date sites of this period in this region.

Despite this pessimism, the north of Britain is far from aceramic. The fingertip impressed jars from Staple Howe have already been mentioned (see above **54**) and other early Iron Age finds from this site comprises angular bowls not dissimilar to contemporary ones from further south (**67**). There is also an element of scored wares in this region at this time and throughout the Iron Age.

Towards the middle Iron Age, there is a range of convex-sided barrel jars with simple rims comparable to those amongst the coarse ware assemblages in southern England and the Midlands. These seem to be long-lived, probably by virtue of their simplicity, and in a coarse fabric with abundant angular inclusions (**68**). Similarly long- lived are more upright jars with high, slack and rounded shoulders and

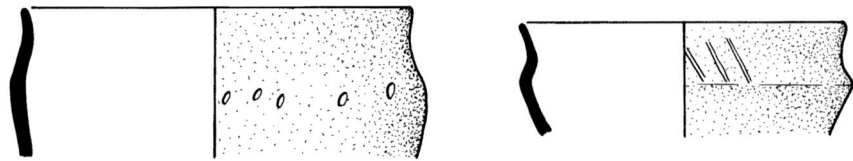

67 *Early Iron Age bowls from Staple Howe, Yorkshire. Scale 1:4. After Brewster 1963*

slightly everted rims. Decoration, other than the scoring mentioned above, is rare and restricted to simple motifs such as fingertip impressions on rims or occasional geometric incision. In the later Iron Age, jars with grooves around the rounded shoulder and bead or short everted rims are common. Fingertip impressions on rims return to fashion, sometimes impressed diagonally to form a cable design. These rims may have internal bevels and recall the Food Vessels of two millennia earlier.

In Yorkshire there are a number of larger 'S'-profiled jars with closed mouths and everted rims. They are generally in a very coarse fabric and tend to be undecorated. These forms continue into the Roman period. North of the Tees the ceramic record is generally poor and is dominated by coarse plain bucket (open) and barrel (closed) forms which continue in use after the Roman conquest and are common on the small enclosed Iron Age and Romano-British native settlements typically found between the Tees and Forth. Despite attempts to place these coarse ceramics into some chronological framework, the paucity of available radiocarbon dates and stratified assemblages has precluded this. As a result, Derek Alexander and Trevor Watkins were merely able to state that at St Germains, East Lothian 'it is only possible to advance a date range [for the pottery] from the middle of the first millennium BC through to the second century AD' (Alexander & Watkins 1998, 226-7, my brackets). This is depressing but unfortunately all too true.

Elsewhere in mainland Scotland, material culture of the later Iron Age, particularly pottery, is sparse and poorly understood. If present on archaeological sites, it tends to be coarse and display a restricted range of bucket and barrel forms under the general, but unhelpful, heading of flat-rimmed wares. This term is unhelpful because we have already encountered it in the preceding periods, even back to the Neolithic, and therefore it has no chronological parameters. Also, paradoxically, the rims of flat-rimmed ware are rarely flat! Instead they are bumpy and often poorly formed. As with almost every rule in archaeology, there are exceptions and the exception in this case is the pottery of the Northern Isles.

In contrast to the Scottish mainland, the pottery of the western and Northern Isles is sometimes decorated and is more varied in form. For example, the sequence from Clickhimin in Shetland stretches from the later Bronze Age right through the Iron Age until the eighth century AD (**69**). The later Bronze Age material comprises coarse barrel urns with abundant steatite opening materials and the rim forms tend to be rounded or slightly pointed. In the early Iron Age, the steatite barrel and bucket urns continue but there is also the introduction of carinated bowls with everted rims which

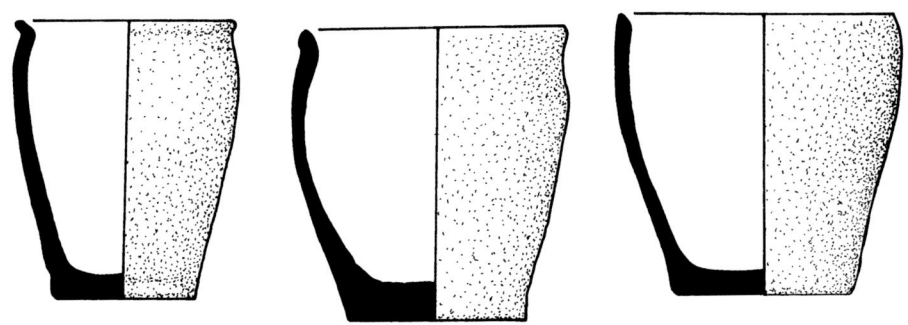

68 *Coarse ware jars from Yorkshire. 1 – Driffield; 2 & 3 – Danes Graves. Scale 1:4. After Brewster 1963*

tend to be finer than the larger vessels. Iron Age elements of the sequence are characterised by high and round shouldered jars with everted rims as well as globular forms. Fingernail impressed cable cordons also appear in this period. In the Broch period, or later Iron Age (first century BC to the second century AD), the assemblage comprises closed vessels with high, rounded shoulders and distinct cordons which may often be fingertip impressed. Other decoration may be incised and comprise fringed triangles similar to Vaul pottery which is discussed below. The Pictish period pottery associated with the wheelhouse occupation of the site is associated with hard, well-fired pots with a range of forms similar to the preceding period but tending towards more globular vessels with less flaring rims. The decoration may be triangular or curvilinear.

Similar pottery exists in the contexts of Hebridean brochs of the later Iron Age (which in northern Scotland continues into what would be the Roman period in southern Britain). These brochs are large, thick-walled defensive towers restricted in their distribution to Scotland and they are particularly common in the North and West. From the Broch at Ballevullin on Tiree was a rich assemblage of decorated pottery (**70**) comprising cordoned jars with fingertip or fingernail impressions as well as vessels with incised decoration. Some of these vessels are fine and well fired while others may be coarser and contain abundant large angular inclusions. The brochs of Dun Mor Vaul and Clettraval produced large and small jars often barrel-shaped or with everted rims, with filled fringed triangles similar to the contemporary material at Clickhimin. The Clettraval assemblage contained barrel jars with finger-moulded cordons and incised arcs. The elaborate nature of this northern material, as already mentioned above, stands in contrast to the stylistically impoverished material of the rest of Scotland.

This book has been primarily concerned with British and Irish insular pottery of the prehistoric period. However, to complete the narrative and take us up to the Roman invasion, mention must be made of Belgic pottery. This fine ware is initially imported to Britain in the first century BC and continues into the Roman period. Local copies are also made of this high-quality pottery. The notable thing about Belgic Ware is that, for the first time in 4000 years, the vessels are wheel-thrown,

The Iron Age: from 600 BC to the Roman Conquest

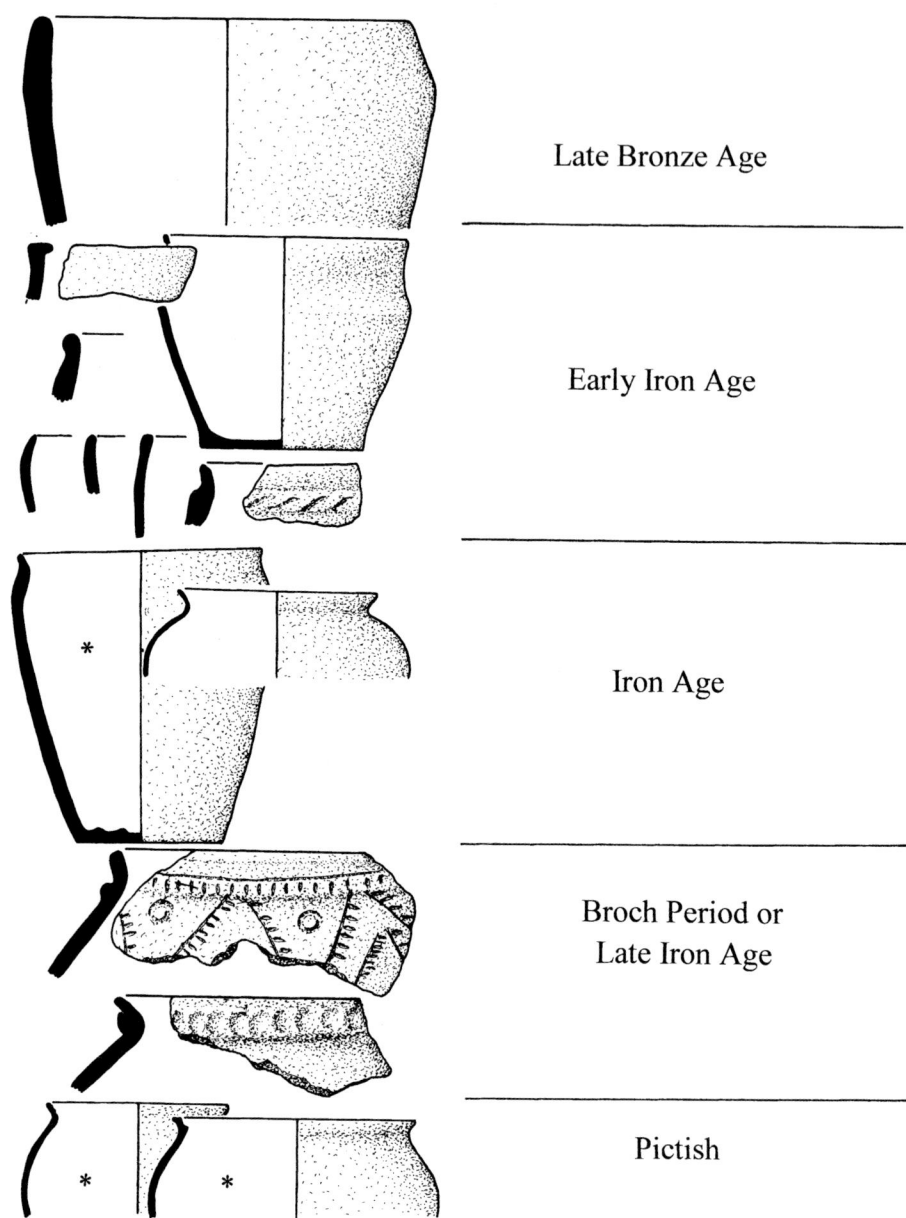

69 *The Clickhimin sequence, Shetland.
Scale 1:4 (sherds marked ★ 1:8). After Hamilton 1968*

The Iron Age: from 600 BC to the Roman Conquest

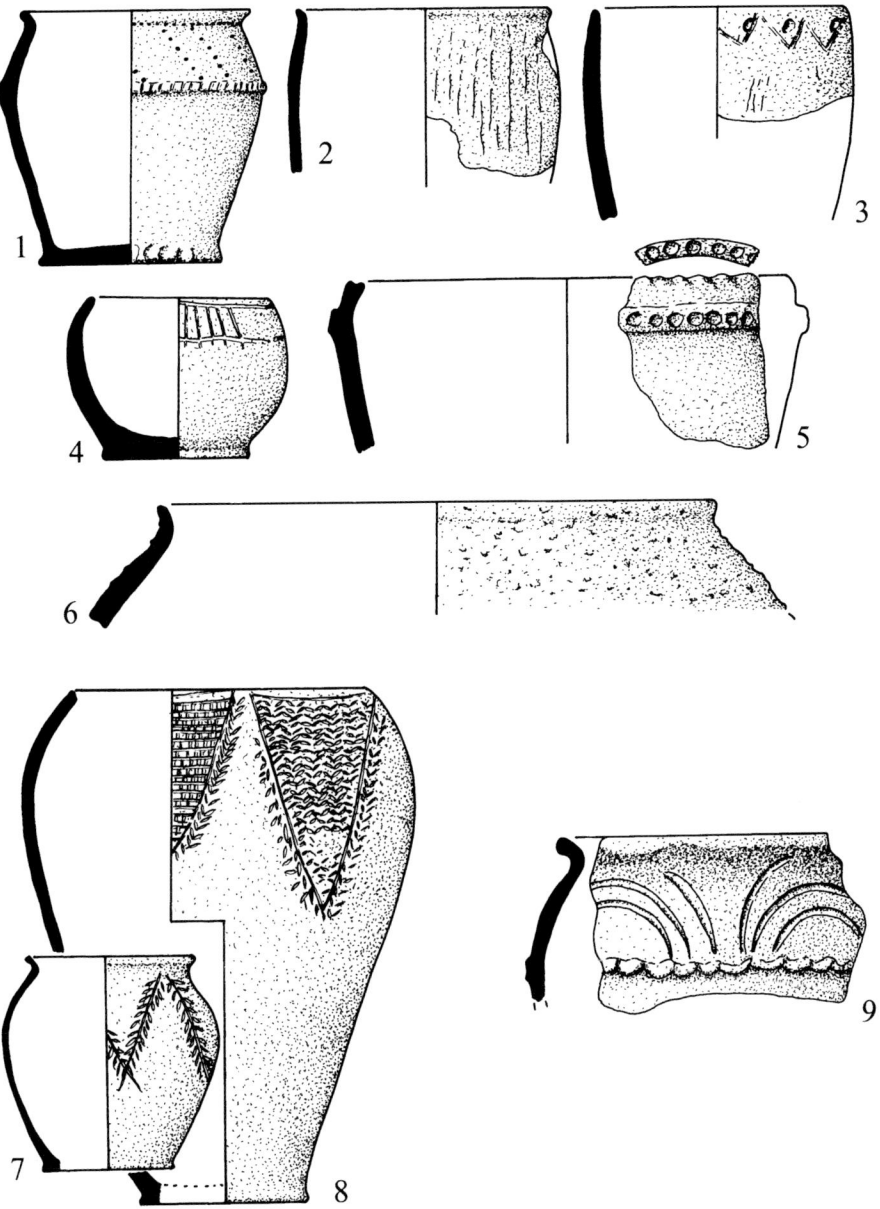

70 *Pottery from the Brochs of the Western Isles. 1-6 – Balevullin. After MacKie 1963; 7-8 – Dun Mor Vaul. After MacKie 1974; 9 – Clettraval. After McKie 1971. 1-6 & 9 – scale 1:4; 7 & 8 – scale 1:6*

The Iron Age: from 600 BC to the Roman Conquest

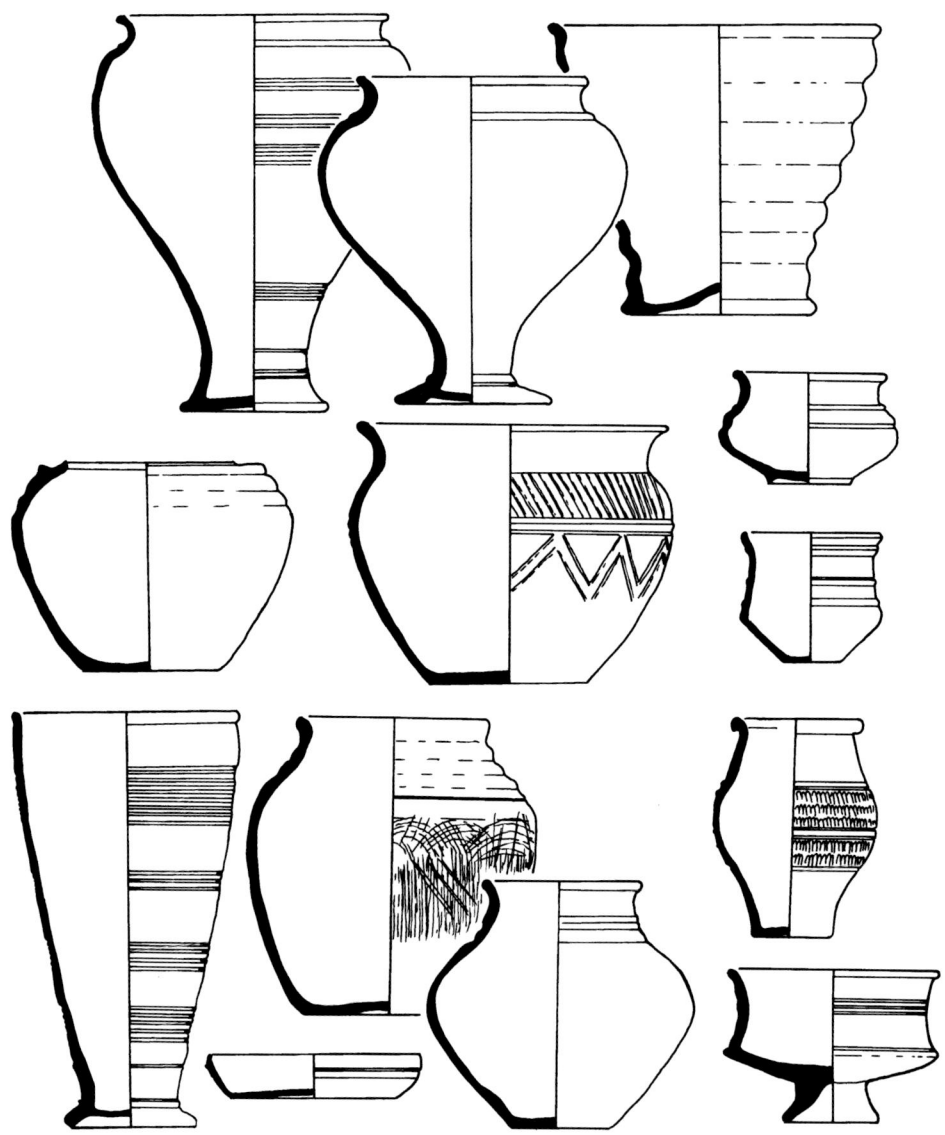

71 *Belgic Pottery from south-eastern England.
Scale 1:4.* After Birchall 1965

which allows fine-walled and elegant forms to be more easily made. Tall pedestalled urns, conical vases, corrugated vases and cordoned pots are all found in Belgic assemblages and this archaeological horizon is often termed the Aylesford-Swarling culture after two sites in Kent. The pottery is so well made and uniform in design that it must represent the work of specialist and accomplished potters. There are also introduced forms such as wheel-thrown lids and *tazze* (singular *tazza*), which are small bipartite cups sitting on a relatively tall pedestalled base. While occurring in domestic contexts, this pottery is also known from some rich cremation burials in south-east England and may be associated with rich metalwork and imported wine-filled amphorae. Rome was on the doorstep.

Conclusion

The last chapter ended with a quote from Barry Cunliffe's book *Iron Age Communities in Britain* in which he indicated that the Iron Age, particularly in southern England, was a time of great diversity and dynamism. It is hoped that some of this variety and innovation has been illustrated above. However in a general and broad work such as this, full justice cannot be given to the complexity of Iron Age ceramics. Cunliffe, for example, devotes over 40 pages of text and 37 pages of pot drawings to his regional groupings based largely on the identification of ceramic style zones, particularly in southern England. As already mentioned, it is tempting to see these style zones, particularly towards the end of the Iron Age, as broadly conforming to tribal territories as documented by classical writers and placenames. In Wessex and the south west, for example, the tribes of the Atrebates, Durotriges, Dumnonii and Dobunni are known from the classical geographers and from the place names of Roman Britain: Exeter, for instance, is Isca Dumnoniorum (Isca of the Dumnonii) and Silchester is Calleva Atrebatum (Calleva of the Atrebates). These territories can be further defined by studying the pottery and pre-Roman coinage to the extent that fairly precise boundaries may be identified (Cunliffe 1993). Pottery however is unlikely to conform so rigidly to political boundaries. Mechanisms such as trade and gift exchange will ensure a blurring of the edges whether it be the pots or their contents that are the more valuable. In southern Britain at least, the advent of Rome lays to rest 4000 years of ceramic development in these islands. That is only half true, of course. The Romans also adopted some local ceramic traditions. Thus the Durotrigian potters continue to work through the Roman occupation as we have already observed. Similarly, Dales Ware cooking pots from north Lincolnshire, Knapton and Huntcliffe Wares from Yorkshire continued to be made, adapted and circulated. The native traditions continue in those regions that were largely unaffected by the invasion, that is the area to the north of Hadrian's Wall; but elsewhere the commercially available mass-produced products of empire dominate the archaeological record.

8 Postscript

We have seen that prehistoric pottery in Britain and Ireland spans some 4000 years of development and that this development is more or less continuous, though varying degrees of external influence can be recognised, particularly in the Iron Age. The technology of pottery is also largely unchanged from the beginnings of the insular traditions around 4000 BC until the introduction of the wheel and kiln shortly before the Roman conquest. Pottery kilns were in use elsewhere in Europe from the very beginnings of the Bronze Age but British and Irish potters would not seem to have had the need for such technology. Without it they were producing perfectly adequate pots that suited the needs of themselves and their clients. We have also highlighted some unanswered questions however. Where are the experimental pieces? Why is there no representational art? Where are our firing sites? Is there a really significant chronological gap between the Impressed Wares of the Neolithic and the Food Vessels and Collared Urns of the Bronze Age and if so, why do the Bronze Age pots resemble the Neolithic ones so strongly? Why do the Iron Age potters of northern Britain not match the level of accomplishment of those in the south and east? Despite having elaborate sequences and regional studies, there is so much about prehistoric pottery that we do not yet know. For me, this is one of the attractions of the discipline.

Archaeologists often get carried away by the construction of intricate typologies. Is this brooch a class 1 or a class 2? Is it class 2a or 2b? What is often forgotten is that such classifications would have meant little or nothing to the people who made or used these artefacts. In contemporary circles, how often have we heard the sentiment 'I've got one like that! It's not the same but very similar.' In other words, we are not classifying contemporary material culture in the same way as we classify the artefacts of the past. I think that this is important because we must constantly remind ourselves that we are supposed to be studying people and that individuals, families and clans, not artefacts, peopled the past. This point made, I would argue that pottery tells us more about prehistoric people than any other type of artefact. It tells us about date, helping us to grasp exactly when the people who made and owned these pots were alive. It can tell us about diet and economy by preserving food residues that might have been absorbed by the porous fabric of the vessel and the seed impressions that might survive in the walls of the pot. It can tell us about the social status of the owner, what type of pot or pots he or she was buried with both in the Bronze Age and the later Iron Age. Ancient weathered sherds can shed light on prehistoric rituals. Fragments of used and broken pottery are often deposited in pits or at monuments as part of some ritual or propitiatory act involving deposition. Pots play a part in burial ritual as well as an essential role in the everyday lives of the living. Pottery can tell us too about regional social divisions by identifying style zones and areas of contact. Trans-regional distributions also hint at trade networks and the larger economy.

What I personally find more fascinating, however, are the special insights that pottery provides into the real people of prehistory. We can recognise individuals. This may be abstract in terms of identifying the works of a single potter or more tangible by allowing us to see the traces and impressions of the actual fingertips, fingernails and even fingerprints of these chronologically remote craftsmen. More than any other aspect of prehistoric archaeology, pottery puts me personally in touch with the real people of the past.

So does the study of pottery have a serious role to play in modern society or is it simply an indulgence of a small number of 'specialists', archaeological trainspotters sharing numbers and details of 'interesting' pots? Well, firstly we are still using pottery and the transformation of clay to ceramic using carefully controlled fire is practised today at both an industrial and craft level. Some societies are still making pottery in a way that has not changed since the Neolithic. Prehistoric pottery therefore has a relevance to and a point of contact with the ceramics we see around us today. I worked with a contemporary craft potter who had never fired his pots in a bonfire before and after the mutually beneficial exchange of knowledge and despite the potter's distinct nervousness, the bonfire firing was totally successful. He liked the surface finish it gave to his pots and he has experimented with the technique since. I also believe that the study of the past can be beneficial to the future and I shall cite just one example.

In 2000, I was invited by Dr Dragos Gheorghiu of the University of Arts in Bucharest to take part in the Vadastra Project. This was a programme of experiment and research into ancient ceramics centred on the village of Vadastra in southern Romania. The firing experiments were not ground-breaking. Much similar work had been carried out in Britain and elsewhere since the 1970s but I was attracted to this project by two elements. Firstly there was the opportunity to experiment with replica kilns and secondly there were children involved. I shall explain.

As mentioned above kilns were in use in Eastern Europe from the late Neolithic-Early Bronze Age transition known as the Copper Age or Chalcolithic. Some kilns have been excavated and we know quite a lot about their structure. I had not experimented with kilns before as all my research involved open-fired pottery, so here was an opportunity to work with a full-scale replica of a 7000-year-old kiln. The Chaloclithic kiln from Cotesti was a simple beehive-shaped structure dug into a hillslope and fired through a flue dug from a platform on the side of the slope. Two men could excavate this small kiln in a day, taking another day to construct the floor and to line the chamber with clay. Our reproduction of this simple kiln worked extremely well and produced some high quality ceramics.

But it was the educational aspect of this project that interested me most. As well as archaeologists, Dr Gheorghiu brought with him to Vadastra contemporary traditional potters and ceramics students who taught simple potting techniques to local school children. They started coiling and ring-building pots just as was done in prehistory. Inevitably we started off with what I described as 'the largest collection of ashtrays in private hands' but gradually pot walls started to grow and forms became more adventurous. By 2001, children as young as 6 years old were beginning to wheel throw pots. I shall never forget one child, too small to reach the kickwheel, having to have the wheel powered by an older, taller friend while he threw a perfectly acceptable small vase. The resulting pots were fired in the local replica kiln.

What I have omitted to mention so far is that Vadastra lies in Oltenia, one of the poorest regions of Romania. There is very little work and people live a subsistence economy. There is no industry and no crafts to speak of. The local villagers need and use pottery and this all has to be bought and imported. Yet on their doorstep lies an excellent source of clay in the riverbank and the chalcolithic technology is simple, easily replicated and extremely effective. Fuel is abundant and the children are eager to learn. All the necessary ingredients for a local industry are to hand and with the right encouragement this industry could be viable. The Neolithic and Chalcolithic ceramics from Vadastra are of a high quality, so why can't the modern inhabitants, some of whom live on top of the actual prehistoric settlement or 'tell' as it is known, re-establish a ceramics industry in this region? I have confidence in this project and pray that it will maintain its momentum.

The study of prehistoric ceramics therefore can have a relevance to the present and indeed to the future; and some of us who gain a fascination from its study are occasionally privileged and fortunate enough to get the opportunity to give something back.

Glosssary of terms

Absorbed residue analysis	Chemical analysis of the fats and other organic residues trapped within the porous fabric of an unglazed vessel (see chapter 1).
Accessory vessels	Pots which accompany burials. Usually believed to have contained provision for the afterlife.
Amphora	Large two-handled storage jar imported from Roman Europe in the final decades of the British prehistoric period. Used for the storage of liquids such as wine or oil.
Assemblage	Collection of pottery from the same archaeological site. Furthermore, the pottery should be from the same phase within the site so that all the different vessels can be considered as broadly contemporary.
Barrel (urn)	A tall vessel whose rim diameter is less than the greatest diameter (see *closed form*).
Barrow	A burial mound usually of the Neolithic and Bronze Age period but also known in the Iron Age, Roman and Saxon eras.
Bowl	A generally bulbous pot whose height is equal to or less than its maximum diameter.
Bucket (urn)	A tall vessel whose rim diameter is or is equal to the greatest diameter (see *open form*).
Carination (Carinated Bowl)	A sharp change of direction or shoulder in a pot's profile (shouldered bowl of the primary Neolithic).
Ceramic	Pottery. Clay that has been through the ceramic change (see chapter 2)
Ceramic change	The point at which the water of chemical composition is driven from the clay particles, usually around 700°C (see chapter 2)
Closed form	A pot whose rim diameter is less than the maximum diameter.
Coil break	Where a vessel has broken along an imperfectly bonded coil, ring or strap (see *coil building*). Sometimes also called a 'false rim' (see chapter 2).
Coil building	Building a pot by means of superimposing cylindrical coils of clay (see chapter 2).

Glossary of terms

Collar	A heavy and deep rim accentuating the mouth of the vessel. Collared Urns of the Bronze Age most commonly exhibit this feature (see chapter 5).
Corpus (pl corpora)	Literally a 'body' of data. In archaeology this is usually a complete collection of artefacts or monuments and can be regional or national. Some discussions of prehistoric pottery can be found in local county corpora – e.g. the Beaker pottery from Kent – or in national lists, e.g. Longworth's 1984 *The Collared Urns of Britain and Ireland*.
Decorative technique	A method of decoration. Twisted cord, incisions, tooling etc. are all examples of decorative techniques, i.e. methods by which decoration is made. These are not to be confused with terms such as lozenges, spirals, herringbone etc. which are all decorative motifs.
Dunting	Cracks formed when the fired pots cool too quickly.
Fire clouds	Black 'blotchy' patches on the surface of a pot caused by the pot being buried in the ash or in close contact with smoking fuel (see chapter 2).
Firing	The process in which clay is heated to such a degree as to become ceramic (see chapter 2).
Gabbroic wares	Pottery made from the Gabbroic clays, notably in Britain from the Lizard peninsula in Cornwall.
Grog	Pieces of crushed pottery mixed with the clay before building a pot.
Inclusions	Pieces of non-clay matter included in the fabric of a pot. These may be naturally occurring (i.e. found naturally in the clay) or deliberately added (see *opening agent*) (see chapter 2).
Jar	A large vessel whose height greatly exceeds the maximum diameter. This term tends to be applied to the large vessels of the Late Bronze and Iron Ages. The term 'Urn' is preferred in the earlier Bronze Age since the main archaeological focus has been on funerary archaeology.
Join void	A thin strip of air between two imperfectly joined coils, rings or straps (see *coil building*) (see chapter 2).
Kiln	A built (or dug) structure in which pots are fired. Not known to have been introduced into Britain until the Roman conquest.

Glossary of terms

Motif	A scheme of decoration. Herringbone, lozenges, spirals etc. are all examples of motifs. These are not to be confused with incision or impression which are decorative techniques.
Omphalos	From the Greek word meaning navel, this is used to refer to small depressions on the base of some vessels, particularly of the middle and later Iron Age. Small cups especially may have omphalos bases.
Open fire	A pit or surface bonfire in which pots may be fired. The temperatures generated by these fires and the firing atmospheres (combustion gases) are more difficult to control than those in kilns. Pottery was fired in open fires throughout British and Irish prehistory.
Open form	A pot whose rim diameter is the maximum diameter.
Opening agent	A non-clay material such as stone or fired clay which is added to the clay prior to the building of a pot. These inclusions form small voids in the fabric to allow the steam from the water of plasticity and water of chemical composition to escape safely (see chapter 2).
Oxidising atmosphere	An oxygen rich atmosphere in the fire or kiln. This will result in the complete combustion of fuel and the pots having a clean yellow or red colour depending on the iron oxides present in the clay.
Petrological analysis	Study of the minerals and rock fragments within the fabric of a pot to try and ascertain the area of manufacture from the geology of these inclusions.
Pinched pots	Pots made by pinching a ball of clay between the thumb and fingers to draw up the sides of the vessels. These pots are generally small and simple but may form the lower portions of larger vessels.
Plastic decoration	Decoration which is applied to or raised from the surface of a pot (see chapter 3).
Radiocarbon dating	A scientific method of dating which relies on the radioactive isotope of carbon (14C), present in all living organisms. When an animal or plant dies, the 14C cannot be replenished and decays at a known rate. By calculating the amount of 14C remaining in a sample the age of the material from death can be estimated.

Glossary of terms

Reducing atmosphere	An atmosphere in which oxygen is scarce or absent. This is almost impossible to achieve in a bonfire or open firing. Under these conditions carbon monoxide is built up. This gas is oxygen-hungry and will take oxygen from the iron oxides within the clay. The result will be dark-coloured pots (brown, grey or black) but must not be confused with sooting or fire clouds (see chapter 2).
Ring building	Building a pot by superimposing cylinders of clay (see chapter 2).
Rustication	The roughening of a surface such as by fingertip impressions or scratching, often as an aid to handling.
Sherd (sometimes shard)	Fragment of pottery
Situla	A large upright vessel often with a high shoulder and upright or flaring neck made of beaten bronze sheets. These vessels are copied in ceramic (Situla jars) at the Bronze-Iron Age transition. The name is from the Latin for 'bucket'.
Slip	A clay in suspension which may be applied to the surfaces of a pot.
Sooting	Carbon being deposited on and in the surface of a pot as a result of it being in proximity to smoking material in the fire. This can be patchy (see *fire clouds*).
Spall (spalling)	Usually roughly circular flake of clay blown out of the wall of the vessel during firing. Normally caused when steam cannot find an escape route through the fabric.
Strap building	Building a pot by superimposing flattened strips of clay (see chapter 2).
Stratigraphy	The study of the layers (strata) and the relationship between features encountered on an archaeological excavation. It is based on the principle that if layer A overlies layer B, then layer A is later. Similarly if ditch 1 cuts ditch 2, then ditch 2 must be earlier than ditch 1. The study of such relationships is fundamental to understanding site sequences and, although the theory is simple enough, factors such as the re-use of earlier features, disturbance of the deposits or the failure of some features to intersect others can severely complicate the issue.

Glossary of terms

Thin section (analysis)	A thin semi-transparent sliver of pottery mounted on a glass microscope slide. It is examined under a microscope to establish the makeup of the fabric and the geological provenance of the clay and inclusions.
Urn	Large vessel whose body height greatly exceeds the maximum diameter. Strictly speaking, this term should only be applied to vessels found with burials but it is more widely applied to early Bronze Age pots of similar types from both sepulchral and settlement contexts. 'Jar' tends to be used in Iron Age studies (see above).
Vase	A pot whose height is greater than its maximum diameter.
Water of chemical composition	Chemical water in the clay molecules which has to be driven off by heat before the clay can become ceramic (see chapter 2).
Water of plasticity	The water between the clay particles which lubricates the particles giving clay its 'squidgy' texture.
Water smoking stage	The point at which the remaining water of plasticity in a dried vessel is driven off by heat. Usually around 200°C (see chapter 2).

Bibliography

Abercromby, J. 1912. *A Study of the Bronze Age Pottery of Great Britain and Ireland and its Associated Grave Goods.* Oxford: Clarendon Press.

Annable, K. & Simpson, D. 1964. *Guide Catalogue to the Neolithic and Bronze Age Antiquities in Devizes Museum.* Devizes: Wiltshire Archaeological and Natural History Society.

ApSimon, A. & Greenfield, E. 1972. The excavation of the Bronze Age and Iron Age settlement at Trevisker Round, St. Eval, Cornwall. *Proceedings of the Prehistoric Society*, 38, 302-81.

Ashmore, P. 1998. Radiocarbon dates for settlements, tombs and ceremonial sites with Grooved Ware in Scotland. In A. Gibson & D. Simpson (eds). *Prehistoric Ritual and Religion*, 139-47. Stroud: Sutton Publishing.

Ashmore, P. 2000. Dating the Neolithic in Orkney. In A Ritchie (ed) *Neolithic Orkney in its European Context*, 299-308. Cambridge: University of Cambridge McDonald Institute for Archaeological Research.

Avery, M. 1982. The Neolithic causewayed enclosure, Abingdon. In H.J. Case & A.W.R Whittle (eds) *Setlement Patterns in the Oxford Region: Excavations at the Abingdon Causewayed Enclosure and Other Sites*, 10-50, Report No 4. London: Council for British Archaeology.

Barclay, G. & Russell-White, C.J. 1993. Excavations in the ceremonial complex of the fourth millennium BC at Balfarg/Balbirnie, Glenrothes, Fife. *Proceedings of the Society of Antiquaries of Scotland*, 123, 43-210.

Barratt, J. C. 1980. The Pottery of the Later Bronze Age in Lowland England. *Proceedings of the Prehistoric Society,* 46, 297-320.

Birchall, A. 1965. The Aylesford-Swarling culture: the problem of the Belgae reconsidered. *Proceedings of the Prehistoric Society*, 31, 241-367.

Brewster, T.C.M. 1963. *The Excavation of Staple Howe.* Malton: East Riding Archaeological Research Committee.

Brindley, A. 1999. Irish Grooved Ware. In R. Cleal & A. MacSween (eds), *Grooved Ware in Britain and Ireland*, 23-35. Oxford: Oxbow Books.

Britnell, W.J., Silvester, R.J., Gibson, A.M., Caseldine, A.E., Hunter, K.L. Johnson, S., Hamilton-Dyer, S. & Vince, A. 1997. A Middle Bronze Age round-house at Glanfeinion, near Llandinam, Powys. *Proceedings of the Prehistoric Society*, 63, 179-98.

Bullied, A. & Gray, H. St. G. 1911. *The Glastonbury Lake Village.* Glastonbury: Glastonbury Antiquarian Society.

Burgess, C.B. 1976a. An early Bronze Age settlement at Kilellan Farm, Islay, Argyll. In C. Burgess & R. Miket (eds), *Settlement and Economy in the Third and Second Millennia BC*, 151-80. BAR 33, Oxford: British Archaeological Reports.

Burgess, C.B. 1976b. Meldon Bridge. A Neolithic defended promontory complex near Peebles. In C. Burgess & R. Miket (eds), *Settlement and Economy in the Third and Second Millennia BC*, 181-208. BAR 33, Oxford: British Archaeological Reports.

Burgess, C.B. 1980. *The Age of Stonehenge*. London: Dent.

Burgess, C.B. 1995. Bronze Age settlements and domestic pottery in northern Britain: some suggestions. In I. Kinnes & G. Varndell (eds), *Unbaked Urns of Rudely Shape. Essays on British and Irish Pottery for Ian Longworth*, 145-58. Oxford: Oxbow Books.

Burrow, S. 1999. The Ronaldsway pottery of the Isle of Man: a study of production, decoration and use. *Proceedings of the Prehistoric Society*, 65, 125-44.

Calder, C.S.T. 1956. Stone Age house sites in Shetland. *Proceedings of the Society of Antiquaries of Scotland*, 84, 340-97.

Calkin, J.B. 1962. The Bournemouth area in the middle and late Bronze Age with the Deverel-Rimbury problem reconsidered. *Archaeological Journal*, 119, 1-65.

Case, H. 1993. Beakers: deconstruction and after. *Proceedings of the Prehistoric Society*, 59, 241-68.

Case, H. 1995. Beakers: loosening a stereotype. In I. Kinnes and G. Varndell (eds) *Unbaked Urns of Rudely Shape. Essays on British and Irish Pottery for Ian Longworth*, 55-67. Oxford: Oxbow Books.

Challis, A.J. & Harding, D.W. 1975. *Later Prehistory from the Trent to the Tyne*. BAR 20. Oxford: British Archaeological Reports.

Childe, V.G. 1931a. The continental affinities of British Neolithic pottery. *Archaeological Journal*, 88, 37-66.

Childe, V.G. 1931b. *Skara Brae*. London: Kegan Paul, Trench, Tubner & Co.

Clark, J.G.D., Higgs, E.S. & Longworth, I.H. 1960. Excavations at the Neolithic site at Hurst Fen, Mildenhall, Suffolk (1954, 1957 and 1958). *Proceedings of the Prehistoric Society*, 26, 202-45.

Clarke, D.L. 1970. *The Beaker Pottery of Great Britain and Ireland* Cambridge: Cambridge University Press.

Cleal, R. 1992. Significant form: ceramic styles in the earlier Neolithic of Southern England. In N. Sharples & A. Sheridan (eds), *Vessels for the Ancestors*, 286-306. Edinburgh: Edinburgh University Press.

Cleal, R.M.J. 1995. Pottery fabrics in Wessex in the fourth to second millennia BC. In I. Kinnes & G. Varndell (eds) *Unbaked urns of Rudely Shape. Essays on British and Irish Pottery for Ian Longworth*, 185-94. Oxford: Oxbow Books.

Cleal, R.M.J., Cooper, J. & Williams, D., 1994. Shells and sherds: Identification of Inclusions in Grooved Ware, with associated Radiocarbon Dates, from Amesbury, Wiltshire. *Proceedings of the Prehistoric Society*, 60, 445-8.

Cowie, T. & MacSween, A. 1999. Grooved ware from Scotland: a review. In R. Cleal & A. MacSween (eds), *Grooved Ware in Britain and Ireland*, 49-56. Oxford: Oxbow Books.

Cunliffe, B. 1987. *Hengistbury Head, Dorset. Volume I, the Prehistoric and Roman Settlement 3500BC – AD500.* Oxford: Oxford University Committee for Archaeology.

Cunliffe, B. 1991. *Iron Age Communities in Braitain.* (3rd edn). London & New York: Routledge.

Cunliffe, B. 1993. *Wessex to AD 1000.* London & New York: Longman.

Davidson, J.L. & Henshall, A.S. 1991. *The Chambered Cairns of Caithness.* Edinburgh: Edinburgh University Press.

Earwood, C. 1989/90. Radiocarbon dating of late Prehistoric wooden vessels. *The Journal of Irish Archaeology*, 5, 37-44.

Earwood, C. 1991/2. A radiocarbon date for early Bronze Age wooden polypod bowls. *The Journal of Irish Archaeology*, 6, 27-8.

Elsdon, S.M. 1975. *Stamp and Roulette-decorated Pottery of the La Tène Period in Eastern England.* BAR 10, Oxford: British Archaeological Reports.

Elsdon, S.M. 1997. *Old Sleaford Revealed.* Monograph 78, Oxford: Oxbow Books.

Evershed, R., Mottram, H., Dudd, S., Charters, S., Stott, A., Gibson, A., Conner, A., Blinkham, P. & Reeves, V. 1997. New criteria for the identification of animal fats preserved in archaeological pottery. *Naturwissenschaften*, 84, 402-6.

Fox, C. 1927. An encrusted urn of the Bronze Age from Wales with notes on the origin and distribution of the type. *Antiquaries Journal*, 7, 115-33.

Garwood, P. 1999. Grooved Ware in Southern Britain: chronology and interpretation. In R. Cleal & A. MacSween (eds), *Grooved Ware in Britain and Ireland*, 145-76. Oxford: Oxbow Books.

Gibson, A.M. 1982. *Beaker Domestic Sites: A Study in the Domestic Pottery of the Late Third and Early Second Millennia BC in the British Isles.* BAR 107, Oxford: British Archaeological Reports.

Gibson, A.M. 1986. The excavation of an experimental firing area at Stamford Hall, Leicester, 1985. *Bulletin of the Experimental Firing Group*, 4, 5-14.

Gibson, A.M., 1995a. First impressions: a review of Peterborough Ware in Wales. In I. Kinnes and G. Varndell (eds) *Unbaked Urns of Rudely Shape. Essays on British and Irish Pottery for Ian Longworth*, 23-40. Oxford: Oxbow Books.

Gibson, A.M. 1995b. The Neolithic pottery from Allt Chrisal. In K. Brannigan and P. Foster, 1995. *Barra. Archaeological Research on Ben Tangaval.* 100-15. Sheffield: Academic Press.

Gibson, A.M. 1999. *The Walton Basin Project: Excavation and Survey in a Prehistoric Landscape, 1993-7.* Research report 118, York: Council for British Archaeology.

Gibson, A.M. & Kinnes, I.A. 1997. On the urns of a dilemma: radiocarbon and the Peterborough problem. *Oxford Journal of Archaeology*, 16(1), 65-72.

Gibson, A.M. & Woods, A.J. 1990. *Prehistoric Pottery for the Archaeologist.* Leicester: Leicester University Press.

Gibson, A.M. 2004. Small but perfectly formed? Some observations on the Bronze Age cups of Scotland. In A. Gibson & A. Sheridan (eds) *From Sickles to Circles: Britain and Ireland at the Time of Stonehenge*, 270-288. Stroud: Tempus Publishing.

Greenwell, W. 1877. *British Barrows*; Oxford: Clarendon Press.

Grimes, W.F. 1938. A barrow on Breach Farm, Llanbleddian, Glamorgan. *Proceedings of the Prehistoric Society*, 4, 107-21.

Hamilton, J.R.C. 1968. *Excavations at Clickhimin, Shetland.* Edinburgh: H.M.S.O.

Harding, D.W. 1974. *The Iron Age in Lowland Britain.* London: Routledge, Keegan Paul.

Henshall, A.S. & Davidson, J.L. 1989. *The Chambered Cairns of Orkney.* Edinburgh: Edinburgh University Press.

Jobey, G. 1978. Green Knowe unenclosed platform settlement and Harehope cairn, Peeblesshire. *Proceedings of the Society of Antiquaries of Scotland*, 110, 72-113.

Jones, A. 1999. The world on a plate: ceramics, food technology and cosmology in Neolithic Orkney. In K.D. Thomas (ed) Food technology in its Social Context: Production, Processing and Storage, 55-77. *World Archaeology*, 31 (1).

Jones, A. 2000. Life after death: monument, material culture and social change in Neolithic Orkney. In A. Ritchie (ed), *Neolithic Orkney in its European Setting*, 127-38. Cambridge: McDonald Institute Monographs.

Kavanagh, R.M. 1976. Collared and Cordoned cinerary urns in Ireland. *Proceedings of the Royal Irish Academy*, 76C, 293-403.

Kendrick, T.D. 1925. *The Axe Age.* London: Methuen.

Kinnes, I., Gibson, A., Ambers, J., Bowman, S., Leese, M. & Boast, R., 1991. Radiocarbon dating and British Beakers: The British Museum Programme. *Scottish Archaeological Review*, 8, 35-68.

Kinnes, I.A. & Longworth, I.H. 1985. *Catalogue of the Excavated Prehistoric and Romano-British Material in The Greenwell Collection.* London: British Museum Press.

Langmaid, N. 1978. *Prehistoric Pottery.* Princes Risborough: Shire.

Lanting, J.N. & Waals, J.D. van der, 1972. British Beakers as seen from the continent. *Helinium*, 12, 20-46.

Liddell, D.M. 1929. New light on an old problem. *Antiquity*, 3, 283-91.

Longworth, I.H. 1967. Further discoveries at Brackmont Mill, Brackmont Farm and Tentsmuir, Fife. *Proceedings of the Society of Antiquaries of Scotland*, 99, 60-92.

Longworth, I.H. 1983. The Whinny Liggate Perforated Wall Cup and its affinities. In A. O'Connor & D.V. Clarke (eds), *From the Stone Age to the Forty-Five*, 65-86. Edinburgh: John Donald.

Longworth, I.H. 1984. *Collared urns of the Bronze Age in Great Britain and Ireland.* Cambridge: Cambridge University Press.

MacKie, E. 1963. A dwelling site of the earlier Iron Age at Balevullin, Tiree. *Proceedings of the Society of Antiquaries of Scotland*, 96, 155-83.

MacKie, E. 1971. English migrants and Scottish brochs. *Glasgow Archaeological Journal*, 2, 39-71.

MacKie, E. 1974. *Dn Mor Vaul. An Iron Age Broch on Tiree.* Glasgow: Glasgow Archaeological Society.

MacPherson-Grant, N., 1991. A reappraisal of prehistoric pottery from Canterbury. In *Canterbury's Archaeology 1990/91*, 38-48. Canterbury: Canterbury Archaeological Trust.

Mallory, J, 1991. Excavations at Haughey's Fort: 1989-1990. *Emmania, Bulletin of the Navan Research Group*, 8, 10-26.

Manby, T.G. 1988. The Neolithic in Eastern Yorkshire. In T. Manby (ed) *Archaeology in Eastern Yorkshire: Essays in Honour of T.C.M. Brewster*. 35-88. Sheffield: Department of Archaeology and Prehistory.

Manby, T.G. 1995. Skeuomorphism: some reflections of leather, wood and basketry in early Bronze Age pottery. In I. Kinnes and G. Varndell (eds) *Unbaked Urns of Rudely Shape. Essays on British and Irish Pottery for Ian Longworth*, 81-8. Oxford: Oxbow Books.

May, J. 1996. *Dragonby. Report on Excavations at an Iron Age and Romano-British Settlement in North Lincolnshire*. Oxford: Oxbow Books.

McInnes, I.J. 1969. A Scottish Neolithic pottery sequence. *Scottish Archaeological Forum*, 1, 19-30.

Mercer, R.J. 1981. Excavations at Carn Brae, Illogan, Cornwall, 1970-3. A Neolithic fortified complex of the third millennium BC. *Cornish Archaeology*, 20, 1-204.

Middleton, A. P. 1987. Technological investigation of the coatings of some 'haematite-coated' pottery from southern England. *Archaeometry*, 29, 250-61.

Middleton, A.P. 1995. Prehistoric red-finished pottery from Kent. In I. Kinnes and G. Varndell (eds) *Unbaked Urns of Rudely Shape. Essays on British and Irish Pottery for Ian Longworth*, 203-10. Oxford: Oxbow Books.

Modderman, P. J. R. 1971. Neolithische und Frühbronzezeitliche Siedlungsspuren au Hienheim, Ldkr. Kelheim. *Analectae Praehistorica Leidensia*, 4, 1-25.

Moore, J. & Jennings, D. 1992. *Reading Business Park: A Bronze Age Landscape*. Thames Valley Landscapes: the Kennet Valley, volume I. Oxford: Oxford University Committee for Archaeology.

Morrison, A. 1968. Cinerary urns and pigmy vessels in south-west Scotland. *Transactions of the Dumfriesshire and Galloway Natural History and Antiquarian Society*, 45, 80-140.

Musson, R.C., 1954. An illustrated catalogue of Sussex Beaker and Bronze Age pottery. *Sussex Archaeological Collections*, 92, 106-11.

Musson, C.R. (with W.J. Britnell & A.G. Smith) 1991. *The Breiddin Hillfort: A Later Prehistoric Settlement in the Welsh Marches*. Research Report 76, London: Council for British Archaeology and Cadw: Welsh Historic Monuments.

Needham, S. 1991. *Excavation and Salvage at Runnymede Bridge 1987*. London: British Museum Press.

Needham, S. 1995. A bowl from Maidcross, Suffolk; burials with pottery in the post Deverel-Rimbury period. In I. Kinnes and G. Varndell (eds) *Unbaked Urns of Rudely Shape. Essays on British and Irish Pottery for Ian Longworth*, 159-71. Oxford: Oxbow Books.

Needham, S. 2005. Transforming Beaker Culture in North-West Europe: Processes of Fusion and Fission. *Proceedings of the Prehistoric Society*, 71, 171-218.

O'Riordain, B. & Waddell, J. 1993. *The Funerary Bowls and Vases of the Irish Bronze Age*. Galway: Galway University Press.

Osgood, R., Monks, S. & Toms, J., 2000. *Bronze Age Warfare*. Stroud: Sutton.

Patchett,. F.M. 1944. Cornish Bronze Age pottery. *Archaeological Journal*, 101, 17-49.

Peacock, D.P.S. 1968. A petrological study of certain Iron Age pottery from western England. *Proceedings of the Prehistoric Society*, 34, 414-27.

Peacock, D.P.S. 1982. *Pottery in the Roman World*, London: Longman.
Piggott, S. 1931. The Neolithic pottery of the British Isles. *Archeological Journal*, 88, 67-158.
Piggott, S. 1954. *The Neolithic Cultures of the British Isles*. Cambridge: Cambridge University Press.
Piggott, S. 1962. *The West Kennet Long Barrow*. London: H.M.S.O.
Piggott, S. 1965. *Ancient Europe*. Edinburgh: Edinburgh University Press.
Richards, C. & Thomas, J, 1984. Ritual activity and structured deposition in later Neolithic Wessex. In R. Bradley & J. Gardiner (eds) *Neolithic Studies, A Review of Some Current Research*. 198-218. Report 133, Oxford: British Archaeological Reports
Richards, J. 1990. *The Stonehenge Environs Project*. London: English Heritage.
Scott, G.J. 1964. The chambered cairn at Beacharra, Kintyre, Argyll. *Proceedings of the Prehistoric Society*, 30, 134-58.
Shepard, A.O. 1954. *Ceramics for the Archaeologist*. Washington: Carnegie Institute.
Shepherd, I.A.G. 1986. *Powerful Pots: Beakers in North-east Prehistory*. Aberdeen: University of Aberdeen Anthropological Museum.
Sheridan, A. 1995. Irish Neolithic Pottery: the story in 1995. In I. Kinnes & G. Varndell (eds), *Unbaked Urns of Rudely Shape: Essays on British and Irish Pottery for Ian Longworth*, 3-21, Oxford: Oxbow Books.
Sheridan, A. 2004. Scottish Food Vessel Chronology Revisited. In A. Gibson & A. Sheridan (eds) *From Sickles to Circles: Britain and Ireland at the Time of Stonehenge*, 243-269. Stroud: Tempus.
Simpson, D.D.A. 1965. Food Vessels in south-west Scotland. *Transactions of the Dumfriess and Galloway Natural History and Archaeological Society*, 42, 26-50.
Smith, I.F. 1965, *Windmill Hill and Avebury. Excavations by Alexander Keiller, 1925-1939*. Oxford: Clarendon Press.
Smith, I.F. 1974. The Neolithic. In C. Renfrew (ed) *British Prehistory: A New Outline*, 100-36. London: Duckworth & Co.
Speak, S. & Burgess, C. 1999. Meldon Bridge: a centre of the third millennium BC in Peeblesshire. *Proceedings of the Society of Antiquaries of Scotland*, 129, 1-118.
Stone, J.F.S. 1949. Some grooved-ware pottery from the Woodhenge area. *Proceedings of the Prehistoric Society*, 15, 122-7.
Strachan, R., Ralston, I. & Finlayson, B. 1998. Neolithic and later prehistoric structures, and early medieval metal-working at Blairhall Burn, Amisfield, Dumfriesshire. *Proceedings of the Society of Antiquaries of Scotland*, 128, 55-94.
Threipland, L.M., 1957. An excavation at St. Mawgan-in-Pydar, North Cornwall. *Archaeological Journal*, 113, 33-81.
Tipping, R. 1994. 'Ritual' floral tributes in the Scottish Bronze Age – palynological evidence. *Journal of Archaeological Science*, 21, 133-9.
Tomalin, D. 1995. Cognition, ethnicity and some implications for linguistics in the perception and perpretation of 'Collared Urn art'. In I. Kinnes & G. Varndell (eds), *Unbaked Urns of Rudely Shape: Essays on British and Irish Pottery for Ian Longworth*, 101-12. Oxford: Oxbow Books.
Waddell, J. 1995. The Cordoned Urn tradition. In I. Kinnes & G. Varndell (eds), *Unbaked Urns of Rudely Shape: Essays on British and Irish Pottery for Ian Longworth*, 113-22. Oxford: Oxbow Books.

Wainwright, G.J. 1980. A pit burial at Lower Ashmore Farm, Roseash, Devon. *Proceedings of the Devon Archaeological Society*, 38, 13-15.

Wainwright, G.J. & Longworth, I.H. 1971. *Durrington Walls Excavations 1966-1969*. London: Society of Antiquaries.

Warren, S.H., Piggott, S., Clark, J.G.D., Burkitt, M.C., Godwin, H. & M.E. 1936. Archaeology of the submerged land surface of the Essex coast. *Proceedings of the Prehistoric Society*, 2, 178-210.

Whittle, A.W.R. 1977. *The Earlier Neolithic of Southern England and its Continental Background*. BAR Report S35. Oxford: British Archaeological Reports.

Williams, J. L. W. & Jenkins, D.A. 1999. A petrographic investigation of a corpus of Bronze Age cinerary urns from the Isle of Anglesey. *Proceedings of the Prehistoric Society*, 65, 189-230.

Worth, R.H. 1967. The Dartmoor Hut Circles. Reprinted in G.M. Spooner & F.S. Russell (eds), *Worth's Dartmoor*, Newton Abbot: David & Charles.

Index

See also glossary, pp142-5

Abingdon (Oxfordshire) 73
Absorbed residue analysis 14, 24, 27, 104
Accessory vessels *see* miniature vessels
Aldbourne cups *see* miniature vessels
All Cannings Cross 115
Allt Chrisal (Barra) 48, 77
Ardleigh urns *see* Deverel-Rimbury
Ashgrove (Fife) 22
Atrebatic wares 25, 123
Aylesford (Kent) 120
Aylesford-Swarling *see* Belgic

Barrel Urns 107, 110, 130 (see also Deverel-Rimbury)
Basketry 20
Balfarg (Fife) 87
Ballevullin (Tiree) 131
Ballynahatty (Co. Down) 87
Ballyalton bowls 74, 76, 84
Bamborough (Northumberland) 66
Barbush Quarry 75
Barnhouse (Orkney) 84, 87
Beakers 17, 22, 29, 30, 32, 34, 42, 54, 59, 60, 65, 68, 87-93, 99, 107
Belgic pottery 32, 128, 134-5
Bevel 15
Biconical Urn 102-3, 107
Black Burnished ware 25, 123
Bolton House (Northumberland) 66
Bonfires 11, 38, 45
Breach Farm (Glamorgan) 29
Breiddin (Powys) 27, 110
Brochs 131
Bucket Urns 107, 112, 130 (see also Deverel-Rimbury)
Burnishing *see* surface treatments

Carinated Bowls 69-71, 74, 88, 101
Carn Brae (Cornwall) 72

Carneddau (Powys) 30
Carrowkeel ware 74
Causewayed enclosures 19, 31, 60, 71
Ceide Fields (Co Mayo) 69
Celtic art 119
Ceramic change 11, 34
Cheese mould 14
Chinnor (Oxfordshire) 126
Clacton style *see* Grooved ware
Clay 34-5, 44-5
Clamp 44
Clettraval 131-2
Clickhimin (Shetland) 110, 130
Coil building 34, 41-2
Collared Urns 17, 20, 31, 32, 54, 64, 67, 78, 93, 96-99, 107, 137
Corbridge (Northumberland) 20
Cord impressions *see* surface treatments
Cordons *see* surface treatments: applied and raised decoration
Cordoned jar 64
Cordoned Urn 38, 93, 101-2, 107, 110
Cornish Urn
Covesea Ware 110

Dales Ware 135
Decoration *see* surface treatments
Deverel-Rimbury 30, 58, 104-7, 112
Diatoms 36
Downpatrick (Co. Down) 102
Dragonby 126-8
Drimnagh Bowls *see* Ballyalton bowls
Duck-stamped pottery 13, 26, 63, 122
Dundrum bowls 84
Dunting 38, 48
Durrington Walls (Wiltshire) 31, 65, 86
Durrington Walls style *see* Grooved Ware
Durotrigian ware 25, 53, 119, 123, 135

Ebbsfleet see impressed ware
Eilean Domhnuill (Uist) 48
Encrusted Urn *see* Food Vessel Urn
Enlarged Food Vessel *see* Food Vessel Urn
Ertebolle 28

Fengate *see* impressed ware
Fertile Crescent 19
Figurative art 11-12
Figurines 11, 40
Fillers *see* inclusions

Fire 11, 44
Fire clouds 47
Flat-rimmed ware 110, 129, 130
Floral tributes 24
Food Vessel 9, 16, 20, 22, 30, 37, 59, 61, 63, 64, 66, 80, 82, 88, 93-6, 104, 113, 137
Food Vessel Urns 20, 66, 93, 99-101
Frilford bowls 126
Functions of pottery 27

Gabbroic clay 26
Glanfeinion (Powys) 38-9
Glastonbury ware 55, 58, 122, 126
Globular Urns *see* Deverel-Rimbury
Goodlands bowls 74, 81
Grape cups *see* miniature vessels
Grain impressions *see* seed impressions
Greek Geometric Ware 11
Green Knowe (Peeblesshire) 107, 110
Grimston-Lyles Hill ware 69
Grog 32, 36-7
Grooved Ware 19, 24, 27, 31, 32, 59, 64, 84-7, 88, 92, 104

Hallstatt 112
Hambledon Hill (Dorset) 31
Henges 31
Haematite-coated bowls 19, 65-6, 115-6, 117-8
Heathery Burn (Co. Durham) 110
Hebridean bowls 15, 76-7
Hembury ware 26, 49, 72, 103
Hengistbury Head (Dorset) 63-4
Hillforts 109, 117
Horseshoe handles 20, 101, 103
Horton 78-80
Hunsbury bowls 58, 126
Huntcliffe Ware 135

Ile Tatihout (France) 26, 103
Impressed wares 17, 21, 24, 31, 38, 59, 60, 62, 78-82, 84, 88, 96, 137
Impressions *see* surface treatments
Inclusions 25, 31, 35-6, 55, 89, 128
Inlay *see* surface treatments
Irish bowls/vases *see* Food Vessels

Jahrlshof (Shetland) 110
Jars 109ff, 131
Join voids 41
Jura (France) 19

Kilellan Farm (Islay) 92
Kilellan Jars 92-3, 119
Kiln 11, 14, 44, 137
Kimmeridge-Caburn 116
Knapton Ware 135
Knowth (Co Meath) 87

La Tène 13, 61, 119
Langdale Pikes (Cumbria) 25
Leather hard 44
Legis Tor (Devon) 34-5
Linearbandkeramik 69
Lizard (Cornwall) 26, 72
London 50
Longstock (Hants) 20
Loom weights 13
Lowick (Northumberland) 66
Luce Bay 13

Maidcross (Suffolk) 30
Maiden Castle (Dorset) 26
Malvernian ware 26, 63
Meldon Bridge style *see* Impressed wares
Mildenhall (Suffolk) 73
Miniature vessels 29, 64, 104-5
Minoan pottery 11
Mondville (France) 26
Monkton-Minster (Kent) 54
Mortlake (London) 62
Mortlake ware *see* Impressed wares
Moulding 42
Murlough bowls 74
Mycenae (Greece) 11

Nether Swell (Gloucestershire) 13
Neuchâtel (Switzerland) 119
North Mains (Perthshire) 22
Northton (Harris) 61, 76-7, 91-2

Omphalos 16, 118, 128
Opening materials *see* inclusions
Otford (Kent) 54-5, 67
Oxidising 50

Paddle and anvil 40, 42
Painted pottery 29
Pedestalled bases 119
Pen Dinas (Ceredigion) 27

Perforated Wall cups *see* miniature vessels
Peterborough (Cambridgeshire) 112, 126
Peterborough Ware *see* Impressed wares
Pigmy cup *see* miniature vessels
Pinching 34, 40-41
Pits 17
Pit firings *see* bonfires
Pollen 22
Polypod bowls 19
Potter's wheel 33
Potters' marks 67

Radiocarbon dating 17
Reading (Berkshire) 115
Reduction 47, 50
Ring building *see* coil building
Rinyo (Orkney) 86, 87
Rinyo style *see* Grooved Ware
Rinyo-Clacton water *see* Grooved Ware
Romania 11, 13
Ronaldsway 42
Runnymede (Berkshire) 115
Ryton (Tyne and Wear) 66

Sandhills ware 81
Saucepan pots 17, 55, 58, 120-2
Scratched Wares 124, 128
Seed impressions 22, 37, 62-3
Shetland 92-3
Situla jars 112
Skara Brae (Orkney) 84, 87
Sketewan (Perthshire) 24
South Lodge Urns *see* Deverel-Rimbury
Southern Decorated Bowls 74
Spall 44, 48
Spoons 13
Sporon (Slovenia) 11
St Germains (E. Lothian) 130
Standrop Rigg (Northumberland) 107
Staple Howe 13, 112, 129
Stone axes 25, 31, 39
Strap building *see* coil building
Surface treatments 51ff
   Applied and raised decoration 63-4, 84, 112
   Birdbone impressions 60, 78
   Burnishing 65, 74, 128
   Cord impressions 21, 59, 78, 84
   False relief 63

Surface treatments (contd)
  Fingernail/tip impressions 61-2, 78, 112, 115, 130, 131, 138
  Impressions 58, 84, 128
  Incision 55, 74, 110, 113, 121, 124, 130
  Inlay 29, 118, 126
  Raised decoration 63-4, 84
  Rustication 53
  Scoring 58
  Stab and drag 58
  Tooling 55-7
  Toothed comb 34, 59, 90

Tazza 135
Temper *see* inclusions
Timber circles 65
Toothed comb *see* surface treatments
Trevisker ware 26, 35, 49, 103
Twisted cord *see* surface treatments

Unstan bowls 25, 76-7, 87, 88
Urns *see* Barrel Urns, Biconical Urns, Bucket Urns, Collared Urns, Cordoned Urns, Cornish Urns, Food Vessel Urns, Trevisker Urns, Wessex Handled urns

Vadastra (Romania) 138-9
Vaul ware 131

Walton Basin (Powys) 24, 27, 31
Water
  of chemical composition 38, 44, 50
  of plasticity 37, 44, 45
Water smoking 11, 44
Wessex Handled Urns 93, 101, 103, 107
West Harling (Norfolk) 112
Wether Hill (Northumberland) 22, 63
Whipped cord *see* surface treatments
Whitehawk (Sussex) 73
Windmill Hill (Wiltshire) 19, 60, 72, 73
Windmill Hill pottery 25, 72
Winterslow (Wiltshire) 67
Witham (Lincolnshire) 120
Woodhenge (Wiltshire) 86
Woodlands style *see* Grooved Ware

Yorkshire vase *see* Food Vessel